This Book is the property of

_____

Name

_____

_____

Phone Number or Email

Understanding Your DNA and Mind

Bob Ainuu Afamasaga

iUniverse, Inc.
New York   Bloomington

Understanding Your DNA and Mind

iUniverse books may be ordered through booksellers or by contacting:

iUniverse
1663 Liberty Drive
Bloomington, IN 47403
www.iuniverse.com
1-800-Authors (1-800-288-4677)

ISBN: 978-1-4401-1301-7 (pbk)
ISBN: 978-1-4401-1302-4 (ebk)

Printed in the United States of America

iUniverse rev. date: 1/26/09

ACKNOWLEDGEMENTS

I am grateful to ALL my friends who stood by me during trials. It is during these trials that the **TSF-24 MIND and TSF-24 BODY System™** came into conception. **The TSF-24 MIND** is discussed in this book *"Understanding Your DNA and MIND."* The **TSF-24 BODY System** is discussed in the next book, *"Understanding Your AMINO ACIDS (Protein) and BODY."*

I am grateful and thankful for the works of such minds such as **Dr. Howard Gardner, Dr. Abraham Maslow, Dr. Robert Anthony, Anthony Robbins, Bob Proctor, Dr. Robert Dew, Dr. Peter D'Adamo, Dr. Joe Dispenza, Dr. David Keirsey, Dr. George Boeree, Dr. Daniel Goleman, Dr. Joni E. Johnson, Walter McKenzie, Linda V. Beren, Myers-Briggs, Dr. Robert Sternberg, Wallace Wattles, Jim Rohn, Brian Tracy, Vic Johnson, Roger Sperry,** and **Mark Joyner,** to name a few, who have written about parts or pieces of the TSF-24. At times I have used or quoted some of their works in this book, and at other times, I have only read some of their writings, which did impact the contents of this book. None of them have endorsed my work but I am very grateful for them.

I am grateful for all those at iUniverse who made this project become a reality; cover designer Luiza Kleina, interior designer Ian Brewer,… and my PSA Liesl Schapker. THANKS A MILLION TO ALL OF YOU!

PREFACE

For thousands of years, man has quested to discover secrets to unlock formulas or sciences of life.

Many of these secrets have been discovered and are now advancing life in the fields of science, communication, transportation, and medicine, to name a few. One of these secrets was the discovery of energy and mass by Albert Einstein; $E=MC^2$ is the same thing as $M=E/C^2$.

This phenomenal discovery by Einstein revolutionized many fields of study, but also shed light to our understanding of the pursuit of wealth and success.

Another phenomenal discovery is the "24 Human DNA and MIND" sequences which will revolutionized many fi eld of studies, from psychology, medicine, genetics, nutrition's, dieting, business,... etc.. You get to see and discover the "24 Human DNA and MIND" sequences or short "TSF-24" in this book.

TSF-24 reveals the NEW treatment or solution model which is based on the concept that our Brain can change our Environment (information, people, physical); Lifestyle (money earning abilities), Health and Fitness (Diet) which influences the activities of your DNA or genes to change you. In other words, our Blood Types, Body Types, Temperaments, personalities and so forth are not predetermined by our parents DNA as currently taught in school.

The current model is that scientist examined the DNA or genes to discovered illnesses or diseases and from this discovery change our environment, lifestyle, health and fitness. Therefore, changing your brain which changes you! This model is opposite the approach you will discover in this book.

The foundation of this book is based on the author's discovery of the 24 Human DNA Sequences which is part of the Universal Genetic Code of 64 DNA Sequence initially discovered by Watson, Wilkins, Franklin, and Crick. This Universal Genetic Code of 64 Sequence belongs to ALL living organism.

The author believes that every living organism has its own DNA Sequence or language which is derived from Universal Genetic Code.

This book is about the 24 Human DNA Sequence or language and how it will help you create your success. Here are some first grounds concepts created by this book and the TSF-24Success System;

1. demonstrate that the mind and body are the same

2. all females think the same

3. all males think the same

4. your blood type demonstrates how you use your brain and there are 48 blood types (24 MIND, 24 BODY) and body types

5. **24 sub-brains and personalities combinations.**

6. **24 Human DNA Sequence**

7. **24 RNA Sequence**

8. **24 main Amino Acids**

9. **3 cell types or tissues which is the body's building foundation and relates to Blood Types**

10. **4 major school of psychology and treatment**

11. **and more which all relates to helping you become successful in whatever your are pursuing.**

Millions of books have been written about the subject of wealth, success, and rich. All of these writings, I present, can be categorized into *four schools of thought which is managed and control by each specific area of the brain or DNA.*

Believe it or not, your brain is the center of your universe. If you don't understand how your brain works, you will continue to face the many challenges of life – success and wealth will be elusive. The field of epigenetic will help us with this understanding.

1. **The Right Brain:** Guanine, Hydrogen, Humanist/ Sociocultural School of Psychology, Superconscious,

Social or Creative Intelligence, Spirit, Extrovert, Idealist, Endomorph, and Blood Type B

2. **The Left Brain:** Cytosine, Nitrogen, Cognitive School of Psychology, Conscious, Intellectual or Analytical Intelligence or Mind, Introvert, Rationals, Ectomorph, and Blood Type A

3. **The Brainstem:** Adenine, Carbon, Behaviorist School of Psychology, Nonconscious, Physiological (Bodily-Kinesthetic) or Practical or Instinctual Intelligence, Body/ Soul, Sensovert, Guardian, Mesomorph, and Blood Type O.

4. **The Mid-brain:** Thymine, Oxygen, Psychodynamic (Analyst) School of Psychology, Subconscious, Emotional or Successful Intelligence, figurative Heart, Emotiovert, Artisan, Ecto-endomorph, and Blood Type AB.

I will use these terms interchangeably throughout this "Reader's Digest" format book, as they all represent the same school of thought for each category. **These four schools of thought are definitive, as they demonstrate or represent the foundation of our genes or DNA..**

I will be using these same definitions throughout. **Ideas and concepts presented <u>will</u> be repetitive as to "bring them home" (i.e., convey my intent) to the reader the convergence of ALL schools of thought under each specific area of the brain – whether it's pure science, psychology, religion…etc.**

ALL your thoughts, actions, behavior and so forth are governed by the four areas of your brain or DNA. <u>My purpose is to catalyze new thinking and to move away from traditional thinking and practices (or intellectual dishonesty) whether it's in psychology, medicine, science, marketing and so forth.</u>

Numerous existed researches are based on the two hemispheres of the brain (Left, Right) but neglecting the existence of the other two - Stem and Mid. Many researchers have accidentally discovered its function but not directly linked it to the Stem or Midbrain. <u>The last two is the missing link to our pursuit of understanding in all areas of life.</u>

You are wired to behave in a specific way, depending on your brain dominant and genetics. This affects everything that you do, whether knowingly or unknowingly including your pursuit of success in any endeavor. The great news is that you can rewire yourself to create the person you desire. The study of epigenetic is giving us direction to this endeavor.

Prior to the beginning of the twentieth century little was actually known about the brain. In the late 1950's and early 1960's some significant research was conducted by Roger Sperry. Sperry's work, which later earned him the Nobel Prize for Medicine in 1981, clearly showed that the brain is divided into two major parts or hemispheres, the *right brain* and the *left brain.* His research also identified that each of the parts of the brain specializes in its own style of thinking and has different capabilities.[1]

Roger Sperry's work separated the Neomammalian brain in to two hemispheres – **Left and Right.**

According to research pioneered by Paul MacLean, M.D., the human brain has three sub-brains – the *Paleomammalian* **(Limbic System or Mid Brain),** *Reptilian* **(Stem)** and *Neomammalian (Right and Left Brain)*[2]. **This is the foundation this whole book is based on –** *these four sub-brains which parallel to each DNA base. There is no literature available in the medical field or sciences to suggest what I am proposing here. The content of this book is the author's conclusion of connecting ALL the dots of what's available out there!*

In the 50s, James Watson, Francis Crick, and Maurice Wilkins deciphered the DNA code. In 2008, the discovery of the 24 Human DNA and MIND sequences took the above Nobel Prize recipient's collective work to the next level. Now, discovered that each base (Guanine, Cytosine, Adenine, Thymine) of the DNA is controlled and managed by each specific sub-brain (Right, Left, Stem, Mid) or vice versa. The DNA is billions of miniature or micro MINDs (brain) at the cellular level. The MIND (brain) is all DNAs in one at the macro or organ level.

Life consists of the interplay of two kinds of chemicals: **DNA and Proteins.** DNA is what biologist called **genotype** *which represents information's, replications, breeding, sex…etc.* **Protein** is what biologist called **phenotype** *which represent chemistry, living, breathing, metabolism and behavior. Neither can exist without the other.*

In other words, life consist of the interplay of two kinds of organs: **MIND (brain) and BODY.** *Neither can exist without the other. Neither the chemicals nor organs an initiate a chemical reaction or process by itself. A chemical substance called RNA links the two worlds of DNA and Proteins. A thought process called CONSCIENCE links the two worlds of the MIND and BODY together.*

The discussion of DNA is a discussion of the MIND (brain) at the cellular level. The discussion of the MIND is a discussion of the DNA at the organ level.

1. **The Right Brain:** The right half of the Neomammalian brain. The right brain functions *in a non-verbal manner and excels in visual, spatial, existential, spiritual, perceptual, creative and **intuitive information.***

Humanist and Sociocultural psychologists such as **Carl Rogers, Abraham Maslow,** to name a few, who studied the mind, unbeknownst to them were observing behaviors controlled and managed by the right hemisphere of the brain. Some psychologist called this area of the brain the "preconscious" or "**superconscious mind**" because its activities are above or faster than the conscious mind.

Many times faster than the conscious mind, the "preconscious" processor continually scans billions of bits of data, determining what is important and what is not. When it notes something important, it immediately signals the conscious mind *(left Brain)* to pay attention.[3]

Psychologist Howard Gardner in his discovery of Multiple Intelligence within humans discussed *Spatial, Musical, Existential, Spiritual and Personal* intelligences[4] which are the domain of the right brain. Within his *personal intelligence* explanation is Interpersonal Intelligence which is the same as **Social Intelligence**.

In 2006, psychologist, Dr. Daniel Goleman discussed **Interpersonal Intelligence** in more detailed (as Gardner's labeled it) in his book titled, **Social Intelligence: the New Science of Human Relationships.** In a nutshell, Dr. Goleman said that our success or anyone's success in any endeavor is dependent upon connecting or synergizing with those around us, because our brains are designed that way!

In religion, when people are discussing concepts of worshiping with **"Spirit"** or **"Strength"** or the realm of supernatural, they are tapping in to the function or the interest of the right brain (intuitive). **The Spirit or Strength within the person is the same concept and is manifestation of the Right Brain. The "Spirit" should NOT be confused with the "Soul" which is governed by the Stem brain.**

"In every human being, whether emperor or cowboy, prince or pauper, philosopher or slave, there is a mysterious something which he neither understood nor controls." Barton in <u>What Can A Man Believe?</u>[15]

2. **The Left Brain: The left half of the neomammillian brain.** The left brain is associated with *verbal, logical, and analytical thinking*. If you reflect back upon your own educational training, we have been traditionally taught to master the 3 R's: reading, writing and arithmetic -- the domain and strength of the left brain.

Cognitive Psychologist such as **Norbert Wiener, Alan M. Turing, Ludwig von Bertalanffy, Noam Chomsky, Jean Piaget, Donald O. Hebb, and George A. Miller to name a few** have been studying and observing behavior controlled and managed by the left hemisphere of the brain. They were fascinated by the **"Conscious" mind and "Intellectual Intelligence."**

Psychologist Gardner discussed **Linguistic and Logical-Mathematical intelligence** which are functions of the left hemisphere brain. He discussed intellectual intelligence as a weak measurement of intelligence.

Intellectual Intelligence is very familiar to all of us with the concept of the Intelligence Quotient (IQ); a standard IQ test which measures raw intelligence, including abilities such as logic (reasoning and analyzing) skills, reading, and writing.

In fact, educational systems use this testing as a measuring tool and benchmark. Based on this school of thought, **your IQ is seen as a strong indicator of the level of success you could attain in life.** It is suggested that, the higher your IQ--the more potential it is that you will be very successful in life.

In religion, the discussion of the **"Mind"** is basically referring to the function of the left brain and its faculties. **The Mind is the manifestation of the Left Brain.**

3. **The Stem Brain: The Reptillian brain.** The brain stem plays a vital role in basic *attention, arousal,* and *consciousness.* All information to and from our body *passes through the brain stem on the way to or from the brain.* The responses of the body to external stimuli are the function of the stem brain.

Behavioral, Evolutionary, and Biological psychologist such as **Ivan Pavlov, Edward Lee Thorndike, John Broadus Watson, Herbert Spencer,** and their followers were observing and studying **"nonconscious"** or **"physiological intelligence"** functions or behaviors controlled and managed by this part of the brain.

Psychologist Gardner's labeled the intelligence from this specific area of the brain as **Bodily-Kinesthetic intelligence and naturalist.**

The same area of the brain and its function is discussed in the realm of religion as **"Body"** or **"Soul." This is not to be confused with the "Spirit" which is in the domain of the Right brain. The "Body" or "Soul" is the manifestation of the Stem Brain.**

4. **The Mid Brain (Limbic System). Paleomammalian brain.** The Mid Brain is also called the emotional brain. Sometimes it is called the chemical brain as well because it is responsible for regulating many different *internal stages – body temperature, blood sugar, blood pressure, digestion, hormone levels and many other processes.*[6]

Psychodynamic psychologists such as **Sigmund Freud (founder of this school of thought), Harry Stack Sullivan, Carl Jung, Erik Erikson, Melanie Klein, Margaret Mahler, Jacques Lacan, and Heinz Kohut,** among many others unbeknownst to them were observing and studying behavior controlled and managed by this area of the brain. The above experts popularized such words as unconscious or subconscious.

"Subconscious" - or the "Being" school of thought teaches that you will never get anything "above" (i.e., more than you have), or never exceed the image you hold of yourself in your subconscious. This image of yourself (or internal representation of "self") creates how you feel about your life and attracts all external elements to match it.

Dr. Robert Anthony said the following in his *"The Secret of Deliberate Creation"* program, *"Quantum Physics,"* ...why self-help books and positive thinking do not work...it has very little to do with *what we think*, it really is all about *how we feel....* In fact, Think and Grow Rich should be re-titled, "Feel and Grow Rich."

Multiple intelligence expert psychologists Howard Gardner discussed **Intrapersonal intelligence** as part of his Personal intelligence concept, which is the same concept, as **"Emotional Intelligence"** that Dr. Daniel Goleman discussed in detailed in his book titled, "Emotional Intelligence: Why It Can Matter More Than IQ." This intelligence is in the domain of the Midbrain.

In religion, the discussion of the **Heart or Figurative Heart** is within the realm of the Midbrain activities. **In other words, the figurative Heart is the manifestation of the Mid Brain.**

So which of these schools of thought will help a person to understand themselves in any endeavor? The answer lies within all four of the schools of thought. They are all correct in their arguments or discussions. They each explain the separate creative or intelligence powers that you possess – *the Secret "Total Success Formula" (TSF:24)*!

Yes, you have inborn or innate resources or DNAs. You own these resources. It is just that no one has told you that. It is the lack of awareness of these four powers (or DNA Sequence) that, I purport, is the culprit to why you are achieving anything less than everything you desire or why you are not getting well from your psychological or other treatment related to the brain.

If you are not getting anything you desire or need, or have interest and intent -- at will, it means your four sub-brains (or DNAs) are not under your control. Indeed, since they are operating in every life "24/7," they could be controlling and managing you. In other words, your powers own you instead of you owning them!

This may sound strange, but this is the truth as I perceive it. **This book is a discovery of *the formula* to understand your four sub-brain; the**

<u>totality of the whole *puzzle of wealth, health, - and success-creation, and psychological help* </u>that **were fragmented, missing, or lost.** Each school of thought independently discussed or combined with another, argues as to the only vehicle of understanding success and wealth creation.

The true creative process for success, health, and wealth in any endeavor or treatment of any brain related illnesses lies within **ALL four** schools of thoughts (or DNAs), as mentioned earlier, and is presented here as the **"Total Success Formula" (TSF-24). - TSF-24 = SU + CN + NC + SB™ or TSF=R+L+S+M.**

I initially set out to rewrite the words and ideas of each author I cited in this book, then I realized--Why "reinvent the wheel?"--when these authors have eloquently articulated individual parts of the **TSF-24.**

I therefore have quoted specific essays relevant to the specific topic discussed. Again, none of these authors have endorsed this book but I am very grateful to each one of them; **Dr. Robert Anthony, Linda V. Beren, Dr. Peter D'Adamo, Dr. Joe Dispenza, Anthony Robbins, Bob Proctor, Darren Hardy, Dr. Howard Gardner, Dr. Daniel Goleman, Dr. George Boeree, Wes Hopper, Dr. David Keirsey, Stuart Licthman, Cesar Millan, Walter McKenzie, Dr. Robert Sternberg, Dr. Joe Vitale, Wallace Wattles, Brian Tracy, Vic Johnson, Dr. J. Robert Dew,** and **Mark Joyner,** for setting the path--for us to use their ideas. It is a privilege and honor to stand on shoulders of these giants.

In an attempt to draw specific attention to ideas, I have used *some italics* and **some bolding,** which are my insertions and not the original author's thinking. Therefore, throughout the whole book, you will find compilations of writings and thoughts of many authors, and researchers in each chapter. They individually shed understanding on parts of **"the puzzle"** that this book will present, and when compiled, will complete the **TSF-24.**

The **TSF-24** teaches you how to balance all four of your powers or brain, so that you can fulfill your dreams, ideas, and deepest wishes; *and also, I intend it as a personal help to anyone who is seeking or looking for help emotionally, physically, and psychologically.*

This book offers the **TSF-24** that successful, healthy, and wealthy person who has lived, uses to discover (either by trial and error, or deliberately), how to understand wealth and happiness they so desire to enjoy. NOW, it is your turn to enjoy whatever your mind finds of interest, your spirit intends or inspires, your body needs, or your heart desires, by understanding the **TSF-24**. Before, you begin your journey; discover your personal TSF-24 genetic formula by following the **4 Steps Method** below.

1. Take the "Do You Know WHO YOU ARE? Survey" to see your customized **TSF and your intelligences based on Dr. Howard Gardner's Multiple Intelligences Theory.** The Survey was created by Walter McKenzie of http://surfaquarium.com based on Dr. Gardners work but I have modified it to accomplish my purpose in this book. The Survey demonstrates the order how you use your brain - which intelligences that you use the most and which you use the least. Next page over. Also, there is a Survey for Teenagers and a Survey for age 8 years and less (great survey for parents to understand their children) at www.AreYouAHuman.Com .

2. Get your Blood Type Test results, A MUST! Your Blood Type whether it's A, B, O tells a lot how to understand your success and failures but more about your health. **You have two Blood Types. One is the MIND and other the BODY.** It's who you are!

3. Confi rm BOTH Step 1 and Step 2 with the **"24 Human DNA Table"** at Appendix IV to see the Blood and Brain Connection presented!

4. Read this book to understand your personal genetic "TSF." Your Brain and Blood at work for you!

It's very important that you do the above **4 Steps** before you begin your journey!

"Do you know who you are? Survey [z]

Part I

Complete each section by placing a "1" next to each statement you feel accurately describes you. If you do not identify with a statement, leave the space provided blank. Then total the column in each section. See Example at **Appendix I.**

Section 1
_____ I easily pick up on patterns
_____ I focus in on noise and sounds
_____ Moving to a beat is easy for me
_____ I enjoy making music
_____ I respond to the cadence of poetry
_____ I remember things by putting them in a rhyme
_____ Concentration is difficult for me if there is background noise
_____ Listening to sounds in nature can be very relaxing
_____ Musicals are more engaging to me than dramatic plays
_____ Remembering song lyrics is easy for me
_____ **TOTAL for Section 1**

Section 2
_____ It is important to see my role in the "big picture" of things
_____ I enjoy discussing questions about life
_____ Religion is important to me
_____ I enjoy viewing art work
_____ Relaxation and meditation exercises are rewarding to me
_____ I like traveling to visit inspiring places
_____ I enjoy reading philosophers
_____ Learning new things is easier when I see their real world application
_____ I wonder if there are other forms of intelligent life in the universe
_____ It is important for me to feel connected to people, ideas and beliefs
_____ **TOTAL for Section 2**

Section 3
_____ I learn best interacting with others
_____ I enjoy informal chat and serious discussion

_____ The more the merrier
_____ I often serve as a leader among peers and colleagues
_____ I value relationships more than ideas or accomplishments
_____ Study groups are very productive for me
_____ I am a "team player"
_____ Friends are important to me
_____ I belong to more than three clubs or organizations
_____ I dislike working alone
_____ **TOTAL for Section 3**

Section 4
_____ I can visualize ideas in my mind
_____ Rearranging a room and redecorating are fun for me
_____ I enjoy creating my own works of art
_____ I remember better using graphic organizers
_____ I enjoy all kinds of entertainment media
_____ Charts, graphs and tables help me interpret data
_____ A music video can make me more interested in a song
_____ I can recall things as mental pictures
_____ I am good at reading maps and blueprints
_____ Three dimensional puzzles are fun
_____ **TOTAL for Section 4**

Section 5
_____ I am known for being neat and orderly
_____ Step-by-step directions are a big help
_____ Problem solving comes easily to me
_____ I get easily frustrated with disorganized people
_____ I can complete calculations quickly in my head
_____ Logic puzzles are fun
_____ I can't begin an assignment until I have all my "ducks in a row"
_____ Structure is a good thing
_____ I enjoy troubleshooting something that isn't working properly
_____ Things have to make sense to me or I am dissatisfied
_____ **TOTAL for Section 5**

Section 6
_____ Foreign languages interest me

_____ I enjoy reading books, magazines and web sites
_____ I keep a journal
_____ Word puzzles like crosswords or jumbles are enjoyable
_____ Taking notes helps me remember and understand
_____ I faithfully contact friends through letters and/or e-mail
_____ It is easy for me to explain my ideas to others
_____ I write for pleasure
_____ Puns, anagrams and spoonerisms are fun
_____ I enjoy public speaking and participating in debates
_____ **TOTAL for Section 6**

Section 7
_____ I enjoy categorizing things by common traits
_____ Ecological issues are important to me
_____ Classification helps me make sense of new data
_____ I enjoy working in a garden
_____ I believe preserving our National Parks is important
_____ Putting things in hierarchies makes sense to me
_____ Animals are important in my life
_____ My home has a recycling system in place
_____ I enjoy studying biology, botany and/or zoology
_____ I pick up on subtle differences in meaning
_____ **TOTAL for Section 7**

Section 8
_____ I learn by doing
_____ I enjoy making things with my hands
_____ Sports are a part of my life
_____ I use gestures and non-verbal cues when I communicate
_____ Demonstrating is better than explaining
_____ I love to dance
_____ I like working with tools
_____ Inactivity can make me more tired than being very busy
_____ Hands-on activities are fun
_____ I live an active lifestyle
_____ **TOTAL for Section 8**

Section 9
_____ My attitude effects how I learn
_____ I like to be involved in causes that help others
_____ I am keenly aware of my moral beliefs

_____ I learn best when I have an emotional attachment to the subject

_____ Fairness is important to me

_____ Social justice issues interest me

_____ Working alone can be just as productive as working in a group

_____ I need to know why I should do something before I agree to do it

_____ When I believe in something I give more effort towards it

_____ I am willing to protest or sign a petition to right a wrong

_____ **TOTAL for Section** 9

Part II
Now carry forward your total from each Section and multiply by 10 (See Table below). Then,

- Add 1 to 4 and divide by 4. This will give you the true score the for **Right Brain area.**
- Add 5 to 6 and divide by 2. This will give you the true score for the **Left Brain area.**
- Add 7 and 8 and divide by 2. This will give you the true score for **Stem Brain area.**
- 9 is a true score for the **Mid Brain.**

You will learn all about the Right, Left, Stem, and Mid brain throughout the book and how this is related to your great success.

SECTION	TOTAL FORWARD	MULTIPLY	SCORE	TOTAL SCORE
1		X10		N/A
2		X10		N/A
3		X10		N/A
4		X10		N/A
		Total 1-4		/4=
5		X10		N/A
6		X10		N/A
		Total 5-6		/2=
7		X10		N/A
8		X10		N/A
		Total 7-8		/2 =
9		X10		N/A
		Total 9		/1

Part III
Now determine how you use your brain profile!
Key:
Section 1 – This suggests your Musical strength
Section 2 – This illustrates your Existential strength
Section 3 – This shows your Interpersonal strength (social)
Section 4 – This suggests your Visual strength
Section 5 – This indicates your Logical strength
Section 6 – This indicates your Verbal strength
Section 7 – This reflects your Naturalist strength
Section 8 – This tells your Kinesthetic strength
Section 9 –This reflects your Intrapersonal strength (emotional)

Remember:

□ Everyone has all the intelligences!

□ You can strengthen intelligence!

□ This inventory is meant as a snapshot in time – it can change!

□ This Survey is meant to empower YOU!

From the Survey Table above, input the Total (after division to find the average) Scores in the **TABLE 1** below.

Then, input scores from **TABLE 1** to **TABLE 2** from the Highest to the lowest score. Highest score is the **Dominant,** next highest is **Auxiliary,** next is **Tertiary** and lowest, Inferior.

TABLE 1 - The Whole Brain Approach			
Right - Social Intelligence	Left - Intellectual Intelligence	Stem - Practical Intelligence	Mid - Emotional Intelligence
Sec. 1-4	Sec. 5-6	Sec. 7-8	Sec. 9

Below is an example of how the TABLE 2 is completed. The order "how" you write them is very important because you get to see "how" you use your brain or "how" your brain works.

The Whole Brain Approach Here's your TSF below! Example				
	Dominant	Auxiliary	Tertiary	Inferior
Brain Label	Mid	Right	Left	Stem
Score	60	45	30	10

The above is the example of "how" you complete TABLE 2 below.

TABLE 2 - The Whole Brain Approach Here's your TSF below!				
	Dominant	Auxiliary	Tertiary	Inferior
Brain Label				
Score				

Look at your results above. Transfer your results from TABLE 2 to TABLE 3 below. This is a great place to start discovering what's holding you back from having the life that you always intend, want, need, and desire. Dr. Gardner's MI Models demonstrate which sub-brain that you use the most and more than likely is your dominant sub-brain. Your dominant sub-brain is your main Temperament, Blood Type or attitude to how you deal with life. Your personality is a "recombination" of the sub-brains or temperaments. You will learn all about this in this book.

This is the real culprit to why you are not successful in all areas of your life – socially, psychologically, physiologically and emotionally. Collective neural activities of these two areas of your brain are the cause. You have to rewire your inferior sub-brain first, .

TABLE 3 - The Whole Brain Approach Input your scores here again!				
	Dominant	Auxiliary	Tertiary	Inferior
Brain Label				
Score				

Your Blood Type will determine your real dominant sub-brain or main Temperament above. It's BOTH the Dominant or Auxiliary of the Survey result. Go see your Doctor or medical professional to get your Blood Type if you don't know what it is. IT'S VERY IMPORTANT THAT YOU KNOW THIS BEFORE YOU READ THE BOOK.

Your result above shows how you used your brain based on the work by psychologist, Dr. Howard Gardner and survey created by Mr. Walter McKenzie. The accuracy of your result is dependent on how you answer each question honestly. Your above result should be verified with the "Human Genetic Periodic Table (part of the Table is listed below)." Both results from the "Human Genetic Periodic Table" and your Blood Type must match, except those who have Mid brain results. This demonstrates that your Blood Type shows how you used your mind. By knowing your Blood Type, you know how you use you mind. Therefore, you know your strengths and weaknesses.

For example, how to read the Table below.

1			2			3		
4 Sub-Brain: Right, Left, Stem, Mid **24 Sub-Brains and Personalities**			**4 Blood Types:** A, B, O, ABO **24 Blood Types: (48-24 MIND and 24 BODY Types**			**24** **Universal Personalities** (Myers-Briggs, Dr. Jung & Dr. Kiersey, Socionic)		
							MIND	**BODY**
R	L	RLMS	B	A	*B+*	A+	**INFJ** Counselor	***ENTP*** *Visionary*
		RLSM			*B+*	A+	**INFP** Idealist ,	***ENTJ*** *Executive*
	S	RSLM		O	*B+*	O+	**ENFP** Inspirer	***ESTJ*** *Guardian*
		RSML			*B+*	O+	**ENFJ** Teacher	***ESFJ*** *Provider*
	M	RMSL		ABO	*B+-*	AB- O+-	**ENFJ Teacher ,**	***ESTP*** *Promote* ***ESTJ*** *Guardian*
		RMLS			*B+-*	*AB- A+-*	**INFJ** Counselor,	***ESFP*** *Performer* ***ENTJ*** *Executive*
L	R	LRSM	A	B	*A+*	*B+*	**ENTJ** Executive	***INFP*** *Idealist*
		LRMS			*A+*	*B+*	**ENTP** Visionary	***INFJ*** *Counselor*
	S	LSRM		O	*A+*	O+	**INTJ** Scientist	***ISFJ*** *Protector*
		LSMR			*A+*	O+	**INTP** Architect	***ISTJ*** *Inspector*
	M	LMRS		ABO	A+-	AB- B+-	**ENTJ** Executive,	***ISFP*** *Composer,* ***INFP*** *Idealist*
		LMSR			A+-	AB- O+-	**INTJ** Scientist	***ISTP*** *Mechanic* ***ISFJ*** *Protector* ,
S	L	SLRM	O	A	*O+*	A+	**ISFJ** Protector	***INTJ*** *Scientist*
		SLMR			*O+*	A+	**ISTJ** Inspector	***INTP*** *Architect*
	R	SRLM		B	*O+*	B+	**ESTJ** Guardian	***ENFP*** *Inspirer*
		SRML			*O+*	B+	**1ESFJ** Provider	***ENFJ*** *Teacher*
	M	SMLR		ABO	O+-	AB- A+-	**ISTJ** Inspector	***ISTP*** Mechanic, **INTP** Architect,
		SMRL			O+-	AB- B+-	**ESFJ** Provider	***ESTP*** *Promoter* ***ENFJ*** *Teacher* ,

M			BO					
M	S	MSLR	BO	O	AB- O+-	A+-	**ISTP** Mechanic, **ISFJ** Protector,	*INTJ Scientist*
		MSRL			AB- O+-	B+-	**ESTP** Promoter **ESTJ** Guardian	***ENFJ Teacher***
	L	MLSR		A	AB- A+-	O+-	**ISTP** Mechanic, **INTP** Architect,	*ISTJ Inspector*
		MLRS			AB- A+-	B+-	**ESFP** Performer **ENTJ** Executive,	*INFJ Counselor*
	R	MRSL		B	AB- B+-	O+-	***ESTP Promoter*** ***ENFJ Teacher*** ,	**ESFJ** Provider
		MRLS			AB- B+-	A+-	***ISFP Composer*** ***INFP Idealist***	**ENTJ** Executive,

These strengths and weaknesses are predetermined by your MIND sequence that you discovered in your Survey. All sub-brain (MIND/DNA) or (PROTEIN/BODY) sequences are predetermined at birth. The fetus chooses 1 of the 24 MIND (DNA) sequence to protect itself and this creates you! Each sequence has TWO Blood types. One Blood Type is from your mother side (maternal) and one from your father side (paternal). The first Blood Type is from father and second is from the mother. In order words, the Blood Type for the MIND is paternal and Blood Type for the BODY is maternal. Which one will be dominant depends on what the fetus (or person) use to care and protect itself throughout life.

The type or kind of work, environment, diet and pursuit in life dictates which one of your Blood Types or sub-brain will be dominant. The MIND takes over the BODY or vice versa. or both.

Again, the Column 2a Blood Type result represents "How" your use your MIND. This is demonstrated from your Survey results. If your Survey and Blood Type result matched the FIRST BLOOD TYPE RESULT IN COLUMN 2a, then what this mean is that your MIND is running your Life. Your THINKING is the main control of your life, whether it is done thought your Left (A+-), Right (B+-), Stem (O+-) or Mid (AB+-) brain. Your THINKING influences, and affects all your daily activities. You are consciously creating ALL your ACTIONS through your THINKING! Your THINKING and Blood Type here is your father's!

For example, your Blood Type test result is A+ and Survey result is LSRM. As you check COLUMN 1 and COLUMN 2, you would see a matched of your Blood Type result, A+ and A+ result in COLUMN 2a with Survey. This person is an INTROVERT and creates his/her life ACTIONS or ACTIVITIES daily by his/her THOUGHTS.

The Column 2b represents "How" you use your BODY and is demonstrated by your actual Blood Type test results. If your Blood Type result do not matched the Survey result but matched SECOND BLOOD TYPE in COLUMN 2b, then what this means is your BODY is running your Life. Your daily THINKING, ACTIONS or ACTIVITIES are governed and directed by information or data stored in your BODY whether it is in your Left (A+-), Right (B+-), Stem (O+-) or Mid (AB+-) brain. These data or information has been passed down to you through your genes and also knowledge you acquired through learning, observation and experience. Your ACTIONS or ACTIVITIES and Blood Type here is your mother's!

For example, your Blood Type test result is O+ and Survey result is LSRM. As you check COLUMN 1 and COLUMN 2b, you would see COLUMN 2b your Blood Type result, O+ and A+ result in COLUMN 2a for Survey. This person's life is run by his/her BODY. This person is a SENSOVERT and his/her life THINKING, ACTIONS or ACTIVITIES daily are created by information or data stored in her/his Right, Left, Stem, and Mid brain.

The next Column is 24 Universal Personalities Profiles. The Profile next to your Blood Type row is your personality profile. If you Blood Type result is in the MIND column, then your Profile will in the MIND column also. Same with the BODY results.

Details of the above Survey and Blood Type results will be explained throughout the book.

CHAPTER 1

INTRODUCTION

"Man's greatness lies in the power of his thoughts"
Anonymous

"The mind is the man, and knowledge mind; a man is but what he knoweth." Francis Bacon[8]

"Thoughts are free and subject to no rule. On them rests the freedom of man, and they tower above the light of nature...create a new heaven, a new firmament, a new source of energy from which new arts flow." Paracelsus[9]

"For as a man thinketh in his heart, so is he."[10]

Wow, those are powerful thoughts! For over fifty years I have pursued understanding of this principle--the power of our thoughts.

It was during my personal trials that I began to see and understand what the previous writers were talking about.

Vic Johnson described best what I was experiencing in the following essay from his e-Meditation Series.[11]

"You are today where your thoughts have brought you; you will be tomorrow where your thoughts take you." **Above Life's Turmoil**

This principle was not easy for me to accept and I fought it for a long time. As miserable as my life was at the time, *I learned this concept*: I was certain that there was no way that it was due to the thoughts that I had held. There were too many other reasons why things had gone bad--my ex-spouse, I'm a minority, the economy, a client who had wronged me, and on, and on, and on. Since I was not responsible for my "bad luck," then certainly my thoughts had nothing to do with it.

But I was wrong. Like the biblical Job who said, "The thing I feared most has come upon me..."[12] I, too, had thought myself to where I was.

1

Dr. Walter Doyle Staples, writing in <u>Think like a Winner</u>! says, "I credit one simple concept with getting me started on my journey into self-discovery. After a great deal of study and contemplation, I came to the conclusion that **people have in their lives today exactly what they keep telling their mind they want."**

Like Dr. Staples, it was a moment of great illumination for me! The logical side of me said, "if you and you alone can think yourself into such a mess, then surely you and you alone can think yourself out of it."

That is what I did. It was not overnight and it was not easy, but it was a sure thing! By accepting all of the responsibility for where I was at and acknowledging it, and all of the responsibility for where I was going, I experienced a tremendous "joy" and "freedom" because I knew in my "knower" (head), that if I got myself into the predicament, I could get myself out.

I was blown away by that thought. It was a great moment of illumination and enlightenment for me!

When I read the essay from Vic Johnson[13] for the first time, I experienced that tremendous joy and freedom, because I stopped lying to myself--that everyone else was responsible for what is happening to me. We each individually created, allowed, invited, and attracted whatever is in our lives.

The truth of the matter is, I have created, allowed, invited, and attracted everything that has happened to me either by choice or default. I am the culprit!

When I stopped lying to myself and everyone else, then I came to the realization that if I got myself into this predicament, I am the only person who could get me out. Wow!

There lies one of the secret principles of success--**accepting where you are at, taking personal responsibility for whatever has happened up to that point, and make immediate changes!**

You created, allowed, invited, and attracted who you are! Wow, this is hard to swallow--and even harder to accept. I had to search deep within myself on where to begin my journey upon discovering this fact.

My inspiration and journey began into the ancient writings of the Middle East, such as the Holy Writings (i.e. Scriptures) [14]. I had many great inspirations along the way from them, such wisdom as *"As a man thinketh, he becomes,* [15]*" The heart is more treacherous than anything else and is desperate...,* [16]*"*(paraphrased) *"The body is always inclined to do what is wrong,"* [17] and *"...Due to the abundance of dynamic energy, he also being vigorous in power, not one [of them] is missing...."* [18]--for sources of strength.

These were the core principles and foundations of what I discovered as attributes to many people's success.

Hundreds of thousands of books have been written about success and how to achieve it.

*I am grateful for all the thinkers and writers throughout the centuries, for each (or all) have pieces of the puzzle of the **TSF**--for which I have had the joy of putting together for the past fifty years and, until now, finally understand its magnitude*

All the contents of this book and any wisdom therein, have passed through generation after generation. As the wise man once said, "There is no new wisdom (thing) under the sun." [19]

All that I am presenting here has already existed in the unlimited possibilities of knowledge of the universe. I am just a tool to present this information to those who quest for it. For example, one of the "four powers" discussed in this book is your "Subconscious," (or the figurative "Heart," or Emotional Intelligence)--the center where your success or failure is created.

As quantum physics shows, I believe, "how you feel" not "what you think" creates what you want. It is in the figurative "Heart" or "Subconscious" where your new and old habits are stored; so, whatever is stored there--that is your autopilot for creating your life now! Your emotional responses to life's situations are dependent on what is stored there.

True, the **other three powers of intelligence are needed to complete the process.** One power cannot affect complete and lasting success alone without the others. However, your "Subconscious" or autopilot works when there is no time for deliberate conscious thought. It works "behind the scenes" of your deliberate thoughts and actions.

It is interesting to note that the four powers of intelligence, in which the four schools of thought are founded on, are parallel to the four areas of your brain as I stated earlier in the Preface.

It is time to explain the previous concepts in terms of the four areas of your brain. Your powers are stored in four areas of your brain--Left, Right, Mid, and Stem (Brainstem). The "Subconscious" is the information stored in your Mid-brain and, at any given moment, it is in harmony or in conflict with information in your three other parts of your brain!

Your brain is phenomenally built to share or shift your powers when any of its components are incapacitated. "It was once believed to be just 'lumps of lonely gray matter,' which now turn out to be complex, inter-looped, Wi-Fi octopi, with invisible tentacles slithering in all directions, at every moment, constantly picking up messages we are not aware of, and prompting reactions...."[20]

Thus, **the key to creating success in any endeavor you pursue in life, is to understand and harmonize all four areas of your brain--**to point them in one direction instead of four directions. In other words, you must **harmonize** all four powers to create and harness your "superpower force" to achieve what you want to accomplish. If you are now confused, then continue reading.

The TSF-24 will show you exactly how, what, when, and why wealth and success are yours. The formula is now available to YOU--to **CREATE, ALLOW, INVITE,** and **ATTRACT** everything you want in life for yourself and family!

You are now taking a journey that will profoundly change your life.

Again, in this book I will offer you a no-nonsense, practical, scientific way, which people who are both physically and/or

spiritually wealthy--indeed, all successful people, practice knowingly or unknowingly to create anything they want. The "Secret" is, they all possess and own their four powers of intelligence by practicing the **TSF-24**! The current US President, unknowingly practice this formula by harmonizing all four areas of his brain to deliver success to himself.

Now, **your desires, needs, intents, and interests, will be brought to you--at will.**

The **TSF-24** is like adding $2 + 2 = 4$ -- **as long as you follow the formula, and do not change anything, the results will be guaranteed.** You will own all four powers of your intelligence by operating your whole brain harmoniously.

The order or sequence of how the formula is applied must be adhered to or else you will NOT get the results of success.

Everything you are about to learn is based on proven psychological and neuroscience studies, wisdom that has been passed down for thousands of years, and timeless principles for success.

Does this formula really work? YES, if it work for Barack Obama, then it will work for you. Ask the most successful people you know how they achieved their success. If you don't know any, then try the formula and **see the results yourself.**

I respect your intelligence more than just to tell you that the formula works, and then expect you to believe me. **The only proof that this formula works is the results you will experience if you apply it.** Nothing will be as convincing as seeing your own results.

If you are like me, you have probably purchased hundreds or even thousands of dollars worth of self-help books, audio programs, and seminars, to improve your performance and change your life. After completing them, you were highly motivated and even made changes, only to find that **within a few days or a few weeks you were right back to where you were before!**

Why is that? It is because **permanent and lasting changes depend on all those four areas: the Heart, Mind, Spirit (Strenght), and Body(Soul) (Superconscious, Conscious, Subconscious, and Nonconscious)**--of all **four intelligences: Social, Intellectual, Physiological, and Emotional--being balanced and harmonized**. A solution aimed at less than all four areas can result in effects that are limited in scope and duration.

Dr. Robert Anthony said that "...the solutions are often like putting frosting on a spoiled cake. No matter how good the frosting looks, we have to deal with what's underneath the frosting. The frosting is *good associations*, positive and right thinking or intelligence, and the cake is our unworkable beliefs *or paradigms* that keep us from producing positive and right results."[21]

Millions of people, who for the past thousands of years, have used part or all of this formula by trial and error, or even by accident, have created success for themselves and their families.

For example, numerous great thinkers or minds such as James Allen, author of <u>As A Man Thinketh</u>,[22] Wallace Wattles for <u>The Science of Getting Rich</u>,[23] Napoleon Hill for the <u>Think and Grow Rich</u> series have covered some of the concepts of the **TSF**. Their writings have changed the business world and created millionaires and successful people, generation after generation.

Imagine people--implementing <u>part</u> of the **TSF** and still creating success for themselves!

Now, it is ALL here in the *TSF-24 MINDSuccess™ and BODYSuccess System™* **in which this book is part and an easy to follow, step-by-step formula!** The **TSF-24** will give you understanding how your brain works.

It is about taking your ideas and dreams and turning them into reality using the TSF-24; understanding how the four areas of your brain work and understanding their operations at will.

Yes, **you possess "four sub-brains"--or four intelligent capacities or DNAs**. Scientists are now discovering that your brain has four areas that affect everything you do. This is where your intelligences to understand, reside.

If you are looking for an inspirational book with light doses of positive thinking and laced with colorful case histories that take up valuable time and space, this is not the book and program for you. However, **if you are looking for a no-nonsense, proven methodology, implemented by successful people that goes beyond positive thinking, then this book will be of great value to you**[24].

You have in your hands information to understand how to create your success that will enable you to go beyond positive thinking *to produce the results you desire.* This understanding has been used by successful, rich, and wealthy people who have lived.

Just to name a few other modern day people who are using or have used the formula to create their wealth and success are: William Gates (USA), Warren Buffet (USA), Carlos Slim Helu (Mexico), Ingvar Kampprad (Sweden), Lakshmi Mittal (United Kingdom), Paul Allen (USA), Bernard Arnualt (France), Prince Alwaleed Bin Talal Alsaud (Saudi Arabia), Kenneth Thompson (Canada), Li Ka-shing (Hong Kong), Roman Abramovich (United Kingdom), Michael Dell (USA), Karl Albrecht (Germany), Shedon Adelson (USA), Liliane Bettencourt (France). Lawrence Ellison (USA), Christy Walton (USA), Jim Walton (USA), S Ronson Walton (USA), Helen Walton (USA), Theo Albrecht (Germany), Amancio Ortega (Spain), Steven Ballmer (USA), Azim Premji (India), and Oprah Winfrey (USA).

Notice, I used the word "wealth" instead of "riches." There is a difference between the two concepts.

The 2006 issue of *Forbes* magazine listed a record number of 793 billionaires worth a combined $2.6 trillion, up 18% since March 2005, and their average net worth being $3.3 billion. **Please note! Some of them are** *wealthy,* **and others are** *rich.*

This is the difference. When you become *rich,* money owns you and is the sole purpose of your existence. Money rebels from you. You continued to go after it to keep it. *You have used some part of the TSF to achieve your success.* Your happiness is defined by external means to satisfy your inner being; money cannot bring that satisfaction to you. More than likely, your riches will disappear with you when you pass away or even earlier than that; it is unlikely it will last much beyond your children.

If your target is to become *wealthy*, then money is a protection to you and your family. Money loves you. Money is attracted to you. Money is a servant to you. Money is not your life and purpose of your existence. You will leave a legacy for your children and the world to follow. Your wealth will transfer to others who will keep your legacy alive, generation after generation.

The **TSF-24** is practiced by those who are *wealthy* like William Gates, Oprah Winfrey, and Warren Buffet; three perfect examples of the wealthiest people in the world. So, if you want to be *wealthy*, and be successful in any pursuit of life, follow the **TSF-24.** The universal **TSF-24** can be applied to any pursuit of life, not just money. **SUCCESS is finding contentment and happiness in whatever you pursue in life, not just money!**

This endeavor will require a commitment on your part--but in the end; it will be worth every minute you have invested in understanding how your mind works.

CHAPTER 2

WHY YOU ARE NOT SUCCESSFUL, WEALTHY OR HEALTHY?

Ok, name something you want. It can be a weight-loss goal, a money goal, a sales quota, a new house, a relationship…, etc. It is entirely up to you.

Now let me ask you a blunt question. **Why don't you have it yet?**

Why don't you have the thinner body, or more money, or whatever it is you said you wanted?

Well? Now let me tell you something shocking. The fault is not with the economy, your parents, your spouse, your neighbors, your mayor, the president or anyone or anything outside of you.

There is only one answer to my question of, "Why don't you have it yet?"

I'll tell you what it is in a minute. Have you ever wondered why so many people have so much trouble getting what they truly want?

Have you considered that there could be an easier way through life? Have you ever felt that life was just too much of a struggle?

Most of us have, at one time or another, just felt that life was a "royal" pain. But the liberating truth is this--life does not have to be that way. What is the answer to why you have not achieved your goals yet?

It is in your own mind and body. No, it is not in your thoughts or not in your conscious mind (or intellectual intelligence). You probably already know of highly intelligent people who are homeless or unsuccessful--so, success is more than just having a high IQ.

The roadblock is deeper. **It is in your whole brain. It lies within all four areas of your brain--Right, Left, Stem, and Mid-brain or Spirit, Mind, Soul, and Heart or your DNA. But more specifically, what is called your Tertiary and Inferior Temperament or Sub-Brain is the**

main culprit! That's your pessimistic self! Identify those two in your brain and understand it with the other two.

Put in another way, all four areas of intelligence associated with each area of your brain must be understood and balanced.

In short, if there is something you are trying to achieve (you name it), and you are not achieving it--chances are the figurative "Heart" (or subconscious or emotional intelligence) part of your brain holds some contradictory intentions for you and is not harmonized with other areas of your brain. Said another way--you want something and it does not.

If you are a typical person, you are constantly giving yourself contradictory instructions, like "I want to lose weight," "I want that delicious pie," or "I am going to be successful in my job," and "I am not smart enough to be successful because my family said so."

Those statements are going different directions. After years' of such frustrating and contradictory messages, your subconscious (Mid Brain) gives up and starts to disregard what you consciously (Left Brain) want.

In other words, you cancelled out your own request. You said, "I want money," but right after that you said (or thought), "I don't deserve it," or "Money never comes to me," or *some similar limiting belief.* As a result, you usually did not get what you wanted! But I have good news for you!

All that is about to end. You can change the expression of your genes or DNA to turn on successful and turn off unsuccessful ones (epigenetic)! You are about to learn how your understanding <u>of your sub-brains and intelligence</u> --allows, creates, invites, and attracts whatever you desire.

Now you will be able to understand your subconscious mind (Mid Brain or figurative Heart), your conscious (Left Brain) mind, superconscious (Strenght or Spirit), and nonconscious mind (Soul or Body)--or saying it another way, now you can understand <u>your emotional intelligence</u> along with your <u>intellectual, physical,</u> and <u>social intelligence.</u>

You are about to understand how your mind works! By understanding how all four areas of your brain work together, you will be able to manage all four of your sub-brains..

Again, understanding how your WHOLE brain works will help you to get whatever you desire, need, have interest in, or intend. But in order for you to accomplish that, you need to know your four sub-brains that makes up your whole brain. Then after that decide if you are more *right-, left-, (brain), brainstem-, or midbrain*-inclined. This is one of the reasons why so many people cannot achieve what they are pursuing in their lives after reading and studying materials, because they are not understanding the information or the information does not related to their brain preference. **They are using the wrong side of their brain to decipher the information or the information doesn't relate to their brain preference.!!**

The **TSF-24** can be adapted to fit you personally, and whether you are dominant in any of these four parts, is the first level of customizing your formula. In fact it is made it easy for you. In the Temperaments, Interactions Styles and Personality Chapter, you will discover your specific mind set or the order how your brain works.

Once when you determine your brain dominance and the order of how your mind works, you now have a beginning place to begin rewiring or reinventing yourself to the person you want to become. The excuse that "old dogs cannot learn new tricks" is a lie!

Know how each part of your brain works, and then you are on your way to control and managing it. You have already discovered the order how your mind work from the Survey at the beginning of the book. That is your personal formula. Remember and memorize that formula or sequence because that is "how" you mind works and order of "how" your DNA sequence works.

As you read the next Chapter, understand how each of your sub-brain works.

CHAPTER 3

THE FOUR BRAINS

"The human brain presents the ultimate riddle: how can a mass of tissue with the consistency of raw egg be responsible for your 'mind,' your thoughts, your personality, your memories and feelings, and even your actual consciousness?" —*Professor Susan A. Greenfield, The Human Mind Explained.*

"The brain is the most difficult part of the body to study," observes *E. Fuller Torrey, a psychiatrist at the U.S. National Institute of Mental Health. "We carry it around in this box on our shoulders that's very inconvenient for research."*

It's the key to your success, wealth and health. YOUR brain regulates how your body operates. It enables you to learn new concepts, even new languages, and it stores and recalls the memories of your lifetime. Yet, neurobiologist James Bower admits: "We really don't know what kind of machine the brain is." Neuroscientist Richard F. Thompson agrees: "There is far more to be learned than we know now." So great is the interest in unraveling the brain's mysteries that the U.S. Congress declared the '90's to be the Decade of the Brain.[25]

Hold on to your brains as you will discover its marvelous and fascinating functions. Carry this book around and read it over and over again and again until you understand how your brain works. IT'S THE KEY TO YOUR GREATNESS AND SUCCESS!

A GLIMPSE INSIDE YOUR HEAD

"Your body, mind, internal and external environment is the manifestation of what is inside your head. You are what you are as a result of what's in your head."[26]

You are born with either a male or female brain. Scientific researched has confirmed this. Medical Doctor Louann Brizendine in her book titled "Female Brain" make the above case.

The female brain compare to the male brain has a larger CORPUS CALLOSUM which facilitates the communication between the

RIGHT and LEFT hemisphere. This function distinguished the female from the male brain[27]. Female brains first, always process any information or data through her intuition, follow by analyzing it for logic .

The male brain compare to the female has a larger hypothalmus in the Mid brain and Stem which facilitates communications between those two sub-brains[28]. This distinguished the male from the female that first, always think through emotionally or non-emotional based on knowledge acquired through learning, observation, and experience.

The male brain complement the female brain and vice versa. The strength of female brain is the weakness of the male brain. The strength of the male brain is the weakness of the female brain. Females ALWAYS think through the MIND (Right/Left), follow by the BODY(Stem/Mid). Men ALWAYS think through the BODY (Stem/Mid)follow by the MIND (Left/Right).

Any confusion or other expressions of who you became are your choice with the help of epigenetic which is influence by diet, environment and lifestyle. There are major differences in both genders as noted above. Our discussion here is about the brain in general of both sexes.[29]

Let's take a quick tour or looked in to the four brains inside your head, and understand how they are related to each other. It's their total cooperation amongst each other that creates the success formula for your success, wealth and health. The four sub-brains are – 1. *Brainstem and cerebellum, 2. Midbrain, 3. Right and 4. Left (Neocortex or Cerebrum).*

These four Sub-Brains controls and managed every activity in the DNA before they manifest itself or become visible at about three weeks of gestation. By week four, major regions of the human brain can be recognized in primitive form, including the forebrain (Right and Left), midbrain, and hindbrain (Stem).[30]

Who you become is determined by the order "how" these four sub-brains arranged itself in your genes as a respond to the diet, environment and lifestyle of your mother in your prenatal existence. There are only 24 combinations and this is the alphabet of life – L, R, S, M which parallel the DNA.

As I mentioned earlier, your DNA activities are controlled and managed by your four sub-brains which corresponds to the four nucleotides that makes up the DNA.

The nucleotide with amino acids creates protein molecules. Proteins come in a wide range of shapes and sizes, and play a wide range of roles in the life of a cell. Some proteins are strong and rigid, and form the building blocks for muscles, tendons, and fingernails. Other protein or enzymes catalyze a large number of chemical reactions such as digestions of food or the synthesis of hormones. Other carries oxygen in the blood, while still others form the protein spools around which the DNA wraps in a chromosome.[31]

The Table below shows how the four nucleotides in the DNA parallel to each area of the four sub-brains that controls and managed it.[32]

1st Base	2nd Base				3rd Base
	G Right	**C** Left	**A** Stem	**T** Mid	
G Right	Gly Gly Gly Gly	Ala Ala Ala Ala	Asp Asp Glu Glu	Val Val Val Val	G-Right C-Left A-Stem T- Mid
C Left	Arg Arg Arg Arg	Pro Pro Pro Pro	His His His His	Leu Leu Leu Leu	G-Right C-Left A-Stem T- Mid
A Stem	Ser Ser Arg Arg	Thr Thr Thr Thr	Asn Asn Lys Lys	Met Ile Ile Ile	G-Right C-Left A-Stem T - Mid
T Mid	Cys Cys STOP Trp	Ser Ser Ser Ser	Tyr Tyr STOP STOP	Phe Phe Leu Lue	G-Right C-Left A-Stem T - Mid

The 24 series or sequence combinations of nucleotides (or bases) in the DNA prescribes or dictates for specific amino acid in the protein chain or gives a stop transcribing signal. This sequence determines your dominant temperament, blood type, body type and all characteristic which you will learn later in the book. The bases are always read fro left to right.) The chain usually starts with **AUG** (Stem, Mid, and Right data) or Methionine (Met). Abbreviations used: <u>**A**, adenine; **G**, guanine; **C**,</u>

<u>Cytosine</u>; **T, thymine** (or U, uracil in RNA). **Ala,** alanine; **Arg,** arginine; **Asn,** asparagine; **Asp,** aspartic acid; **Cys,** cysteine; **Gln,** glutamine; **Glu,** glutamic acid; **Gly,** glycine; **His,** histidine; **Ile,** isoleucine; **Leu,** leucine; **Lys,** lysine; **Met,** methionine; **Phe,** phenylalanine; **Pro,** proline; **Ser,** serine; **Thr,** threonine; **Trp,** tryptophan; **Tyr,** tyrosine; **Val,** valine.[33] There are actually 24 main Amino Acids, not 20 as currently understood.

Biology, Molecular Biology or a Genetic teacher will be able to explain you the above information and Table. For our discussion in this book, the four sub-brains controls and managed the activities of each corresponding nucleotide of the DNA and its processes. The sequence of which protein to be created first, second and so forth is ALL governed by the sub-brain that will protect the fetus or embryo during its prenatal existence. These dominant cells or proteins are dictated by the sub-brain that will be dominant.

The information below about each part of the brain below was from the work of Dr. Joe Dispenza[34] and Dr. P. MacLean[35]. The graphics were courtesy of **EnchantedLearning.com.**

1. The Brainstem and Cerebellum:[36] or the Nonconscious Mind.

The first brain of the four sub-brains in your head to develop is the Brainstem and cerebellum. It's the seat of your nonconscious mind, soul/body, physiological, instinctual, practical, and kines-thetic intelligence. It primarily *supports the basic life functions, in-cluding the maintenance and control to the heart rate and breathing.* It also regulates our various levels of wakefulness and sleep. Both *wakefulness* and levels of *alertness* are con-trolled by the brainstem to a greater extent than by the higher centers of the neocortex (Left and Right).

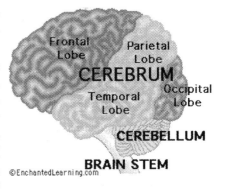

The *cerebellum or little brain* is also part of our first brain. Its wrinkles and folds give it a distinct appearance. Relative large compare to other brain structures, it is a three-lobed structure attached to the brainstem at the very back of the skull, underneath the hindmost area of the neocortex.

Recent functions brain scans reveal that the cerebellum is the brain's most active area. Scientist believes that the cerebellum is responsible for *balance, coordinating movement; the cerebellum performs both a motor (excitatory) function as well as braking (inhibitory) function.*

Certain types of simple actions and responses are learned, coordinated, memorized, and stored in the cerebellum. After a skill is learned and memorized – wired to the cerebellum – our body can perform the action automatically with little conscious thought. Hardwired attitudes, emotional reactions, repeated actions, habits, conditioned behaviors, unconscious or nonconscious reflexes, and skill that we mastered are all connected to and memorized in the cerebellum.[37]

2. The Midbrain or the Subconscious Mind:

The second sub-brain to develop is the Midbrain. It's your subconscious mind, figurative heart, and emotional intelligences area. It locates directly in the middle of the brain. One of the many terms for this area is the limbic system. Situated just above the brainstem, the midbrain in an adult is about the size of an apricot.

Although the midbrain occupies one-fifth of the volume of the brain, its influence on the behaviors is extensive, which is why it is also known as the *emotional brain.* It is also called the *chemical brain* because it is responsible for regulating many internal states.

It is our midbrain that performs all those marvels that we usually take for granted, *automatically maintaining and controlling body temperature, blood sugar levels, blood pressure, digestion, hormone levels and innumerable other process. The midbrain also adjusts and maintains our internal state to compensate for changes in our external world.*

The midbrain is primary composed of the **thalamus, hypothalamus, pituitary, pineal gland, hippocampus, amygdala, and basal ganglia.**

1. Thalamus (Part of the id):

The thalamus is the meeting point for almost all nerves that connect one part of the brain to another part of the brain, the body to the brain, and the brain to the body. The thalamus name is derived from the Greek word meaning "inner chamber" is the oldest and largest part of the midbrain. A collection of nerve cell nuclei that meet at the central junction point, it is made up of two distinct centers, one on each side of the midbrain.

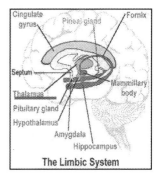

Think of the thalamus as a switchboard or air traffic control tower that can connect any part of the brain and the body. There is not one signal from the environment that does not pass through the thalamus. The sensory organs (ears, eyes, skin, tongue, and nose) send messages to the thalamus, which relays them to their final destination in the neocortex or the conscious brain (left brain).

At the same time, the thalamus can send signals to other areas of the brain so as to alert or inhibit different brain systems. In this way, the thalamus processes sensory information from the external world, identifies and sorts the input into the appropriate category, and transmits this data to the many conscious centers in the cerebral cortex.

2. Hypothalamus (Part of Ego or Conscience):

This area of the midbrain is a chemical factory that *regulates your body's internal environment and balances your systems with the external world*. It generates the chemical messengers for the entire body. The oldest part of the, limbic system, it can affect any organ or tissue in the body.

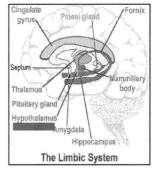

Unlike the **thalamus, which monitors external stimuli**, the main job of the **hypothalamus is to make chemicals call neuropeptides** that keep the internal affairs of the body in balance with references to the external world. It regulates many body functions necessary for survival through the process of homeostasis, the automatic self-righting mechanism that, like a thermostat regulates and maintains the body's chemical balance and internal order. It controls and manages bodily functions such as appetite, thirst, sleep, wakefulness, blood sugar levels, body temperature, heart rate, blood pressure, chemical balance, hormonal balance, sex drive, immune system reactions, and metabolism. It also plays the most important role in your experience of emotions. <u>This is the part of the brain that manufactures the chemicals that allow you to feel the way you were thinking or how you were reacting.</u>

3. Pituitary gland (Part of id):

The pituitary gland secrets chemicals that activates your body's *hormones*. It is often called the master gland, because it governs and controls many vital processes in the body. This pear-shaped gland which hangs off the hypothalamus like a fruit helps in manufacturing most of the hormonal signals created by the hypothalamus to communicate with the body's major glands. The hypothalamus sends both chemical and

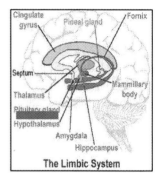

The Limbic System

electrical signals to the pituitary so that it can make certain chemicals that turn on various chemical/hormonal states.

4. Pineal gland (Part of id):

The pineal gland, a tiny, pine cone-shaped structure, sits in the back of the midbrain, above the cerebellum. <u>It chemically regulates our cycles of sleep and wakefulness.</u> **It's the brains internal clock.** Two neurotransmitters are produced in the highest quantities in the human body by the pineal – *serotonin* (prepares the brain to be awake during the hours of daylight) and *melatonin* (prepares the body to

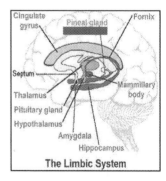

The Limbic System

experience restorative sleep during the hours of darkness and plays a role in causing the brain to dream.)

5. Hippocampus (Part of Super-Ego)

The hippocampus <u>makes long-term memories</u>. We learn from new experiences and form memories thanks to this area of the midbrain. It sort of a clearing house for memory, it classifies incoming information as having either short-term or long-term importance, and files it accordingly. Memories that move in to short term storage pertain to information that we need immediately but can then forget. Shopping

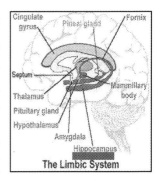

lists, phone numbers that we will call only once, and directions that we will probably never need again are good examples of information that is stored in short-term memory.

In long term memory, the hippocampus stores information that we may need to access repetitively or at will in the future. It stores long-term memories that are involved mostly with our experiences, based on the various types of information our five senses provide.

Whenever we have a new experience, the hippocampus, through the combination of all our senses (seeing, smelling, tasting, feeling, and hearing) allows us to create a new memory. By connecting all this incoming sensory information, the hippocampus will associate a person with a thing, a place with time, a person with an event, and so on. Also, one primary function of the hippocampus is closely related to our search for novelty. This is the part of the brain that is responsible for making the unknown, known.

6. Amygdala (Part of Super-Ego):

The Amygdala is responsible for *alerting the body in survival situations*. It also stores the four highly charged emotions: <u>aggression, joy, sadness and fear</u>. It helps to attached different emotional charges to our long-term memories.

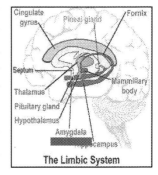

When life threatening situation exist, the amygdale gives a rapid, action-oriented assessment of the external environment. It activates the body to respond even before you are consciously aware of the danger, so we call this a precognitive response.

For example, imagine that you are riding your bicycle in the park whiles listening to your MP3 player, mesmerized by a melody. In an instant, a young child darts out of the bushes and begins to cross your path, right in front of the bike. You amygdala receives vital information that bypasses your neocortex (left and right brain), causing you to hit your rakes even before you are conscious of you actions. This enhanced precognitive reaction may make the different between life and death.

In an intriguing new study, scientist at the University of Wales worked with a blind patient who seems to posses a sixth sense that allows him to recognize sad, angry or happy faces. The researchers concluded that emotions displayed on a human face are registered not in the visual cortex but in the right side amygdala, which sits deep within the brain's temporal lobe. Having memory stored in this area of the brain, which triggers instantaneous responses, could explain much about the sensitivity of some individuals.

7. Basal ganglia (Part of Ego or Conscience):

The basal ganglia <u>integrate thoughts and feelings with physical actions</u>. They are intricate bundles of neurological networks that are interconnected with the neocortex; they are situated in each hemisphere of the midbrain, directly under the neocortex and above the midbrain's deeper structure.

For example, recall a time when you were learning a skill that involved muscle movements, such as riding a bike. In the beginning, you had to think consciously about what you were doing. Every time you practiced, you reinforce neural circuits in your brain that relayed commands to your body relating to balance, coordination, and so on. After much repetition, these neural networks became hardwired and your movements in pedaling the bike and keeping your balance became automatic.

At that point, you basal ganglia, along with your cerebellum took over the coordination of automatic movements. As you rode, the basal ganglia received sensory information from your environment via neocortices, plus commands from your neocortex to move your muscles and orchestrate your actions. Your basal ganglia integrated your thoughts and feelings with your physical actions, smooth out your fine motor movements, and suppressed your body from making random, involuntary movements. In addition to that role, the basal ganglia allows us to control our impulses, to set our idle speed for anxiety and to contribute to our feelings of pleasures and ecstasy.[38]

3. Neocortex Or Cerebral Cortex (Left and Right Brain).

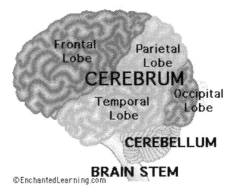

The next sub-brain is the Neocortex (other scholars believed that there are only 3 sub-brain – brainstem midbrain and neocortex or cerebral cortex.) which *is the seat of our consciousness or awareness and of our creativity as a species.* It is our thinking, reasoning brain that allows us to learn and remember everything that we experience from our external world, and then modify our actions to do something better, or different, or to repeat an action the next time, it had a positive result. The Neocortex is composed of two hemispheres – **the Right and Left** which is the other two sub-brain of the four sub-brain of the brain. Nobel Prize winner, Roger Sperry, initiated the study of both hemispheres. These two hemispheres are connected by a "fiber optic "bridge comprise of hundred of millions of neuron called *corpus callosum.* These twin neocortices literally encapsulate the *midbrain and the brainstem.* Each hemisphere is responsible for controlling the opposite side of the body.

The *corpus callosum* is the largest fibrous pathway of neurons in the entire body, totaling approximately 300 millions nerve fibers. Scientist postulate that the *corpus callosum* existed so the two hemispheres (left and right) could communicate with each other through this bridge. Nerve impulses constantly travel back and forth across the *corpus callosium,* giving our brain specialized ability to observe the world from *two different points of view.*

The **Left and Right hemispheres** are further subdivided in to four separate regions known as *lobes.* Therefore, there are two frontal lobes, two parietal lobes, two temporal lobes, and two occipital lobes. Each of these areas process different *sensory information, motor abilities, and mental functions and is assigned to perform different tasks.*[39]

1. The frontal Lobes:

The frontal lobe is the resting place of conscious awareness or consciousness. It is where self-awareness is born. *It allows you to take your emotions and define them in to meanings.* The prefrontal cortex is the laboratory where you paste together thoughts with associations to drive meaning from what you are learning. It gives you the privilege to gain meaning from the external world.

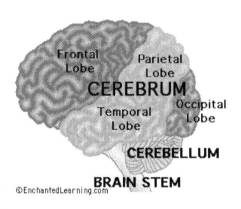

Free will is major keyword we use to describe the frontal lobe. The seat of your free will and self determination, the frontal lobes allows you to choose your every thought and action and in so doing, control your destiny. When this lobe is active, you focus on your desires, create ideas, make conscious decisions, assemble plans, carry out an intentional course of action, and regulate your behavior. The frontal lobes bestowed on human a focused, intentional, creative, willful, decisive, purposeful mind, if we will only put it to use.

The frontal lobes are regionally divided in to subsections that are responsible for numerous related functions. The back of the frontal lobes is the home to the *motor cortex* which exists as a neighboring slice of cortical tissue right in the front of the *sensory cortex.* The motor cortex and sensory cortex are at the dividing line between the *parietal lobe and frontal lobe.*

The *motor cortex* activates all of the voluntary muscles in the body and participates in all your voluntary movement and actions. You activate the motor cortex when you need to take determined actions and control purposeful movements.

The *prefrontal cortex* is a cortical region related to the crowning achievement of your abilities in the areas of consciousness and awareness. This is the brain area that is most active during our important period of consciousness, deliberate concentration. It is this compartment that your true uniqueness as human being exists. This area allows you to supersede the stimulus-response, action-reaction, cause-effect patterns you unconsciously live by day by day.[40]

2. Parietal Lobes:

The *parietal lobes* are located just above each ear and they extend to the top center of the head, reaching the midline of the brain. *It process what you feel with your hands and with your bodies, also called tactile and somatosensory perceptions.* Somatosensory by definition is the information you receive from the body (soma) that you feel (sensory) in the brain. Features such as pressure, temperature, vibration, pain, pleasure, light touch, two-point discrimination, and even the awareness of where your body parts are located without looking at them are all integrated in the somatosensory cortex of the parietal lobes.

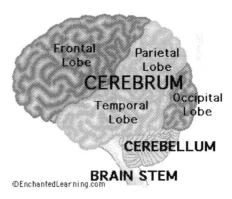

The *parietal lobes* process information from the body received by your peripheral nerves, *mainly from your external environment* and to a lesser degree from your internal environment. Peripheral nerves are those long nerves that act like communication wires, transmitting information from the brain to the body and from the body to the brain.

The entire map of how the body feels can be charted in the sensory cortex of the brain, specifically in the somatosensory areas located in the parietal lobes.[41]

3. The Temporal Lobes:

The temporal lobes are just under the surface of and slightly above each ear. *They are responsible for auditory perception – that is, how you process what you hear.* The auditory lobes are primarily positioned in this quadrant to process all types of sounds. Within these lobes there seem to be thousands of colonies of neurons related to specific aspects

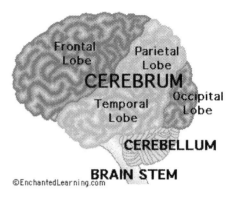

of how we process sounds. Because what we hear is so intricately tied to language, we will define language as a series of specific sounds that a produced for intentional communication, and then comprehensively understood. In other words, what arrives at your ears is a stream of continuous sounds carrying an intention or meaning that is called language.

The temporal lobes are intricately involved in storage of some types of memory and facilitate the making of long term memories. As we know, this takes place through the hippocampus. When there is damage to both the temporal lobes and the hippocampus, many people can not form new memories. Scientist who experiment on the temporal lobes using low voltage electrical stimuli have reported that their subjects experience immediate sensation of dejavu (an uncanny sense f familiarity and memory). Jamais vu (a feeling that a familiar person or place if unfamiliar), heighten spontaneous emotions, and/ or strange reveries or insights.

The temporal lobes also have a visual association center that links what we use to our emotions and memories. It is the store house of many of our visual emotional memories. Once we see something in the external work, our brain uses this association area to process what we see with what we remember and how we feel emotionally. In other words, the temporal lobes process visual symbols with meaning feelings. Most of the millions of learned associations that you have experienced in you lifetime are stored in the temporal lobes' association cortex, to be activated as needed.

The temporal lobes are responsible for language, hearing, (processing sounds), conceptual thinking, and associative memories. The temporal lobes associate most of what we have learned and experience via our senses through out our life to people, places, things, time, and past events in the form of memories. We can associate what we hear, see, feel, taste, and smell, and it is the temporal lobe that facilitates this skill.[42]

4. The Occipital Lobes:

The *occipital lobes* are the vision centers. The *visual cortex,* as it is sometimes described, has six distinct regions that process data from the outside world in order for us to see coherently. This complexity stands to reason, because vision is the sense that human beings rely on the most in order to function in the world. Six distinct layers are 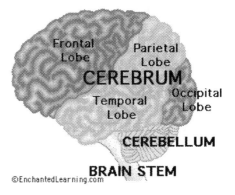 allocated to interpret visual qualities like *light, movement, form, shape, depth, and color.*

The *primary visual* cortex (V1) encounters visual information that your eyes see and consciously process. V1 is organized in such a way that nerve cells are divided up to process different parts of a whole picture. Therefore, when only one small area of the V1 is damaged, we have a visual blind spot, because the nonfunctioning neurons cannot process their part of the picture. When this area is completely damaged, normal sight as we know it is lost. Amazingly, when scientist began studying individuals who were blind in the V1 area, *these subjects not only perceived movement, but could also perceive the shape of the object.*

Distinct geographical locations within the visual cortex process other aspects of sight. Some clusters of neurons perceive only color. Generalization forms and edges are perceived in one area, while specific shapes and patterns (such as the shape of the hand) are recognized in another neural region. Still other nerve cells respond to depth perception, angles, and dimension.

As visual information passes from the eye to the *occipital lobe*, it is processed in a cascade of nerve reactions from the back of the brain to the front, through the six different regions. This why is blind sighted person could still interpret reality through his visual field. The information that made it to his primary cortex was passed to the adjacent areas, which were activated for further processing. Thus while he could not consciously see an object, he could perceive movement, shape, the direction from where the object came, and other aspects of vision.[43]

In summary, the **left and right hemisphere** is composed of; the *frontal lobes* which are *responsible for intentional action as well as focusing our attention.* They coordinate nearly all the functions in the rest of your brain (the motor cortex and language center are part of the frontal lobe).

The *parietal lobes* deals with sensations related to touch and feelings (sensory perception), visual-spatial tasks, and body orientation, and they also coordinate language functions.

The *temporal lobes* process sounds, perception, learning, language, and memory, and they are the centers that process smell. This lobe also includes a region that facilitates our ability to which thoughts to express.

The *occipital lobes* mange visual information and are often called visual cortex. The above is the most researched area of the brain.

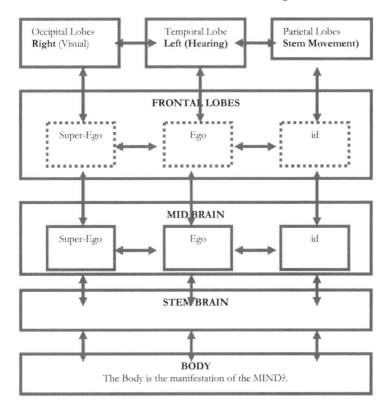

The other two sub-brain; **stem** and **mid** are finally getting some attention in the research community. Although, numerous research data is available in the scientific community about all four sub-brains, *nothing directly links or specifically connects all the dots to four sub-brains and a whole brain approach.*

The above diagram shows a simple or whole brain approach relation between the four sub-brains – Right (Occipital Lobes), Left (Temporal Lobe), Stem (Parietal Lobe), Frontal Lobe (mirrors the Mid Brain), Mid Brain, Stem Brain and Body.

You can see that your BODY is the manifestation of your MIND. Your MIND is the manifestation of your BODY. Your INTERNAL ENVIRONMENT is the manifestation of the MIND and BODY. Your EXTERNAL ENVIRONMENT is the manifestation of your BODY and MIND. ALL four approaches are needed to create success in whatever you are pursuing.

The world population speaks four universal language of the brain. These languages are control and manages by the four sub-brain discussed above. No matter what ethnic, nationality and race you were born to, other humans understand the specific language you speak. Your temperament, interaction style, personality and Blood Type are determined by these four sub-brains. Even, your diet or food that is good for you! These four sub-brains creates the 24 Universal Personalities of the world.

When I discussed these four sub-brains as **social** brain, **intellectual** brain, **bodily-kinesthetic or physiological** brain and **emotional** brain throughout the book, I am referring to the ***collective neural activities*** (For example, the Occipital Lobe for the Right Brain or the Social Brain or Temporal Lobe for the Left Brain or intellectual brain,) ***of that region of the brain as its main trigger point or initiator of those specific activities.*** For example, the **social brain** is control and manages by *right hemisphere of the brain* (frontal, parietal, occipital and temporal lobes);

"...those extensive neural modules that orchestrate our activities as we relate to other people – consist of circuitry that extends far and wide...an early proposal identified structure in the prefrontal area (parietal areas).[44]

So each sub-brain is fluent in its own language with its own *collective neural activities* that supports it. For example, the **right and left** brain are supported by the various lobes –*frontal, parietal, temporal, and occipital*; the **mid** brain is supported by *thalamus, hypothalamus, pituitary gland, pineal gland, hippocampus, and amygdala*; and **stem** brain is supported by *the cerebellum and stem*. These four sub-brains and their collective neural activities determine how you intend, think, behave and desire for things.

BRAIN DIFFERENCES[45]

*Okay, a*re you a *Right-, Left-, Mid-,* or *Stem*-brain dominant thinker? Here is one way to identify *Right*-Brain-inclined from the *Left*-brain-inclined individuals and so forth. The following article below was written by Dr. John Robert Dew[46] and I have added mid and stem brain information into it. The information can be applied to any work environment.

One of the best ways to liven up a room of quality professionals is to press someone for a definition of "*quality.*" The room will quickly ignite into an inferno of disputes about it.

"It's conformance to established requirements (*stem brain*)," one will argue.

"No, its understanding variation in systems (*left brain*)," another will counter.

"You're all wrong," someone will shout. "It's meeting the customer's expectations! (*right brain*)"

"*No, it doing what feels right for the customers and us (mid).*"

The concept of quality is envisioned in different ways by different people because people process information and conceptualizes situations in a variety of ways. Much of this variation in **mental conceptualization or cognition,** and **information processing** results from the relative dominance of one of the four sub-brains in your whole brain.

THE BRAIN-DOMINANCE THEORY

Roger Sperry, a Nobel Prize winner, initiated the study of the relationship between the brain's *right* and *left* hemispheres. Sperry found that the *left* **half of the brain** tends to function by processing information in an analytical, rational, logical, sequential way. The *right* **half of the brain** tends to function by recognizing relationships, integrating and synthesizing information, and arriving at intuitive insights.

In other words, the *left* **side** of your brain deals with a problem or situation by collecting available data, making analyses, and using a rational thinking process to reach a logical conclusion. The *right* **side** of your brain approaches the same problem or situation by making intuitive leaps to answers based on insights and perceptions. The *left* **brain** tends to break information apart for analysis, while the *right* **brain** tends to put information together to synthesize a whole picture.

Research into the brain's function and individuals' brain dominance was further enhanced by Ned Hermann, the former manager of management education at General Electric's Management Development Institute. Hermann developed a brain-dominance profile instrument to help people assess the manner in which they use their brains. Hermann's research suggests that people in various professions tend to be either *left*-brain-, or *right*-brain oriented.

Herman and Sperry missed the other 2 sub-brains and are understandably why because almost 90 percent of people learned by either visual or auditory or both.

Roughly research shows that 75 percent of people are visual (intuitive), 20 percent are auditory *(thinking), 4 percent kinesthetic (senses), and 1 percent is emotional (feelings)*[47].

Managers, for instance, tend to be *left*-brain dominant, focusing on organizing, structuring, and controlling situations. Social workers and psychologist tend to be *right*-brain dominant, drawing on their ability to relate to emotions to achieve insights about situations. *Workers or line staff tends to be stem brain dominant as they prefer doing or carrying out task assignments. Organization or work energy motivator or de-motivator employees are the mid brain dominant as they dictate the mood of the workplace.*

Quality and Brain Dominance[48]

The "*quality*" field, by its very nature, covers a broad range of concepts, tools, and techniques. Some of these concepts, tools, and techniques are clearly in the *left*-brain arena, such as using statistical tools and organizing plans to ensure the quality of projects and processes. Others are in the *right*-brain arena, such as using relationship diagrams to solve problems; forming teams to analyze systems; and applying intuitive concepts such as zero defects. But implementation of what the left and right brain comes up with lies in the jurisdiction of the *mid* and *stem* brain staff.

With such a broad range of concepts and approaches, it should come as no surprise when quality professionals become engaged in rather spirited disputes over how to achieve "*quality*"--and even over the very meaning of the term.

Left-brain-quality professionals might be exasperated with their *right*-brain colleagues because they seem to lack an appreciation for the careful use of data. *Right-brain-quality* professionals might be irritated with their *left*-brain colleagues for being too rigid in their thinking, or too slow to grasp the causes of problems. The *stem* and *mid brain* professionals might be up set with the left and right for not considering them in their policy or process formulation as they are the ones carrying or implementing their ideas. **Of course, all of these positions are relative to how the individual processes information, and defines quality--and no one position is right or wrong.**

The separation of differences amongst *stem, mid, left*-brain and *right*-brain approaches and permeates every area of life; every relationship and every endeavor.

Figure 1: Comparison of Quality Approaches	
Quality professionals who are left-brain dominant prefer to:	**Quality professionals who are right-brain dominant prefer to:**
Solve problems through the use of data.	Solve problems through the understanding of relationships.
Perform statistical analysis of data.	Use "cause and effect" diagrams.
Develop solutions using logical analyses of facts.	Develop solutions using creativity and brainstorming.
Have work done by individuals who are assigned to study a system using an orderly approach.	Have work done by teams that will raise many questions and work multiple issues.
Define quality as conformance to definable requirements that can be measured.	Define quality-based on a holistic concept, such as total quality.
Establish controls in the early stages of a system that will ensure quality is controlled throughout the system's life-cycle.	View quality as a process for continuous improvement in which controls are only temporary.
Improve quality by studying specific variations within a system.	Improve quality by starting with a holistic strategic-quality plan.

Identify root causes of problems by: elaborately categorizing possible causes and using strict rules for questioning.	Identify root causes of problems by using the "five-whys" method, barrier analysis, and process diagrams.

To illustrate, there are four methods commonly used (whether knowingly or unknowingly) to perform root-cause analysis. One approach employs a pre-established set of questions that forces the investigator into using one of the pre-established root-cause categories. This approach typifies a *left-brain* thinking process that values order and systematic steps in developing a solution to a problem.

On the other hand, *right-brain* thinkers will approach root-cause analysis by first trying the **"four-W" method** (i.e., who, what, when, where) to find a solution. This solution might not fit any reestablished set of root-cause categories, but it works. If the "four-w" method does not work, *right-brain* thinkers will use barrier analysis (*or another tool that provides a visual image of the situation*) to "see" where a barrier existed.

Another is the **"how to"** method from the *stem brain* who will approach root-cause analysis to find a solution. This solution might not fit any pre-established set of root-cause categories, but it works when "how to "questions to implementing the solution is answered.

Last, is the *mid brain* approach of answering any **"why"** questions to solutions. "Why" is it done this way, and not this way...Why?...Why... etc?

Another example can be seen in approaches taken by quality auditors. For *left-brain* thinkers, the audit is often a systematic and detailed hunt for any deviation from procedures or requirements, no matter how minute. In many cases, this is exactly what an organization needs from a quality audit. For *right-brain* thinkers, the quality audit is often regarded as a tool for identifying opportunities for continuous improvement. Minor deviations from procedures are not given much attention. For *stem-brain thinkers*, this process slows down or interrupts the work process of serving customer. For the *mid-brain*, this cold process kills the harmonious and fun working atmosphere by creating mistrust and suspicion between company and customers or even among workers..

The hunt is on for "big game,"--where the organization can make breakthroughs in customer satisfaction or cost reduction, product or services improvement, and even company profits. In many cases, this style of auditing is exactly what an organization needs. **Each style is different, and all can add value in certain circumstances.** Each style has its roots in how the auditor thinks.

On a larger scale, the difference between *left-brain* and *right-brain* thinking can be seen in how a quality program is designed. *Left-brain* thinkers tend to value a "cradle-to grave" quality program. They systematically design a program that comes complete with design control, verification of construction and manufacturing, statistical controls, and an audit program.

Right-brain thinkers often value the input of the employees working in the process. They design a quality program by bringing these employees together to identify existing problems, brainstorming solutions, and implementing corrective actions. *Left-brain* program designers bring great skill in developing carefully controlled processes, while *right-brain* program designers get employees excited about quality and motivated to make improvements. Once again, although the approaches are different, both are important.

*What are always missing from any organization discussion of creating or implementing any project are the **stem** and **midbrain** dominant employees. The **stem brain** dominant employees are the doers or the workers who carriers out the mission (left) and vision (right) of the organization. The **mid brain** brings in the fun and energy that drives a project to success or failure quick or slow. .*

*The **midbrain** dominant employees on the other hand are the emotional charged of the organization, either positively or negatively. They will light fire and bring fun to accomplishing the mission and vision of the organization. They dictate the temperature or the mood of the organization.*

WHOLE-BRAIN THINKING

It is vital to recognize your thinking patterns and be cognizant of these patterns' strengths and weaknesses in dealing with information. If you are *right-brain* dominant, you must recognize the usefulness of *left-brain* thinking and appreciate the need to pause and pay attention to planning and organizing data and systems; recognize the *stem brain* as doers or workers interested in carrying out assignments, the *midbrain* as the motivators or the energy engine of the organization.. If you are *left-brain* dominant, you must allow *right-brain* input into your methodical approach to providing quality; and recognized the importance of the *stem brain* for they are the ones that will implement or carry out your methodology, and *midbrain* as energy booster or drainer to the accomplishment of whatever system or method you put in place. If you are *stem brain* dominant, you must recognize that *left-brains* see details in a problem; *right-brains* see the big picture, and *midbrain* gives emotional energy to implementing the solutions. As a *midbrain*, you must recognize that *stem-brain* employees are the group that will get the job done, the *left-brain* are the thinkers, the *right-brain* are the dreamers or visionary and they are the motivators *(mid brain)*, persuading and involving others.

Quality professionals *(or any other professionals)* who choose to deny the validity of other thinking styles will close themselves off from their colleagues and limit their own professional growth by avoiding different tools and concepts to address differing situations. When people cling to their comfortable thinking processes, they restrict themselves in the manner by which they will be able to define a problem or situation. As it is often said among quality professionals, *"If the only tool you have is a hammer, every problem looks like a nail."*

At the most fundamental level, you must be aware of how you think and process information and appreciate other people's different approaches. Truly creative professionals will find ways to incorporate the talents of all four sub-brains to maximize their personal effectiveness.

Although it is not difficult to determine which hemisphere dominates your thinking, identifying ways to harness the power of the other side can be great, so here are some tips:

1. If you are a *right-brain* thinker, you can benefit from training in logical decision-making. By studying statistical processes, for example, you can envision how statistical tools fit into a broad pattern and work to incorporate these tools in appropriate ways. Take a week out of the month and work with your line staff and get to see how they carry or implement company or organization polices. See who are the emotional leaders and spent time to get to know them.

2. If you are a *left-brain* thinker, you can study team processes and high-quality philosophies to ensure that your approach to addressing quality issues has not become too focused on specific problems --or completely reliant on data. You can plan to involve teams and structure brainstorming into the problem-solving process. Take a week out of you work schedule every month to work with your line staff and experience how they carry your organization or company policies. Find out who the company emotional leaders are and get to know them. Commend them for the work they do!

3. If you are a *stem-brain* thinker, you can benefit from training in logical decision-making. By studying statistical processes, for example, you can envision how statistical tools fit into a broad pattern and work to incorporate these tools in appropriate ways and see how left-brain thinkers think. You can study team processes and high-quality philosophies to see how right-brain thinkers think. Get to know your emotional leaders and find out what makes them tick.

4. If you are a *mid-brain* thinker, you can benefit from training in logical decision-making. By studying statistical processes, for example, you can envision how statistical tools fit into a broad pattern and work to incorporate these tools in appropriate ways and see how left-brain thinkers think. You can study team processes and high-quality philosophies to see how right-brain thinkers think. Commend and praise your fellow workers. You are great at this – motivating others.

By effectively harnessing all four sub-brains of the brain's thinking processes, you can shift from one thinking process to another, as the situation warrants. For example, *right-brain* thinking can be used to develop a quality, high-strategic plan. *Left-brain* thinking can be used to analyze a problem. When the problem has been analyzed, *right-brain* processes can be called on to develop possible solutions. *Left-brain* concepts can help plan how to implement a solution into the work system, while *right-brain* thinking can sell the solution to the organization. *Stem-brain* thinking can be used to have hands on testing the solutions. *Midbrain* thinking is used by having fun or energy while implementing the process or solution.

Quality professionals can become comfortable with using certain tools and having certain viewpoints that fit their mental processing. To become more effective in their daily practices, however, they must learn to move out of their comfort zones. Unfortunately, professional growth has often meant "digging a current rut even deeper" by adding to an area of strength. This can be seen in the *right-brain* quality manager whose professional development for this year is to attend another seminar on team building. Rather, this manager needs to attend a *left*-brain seminar, such as on how to establish an audit plan or *stem-brain* seminar on how to carry out orders or instruction or a *midbrain* seminar on how to enjoy or have fun at your work place. . Similarly, the experienced *left*-brain auditor needs to take a seminar on how to lead focus groups, instead of on auditing, to develop a broader range of skills. Likewise, the *stem-brain* and *mid brain* employees must attend seminars in team building, audit plan and similar programs to get familiar with how the other brain dominant employees think.

The old admonishment *"to know thyself"* certainly applies to knowing how you think. *This is the secret.* Often, we are unaware or uncritical of the thinking processes we routinely use to process information and make decisions. We have developed comfortable patterns of thinking that are reinforced in the neural networks of our brains.

To achieve our full potential, however, we must:

1. Examine our own minds. We must become aware of our thinking processes and how they establish the frame of reference that determines how we view the world.

2. Learn how others think and process information. Think of another person whose approach substantially differs from our own. Talk with that person to learn how he or she solves problems and what tools he or she prefers to use. Chances are good that this person's brain dominance is different from your own; you can both learn a lot from each other if you are willing to accept each other's thinking as valid.

3. Adapt, adapt, adapt or adjust, adjust, adjust, adjust how you think to accommodate new learning. You accomplish this by listening to your colleague's ideas and thoughts.

4. Rewire your mind to accommodate new knowledge for greatness and success.

Unfortunately, instead of learning from someone who is different, we tend to avoid them or deny the validity of their knowledge because of our ego. This process, known as "marginalization," allows people to push those who are *"different"* to the edges of their awareness, where the different thinking and different actions will not disturb their comfort zones.

WHETHER YOU BELIEVE IT OR NOT

Those of you who are *left-brain* thinkers will likely want more evidence of the brain-dominance theory. Those of you who are *right-brain* thinkers will likely intuitively grasp or reject the theory offered here. Those of you who are *stem-brain* thinkers' concern are how is this benefit me now. Those of you who are *midbrain thinkers* will want to know what fun activities will this bring in to my life and why should I believe you?

Regardless of whether you believe the brain-dominance theory, growth comes through self-awareness of your thinking processes and through understanding of how your comfortable thinking patterns influence your views, and your ability to learn and perform.

So, whether you believe the dominance brain theory or not, be open-minded to it. You will see, from the premise of this book, that your success is dependent on how you think; i.e. how your whole brain operates. Researched has shown that you have four specific area of you brain that manage and controls you. This book will help ALL -*right, left, stem and mid*-brain groups to achieve success in whatever you plan to pursue.

> **Our educational system, as well as science in general, tends to neglect the nonverbal form of intellect. What it comes down to is that modern society discriminates against the right hemisphere (*and mid, and stem*). Roger Sperry – 1973.**

THE HARMONIZED BRAIN

As we develop our creative skills or intelligence, we must also develop our ability to <u>suspend</u> the *left* brain and to <u>release</u> the *right*; suspend the *right* brain and release the *left*; or suspend the *right* and release the *mid*-brain, or suspend the *mid*-brain and release the *stem*-brain, and so forth. The ultimate goal for all of us is to approach our life and our work using a *"harmonizing"* whole-brain approach.

We cannot make the mistake of thinking that the *left* and *right* brains are two totally separate entities within our bodies. They are connected and <u>do</u> have areas of overlap. They also overlap with *mid*- and *stem*-parts of the brain, *the other two areas.* As you read about the different function of each area of your brain and application within the Quality Professionals; all four perform and carry out functions that create the person you are or have become.

An integrated "understanding" whole-brain approach begins to maximize the untapped potential of the human brain—understand and own all four areas of your brain.

CHAPTER 4

YOUR FOUR POWERS OF CONSCIOUSNESS AND INTELLIGENCE!

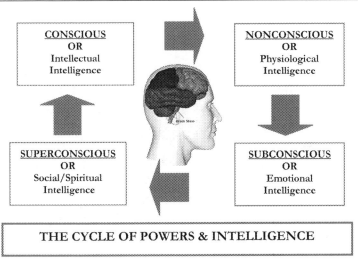

CONSCIOUS OR Intellectual Intelligence		NONCONSCIOUS OR Physiological Intelligence
SUPERCONSCIOUS OR Social/Spiritual Intelligence		SUBCONSCIOUS OR Emotional Intelligence

THE CYCLE OF POWERS & INTELLIGENCE

What are the terms or concepts of superconscious, conscious, nonconscious, and subconscious mean?

The concept of **conscious,** and **unconscious** were not exactly invented by Dr. Sigmund Freud but he was responsible for making it popular. The **conscious mind (intellectual intelligence) is what you are aware of at any particular moment, your present perceptions, memories, thoughts, fantasies, feelings, what have you.**[49] This conscious mind is the function or operates within the realm of the **left** or the **intellectual brain.**

Working closely with the **conscious mind** is what Freud called the **preconscious** mind, what we might today call *"available memory:"* anything that can easily be made conscious, the memories you are not at the moment thinking about but can readily bring to mind.

Dr. Lewicki has also determined that the **preconscious mind** (**superconscious mind**) processing, the inner mind is "comparably more able to process complex knowledge faster and smarter overall

39

than our ability to think (left) and identify meanings of stimuli consciously.[50]

Paul Scheele, author of "Natural Brilliance" and founder of PhotoReading system labels the **superconscious** as **"other-than-conscious"** and **"preconscious processors."** He said, according to educational psychologist Dr. Win Wenger, the database of the **unconscious mind** (what Dr. Win was referring to is what I called the **superconscious** mind)outweighs that of the **conscious mind** by ten billions to one. The pathway into this phenomenal capacity of the mind is called the **"preconscious processors (mind)."** Many times faster than the conscious mind, the **preconscious processor** continually scans billions of bits of data, determining what is important and what is not. When it notes something important, it immediately signals **the conscious mind** to pay attention. The **"preconscious mind"** is also called **superconscious mind** by other writings. I prefer to use the term **superconscious mind** instead of **preconscious or preconscious process** in this writing to mean the same. The **preconscious** mind or what I called the **superconscious** operates within the realm of the <u>right</u> or <u>social brain</u>.

The largest part by far is the **subconscious. This is where the Super-Ego that Freud discusses is wired to the Superconscious or the Right Hemisphere of the brain; the Ego is wired to Conscious or Left Hemisphere, and id is wired to the Nonconscious mind or Stem brain.** The **Subconscious** mind operates within the realm of **mid** or <u>**emotional brain.** The diagram below illustrates how all the consciousness relates to one another.</u>

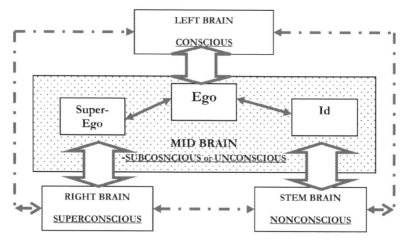

Lastly, skills and information can be acquired **nonconsciously,** according to research done at the cognitive laboratory at Tulsa University. The work done by Dr. Lewicki suggests that human cognitive system **nonconsciously** detects and process information. *This process lies within the realm of the senses, stem or the _instinctual brain_.* His studies over the past decades provide evidence that subjects in experiments have no access to the newly acquired procedural knowledge and no idea that they have learned anything from the stimulus materials, even though the newly acquired knowledge consistently guides their behavior.[51]

Dr. Freud's **unconscious mind** is the same as what I called the **nonconscious mind.** Feud said it includes all the things that are not easily available to awareness, including many things that have their origins there, such as our drives or instincts, and things that are put there because we can't bear to look at them, such as the memories and emotions associated with trauma.

According to Freud, the **unconscious** is the source of our motivations, whether they be simple desires for food or sex, neurotic compulsions, or the motives of an artist or scientist. **And yet, we are often driven to deny or resist becoming conscious of these motives, and they are often available to us only in disguised form**[52] as they are information stored in our DNA and passed down from one generation to another generation.

Pioneer psychologist Carl Jung expands on Freud's concept of **unconscious** and called this **collective consciousness.**

Collective consciousness is what you could call your "**psychic inheritance.**" *It is the reservoir of your experiences as a species, a kind of knowledge we are all born with. And yet we can never be directly conscious of it. It influences all of our experiences and behaviors, most especially the emotional ones, but we only know about it indirectly, by looking at those influences.*[53]

There are some experiences that show the effects of the **collective unconscious** more clearly than others: The experiences of love at first sight, of deja vu (the feeling that you've been here before), or reincarnation (you have lived in a past life or in a another time period), and the immediate recognition of certain symbols and the meanings of certain myths, could all be understood as the sudden conjunction of our **outer reality and the inner reality** of the **collective unconscious.** *Grander examples are the creative experiences shared by artists and musicians all over the world and in all times, or the spiritual experiences of mystics of all religions, or the parallels in dreams, fantasies, mythologies, fairy tales, and literature*[54].

The **collective consciousness** by Dr. Jung and **unconsciousness** that Dr. Freud were discussing are information past down from previous generation in your genes and controlled by your stem brain. The field of epigenetic is explaining how this information in our gene affects us and future generation. An understanding of it helps us turn off information that was past down to us that is causing us to fail in life.

Aside from what is called "time and unforeseen occurrences," "imperfection," and "works of governments," everything that has happened to you, or where you are at in life, are what you created *superconsciously, consciously, nonconsciously,* and *subconsciously,* by using your intelligence.

Pioneer psychologist Carl Jung[55] in his *personality typology* helps us understand how things happen to us which unbeknownst to him was observing **four attitudes** and **four functions** control and manage by each area of the brain *–right, left, stem and mid or DNA base.* Dr. Jung discussed two attitudes (but there are four altogether as I will add the other two to his typology) which he classified as an **extrovert and introvert**. The other two are **Sensovert** and **emotiovert**.

The **extrovert** (social/spiritual) person prefers the *external* world of things, people and activities and is *intuitive.* The **introvert** (intellectual) person prefers their *internal* world of thoughts, feelings, fantasies, dreams, and so on and is *thinking.* The **Sensovert** (instinctual) person prefers things or persons that satisfy their five *senses or body feelings (of present or past) and is sensing.* For example, they will go out to play football not because they want to be with other people or their inner person wants it but because their body senses *(information in DNA)* move them to. The **emotiovert** (emotional) prefers to do things driven by their *emotions (information stored in their subconscious or figurative heart)* and is *feelings.*

The four functions that correspond to the above four attitudes (extrovert, introvert, sensovert, emotiovert) are; *intuitive, thinking, sensing and feelings.*[56]

The first is **intuiting (extrovert)**. Intuiting is a kind of perception that **works outside of the usual conscious processes**. It is **rational** like thinking, but comes from the complex integration of large amounts of information, rather than simple seeing or hearing. Jung said it was like *seeing around corners.*

The second is **thinking (introvert)**. Thinking means evaluating information or ideas rationally, logically. Jung called this a **rational** function, meaning that it involves decision making or judging, rather than simple intake of information.

The third is **sensing (Sensovert)**. Sensing means what it says: getting information by means of the senses – *see, hear, touch, taste and smell.* A sensing person is good at looking and listening and generally getting to know the world. Jung called this one of the **irrational** functions, meaning that it involved judging rather than perception of information.

The fourth is **feeling (emotiovert)**. Feeling, like **sensing**, is a matter of evaluating information, this time by weighing one's overall, emotional response. and it involves perception rather than judging. Feelings are **irrational.**

All **four attitudes and functions** allow, create, invites, and attract your reality. **How is that?** In short:

1. As an **Extrovert,** you *allow* or **accept** the external world into your life through your Superconscious Mind or the *Right* side of your brain to change you. As a spiritual person, you are naturally social or as a social personal, you are naturally spiritual. Daniel Goleman[57] said that your inner state affects and drives the other person *or vice versa.* We are forming brain-to-brain bridges--a two-way traffic system all the time. We actually catch each others emotions like a cold. The more important the relationship, the more potent such a "contagion" will be. A key to understanding this process according to Goleman is the process called "mirror neurons"--neurons whose only job is to recognize a smile and make you smile in return. You can ACCEPT or reject this. For example, if you are an anger-prone

person, you can infect yourself with calmness by spending time with mellower individuals, absorbing less-aggressive behaviors, and thereby sharpening your social intelligence. By ACCEPTING where you are at in life and ALLOWING others and situations to propel you forward by using these "mirror neurons" of your brain to clear any disbeliefs that are holding you back. Infect yourself with a Mentor or Role Model who has achieved the same or similar goal as the one you are pursuing and CLEAR it with the "Universe" or "Infinite Wisdom."

2.   As an **Introvert,** through reason and logic, you *create your reality or world from within* your Conscious mind, or the *Left* side of your brain. Before you can HAVE anything in life, you must CREATE it in your mind first, which becomes an idea, dream, goal, idea, target, or vision! SEE it in your mind's eye.

Golf legend Jack Nicklaus illustrates this concept by having always played a course in his mind before actually beginning a game. He says, *"I never hit a shot, not even in practice, without having a sharp, in-focus picture of it in my head. First, I see the ball where I want it to finish, nice and white, and sitting up on high on the bright green grass. Then the scene quickly changes, and I see the ball going there, its path, trajectory, and shape, even its behavior on landing. Then there is a sort of fade-out, and the next scene shows me making the kind of swing that will turn the previous images into reality."*[58]

ALL great athletes and successful people follow the <u>same method</u> or technique that Jack Nicklaus uses. Therefore, SEE your dream, goal, idea, target, or vision, as **already** happened in your mind's eye first!

3.   As a **Sensovert,** you *invite* your reality or world in to yourself by means of your five senses with your Nonconscious Mind, or the *Stem* of your brain. Your nonconscious mind or body has preprogrammed desires, needs, intentions, and interests (or genetics) that you act on or yield to; thus inviting consequences, results, and effects into your life. Some of these urges or desires may be driving you crazy because you don't understand where they come from but you have free will to choose it. For example, people who engaged in "hooking up" behavior have no intellectual or emotional attachment to the person or stranger they are having

sex with. They place themselves in dangerous situations such as catching AIDS, getting pregnant, or even their own safety or security, all because their body controls them, instead of them controlling it.

"Researchers may have discovered the region that fuels addictions, such as smoking, which may also help other addictions...." Dr. Nasir Naqvi, a doctoral student in the medical scientists' training program, at the University of Iowa Carver College of Medicine said, "...a lot of pleasure that comes out of smoking is *what it does to the body*, rather than nicotine reaching the brain. *Each puff stimulates sensations in the throat, the lungs, the chest,* and these are important for why smoking is pleasurable. We think that when people are craving for cigarettes, they are remembering that type of pleasure, and from this area of the brain, which is known to sense what is going on in the body, and which may play a role in remembering that type of pleasure."[59]

As Dr. Naqvi discovered, your body or physiological intelligence INVITES what gives pleasure (or even pain) to you. You have the power to choose and have them in your life or overcome it by **resolving conflicts which triggers them from your past.**

4.   As an **Emotiovert**, your feelings or emotions *attract* your reality or world by means of your Subconscious Mind, or the *Mid*-section of your brain. As a RESULT of ALLOWING, CREATING, and INVITING, you ATTRACT your heart's desires, your body's needs, your spirit's intentions, and your mind's interests, knowingly or unknowingly, to form the life you are currently living. BELIEVE it or not--it is yours automatically! Be careful what you ALLOW, CREATE, and INVITE into your life, because you will ATTRACT ALL of it. All information you created from your childhood with emotions (good or bad) is stored in this area and is creating the life you have NOW.

A very close friend of mine relates this story to me: After his divorce, he reflected back to all the women who came in to his life. He discovered one common thread about all of them was that they were all bi-sexual. He said he was puzzled by this attraction to these females. But, he finally remembered one day, at the age of 4 ½, he found a Penthouse magazine in his older brother's room.

"I was curious about the picture of the two women on the cover and hid the magazine for myself. Everyday I would hide under my brother's bed and look at the contents of the magazine. I never knew those images would imprint into my heart or subconscious, and attracted that very type of woman into my life."

So, the inclination of your brain whether to the *left-* or *right-*hemisphere, or *stem-*, or *mid-*section, **allows, creates, invites,** and **attracts** everything in to your life by your choice--or by default (with exception of things caused by time and unforeseen occurrences and governments). **This brain inclination for one area to be dominant over the other three was a survival mechanism you created at birth or at an earlier age, depending on your environment, mother's diet, and lifestyle and authority figures in your life**[60]. Whether you believe this or not, it does not make a difference. **It is what it is and researched support this!** Sigmund Freud and the Psychodynamic School of Psychology and epigenetic explain this.

The following excerpt was written by Wallace Wattles in his book, The Science of Getting Rich. **I have included some changes in italics to emphasize new discoveries of wealth and success.**

"We develop our powers *or intelligence superconsciously, consciously, nonconsciously, and subconsciously,* by making use of things in society. Society is so organized that we must have money or material wealth, or spiritual, physical, and emotional health, in order to become happy.

The object of all life is development *of the mind to serve its purpose;* and everything that lives has an inalienable right to all the development that it is capable of attaining.

A person's "right to life" means "...his right to have the freedom and unrestricted use of all the things which may be necessary to his fullest emotional, physical, mental, and spiritual unfoldment , or full development of his/her powers."

There are ONLY four powers or intelligences that we possess;

1. **the power of the spirit/strength or superconscious, or social intelligence ;**

2. the power of the mind or conscious, or intellectual intelligence;

3. the power of the body/soul or nonconscious, or physiological intelligence, and

4. the power of the heart (figurative) or subconscious, or emotional intelligence.

None of these powers or of intelligences is better than the other. All alike are desirable, and not one of the four--heart, body/soul, mind, or spirit, can live fully if either of the others is cut short of full life, expression, and utilization. It is not right or noble to use or live only for the power of heart, and deny mind, body, or sprit. It is wrong to use (or live) for the intellect, and denies physiology (body), social (spirit), or emotional (heart), and so forth.

We are all acquainted with the loathsome consequences of just living for the body/soul (or nonconscious mind), and denying the mind (or conscious), spirit (or superconscious mind), and heart (or subconscious mind).

We see that *real* life means the complete expression of that which the entire person can give forth through spirit, mind, body/soul, and heart.

Wherever there is unexpressed possibility, or a function not performed, there is unsatisfied desire. Desire is possibility seeking expression, or function seeking performance.

A person cannot INVITE, use, or live fully in the power of the body (physiological intelligence), without good or healthy food, comfortable clothing, warm shelter, and without freedom from excessive toil. Rest and recreation are also necessary to one's physical life. Whatever NEEDS the body asks for must be fulfilled.

A person cannot CREATE, use, or live fully in the power of the mind (intellectual intelligence) without books and time to study them, without opportunity for travel and observation, or without intellectual companionship. Whatever the INTEREST of the mind, it must be met.

To CREATE, use, or live fully in the power of the mind, a person must have intellectual recreation, and must be surrounding with all the objects of art and beauty one is capable of using and appreciating.

A person cannot INTEND, use or live to full strength or spirit (social intelligence), without others and is successful only as a person can ALLOW the fact that his strength or success is dependent on others strength aside from himself. "No man is an island."

The synergy of our (and others') strength is what can only bring great success to a person. Dr. Vitale said, "It's the difference between running a marathon alone, or running one with a crowd to cheer your on."

A person cannot ATTRACT, use, or live fully in the power of the Heart (emotional intelligence), unless a must have LOVE.

A person's highest happiness is found in the bestowal of benefits, whether it is emotional, physical, spiritual, or psychological, on those he loves. Love finds its most natural and spontaneous expression in **giving.**

The person who has nothing to give cannot fill their place as a *power of the subconscious, heart,* and *emotional intelligence..* It is in the use of material (physical), emotional, spiritual, and psychological "things," that a person finds full life for his body, develops his mind and heart, and unfolds his strength or spirit. *It is, therefore, of supreme importance to develop and use all of one's four powers of intelligence.*

There is a science of getting anything you want, and it is an exact science, like algebra or arithmetic. These four powers (or intelligence) and certain laws govern the process of acquiring anything.

Once these powers and laws are learned, understood, and obeyed by any person, that person will get anything with mathematical certainty.

The ownership of anything comes as a result of applying the TSF-24.

Those who do these things, as laid out in the **TSF-24**, whether purposefully or accidentally, get what they want; while those who do not, follow--no matter how hard they work, or how able they are--they remain poor, unhappy, and dissatisfied.

It is a **natural law** that **"like causes" always produce "like effects;"** and, therefore, anyone who learns to control and manage their four powers will infallibly get whatever they want.

The following facts show that the previous statement is true:

Getting whatever you want is not a matter of environment. If this is true, the people of one city would all be wealthy, while those of other towns would all be poor; or the inhabitants of one state would roll in wealth, while those of an adjoining state would be in poverty.

But, everywhere we see wealthy and poor living side-by-side in the same environment, and often engaged in the same vocation. For example, when two people are in the same locality, and in the same business, and one gets *wealthy* while the other remains poor, it shows that getting *wealthy* is not primarily a matter of environment.

Some environments may be more favorable than others, but when two people in the same business are in the same neighborhood, and one gets wealthy while the other fails; **it indicates that getting *wealthy* is the result of doing things in a certain way or following a specific formula of success.**

And further, the ability to follow a formula or do things in this certain way is not due solely to the possession of talent, for many people who have great talent remain poor, while other who have very little talent get wealthy.

Studying the people who have got wealthy, we find that they are an average lot in all respects, having no greater talents and abilities than other men. **It is evident that they do not get *wealthy* because they possess talents and abilities that other people do not have, but because they happen to do things in a certain way, or follow a specific formula for success.**

Getting *wealthy* is not the result of saving, or "thrift"; many very penurious people are poor, while free spenders often get *wealthy*. Nor is getting wealthy due to doing things which others fail to do; for two people in the same business often do almost exactly the same things, and one gets wealthy while the other remains poor or becomes bankrupt.

From all these things, **we must come to the conclusion that getting wealthy is the result of <u>doing things in a certain way, or following a specific formula of success.</u>**

If getting wealthy is the result of doing and possessing the four powers, and if "like" causes always produce "like" effects, then any man or woman who can do things in that way can become wealthy, and the whole matter is brought within the domain of exact science.

The question arises here, whether this certain way, or possessing the four powers of intelligence, may be so difficult that only a few may follow it.

This cannot be true, as we have seen so far, as natural ability is concerned; talented people get wealthy or successful, and blockheads get wealthy or successful; intellectually brilliant people get wealthy or successful, and very stupid people get wealthy or successful; physically strong people get wealthy or successful, and weak and sickly people get wealthy or successful.

Some degree of ability to think and understand is, of course, essential; but, in-so-far when natural ability is concerned, **any man or woman who has sense enough to read, understand, and follow, can acquire the four powers, or intelligence, and can certainly get wealthy or successful.**

Also, we have seen that it is not a matter of environment. Location counts for something--one would not go to the heart of the Sahara and expect to do successful business.

Bob Proctor explains the previous teaching of Wallace Wattles of getting wealthy or successful with the importance of understanding the distinct powers you have. *I have included the fourth power in the discussion below.*

Mr. Proctor covers three levels of powers. *I am grateful for the wisdom he has on this subject:*

You will soon become aware that you are constantly **living simultaneously** with four distinct powers of "Being." You naturally posses these four powers and your *sub-brain* correspondingly control and manage each of the specifics.

1. You *are both* a spiritual and *social* person (being/spirit) (*Are you social because you are a spiritual person or are you spiritual because you are a social person? - both*), and your superconscious mind or the *right* side of your brain controls and manages your strength/spirit and social intelligence. *The attribute of LOVE[61] is the embodiment of your superconscious. This LOVE is based on principles and of the mind, not emotions as compare to the Love found in your subconscious mind. The other two attributes are joy and peace.*

5. You have an intellect (a mind), and your conscious mind, or the *left* side of your brain controls and manages your mind and intellectual intelligence. *The attribute of JUSTICE and RESPECT are the embodiment of your conscious mind. The attributes that managed justice and respect are long suffering, kindness, and goodness.*

6. You live in a physical body (body), and your nonconscious mind, or the *stem* side of your brain controls and manages your body and physiological intelligence and senses. *The attribute of POWER is the embodiment of your nonconscious mind. And humility, faith, and self-control managed this power. You MUST be humble to overcome whatever was passed down to you from your past. Humble people are teachable and coachable.*

7. You have emotions, feelings, and beliefs (heart), that attract results, and your subconscious mind or the *mid*-section of your brain controls and manages your heart and emotional intelligence. *The attribute of WISDOM is the embodiment of your subconscious mind. The collective attributes of love, peace, joy, long suffering, kindness, goodness, humility, faith, and self-control are the ingredients or composition of wisdom.*

To understand this abstraction better, you must keep in mind that you simultaneously have four distinct powers of existence, or intelligence, and all four areas of your brain overlap each other – left, right, stem and mid.

Multiple Intelligence psychologist expert, Howard Gardner in his book, "Frames of Mind – The Theory of Multiple Intelligences" and his others works discussed that there are 10 types of intelligences concepts. Only nine was part of the Survey that you took at the beginning of the Book. Interestingly, these various intelligences or multiple intelligences fall within the domain of your four sub-brains.[62]

1. **Right Brain :** *Spatial, Musical, Interpersonal, Existential and Spiritual intelligence*

Spatial intelligence (Visual) involves the potential to recognize and use the patterns of wide space and more confined areas.

Musical intelligence involves skill in the performance, composition, and appreciation of musical patterns. It encompasses the capacity to recognize and compose musical pitches, tones, and rhythms. According to Howard Gardner musical intelligence runs in an almost structural parallel to linguistic intelligence.

Interpersonal intelligence or social intelligence is concerned with the capacity to understand the intentions, motivations and desires of other people. It allows people to work effectively with others. Educators, salespeople, religious and political leaders and counselors all need a well-developed interpersonal intelligence.

Existential intelligence, a concern with 'ultimate issues', is, thus, the next possibility that Howard Gardner considers - and he argues that it 'scores reasonably well on the criteria'. However, empirical evidence is sparse - and although a ninth intelligence might be attractive, Howard Gardner is not disposed to add it to the list. 'I find the phenomenon perplexing enough and the distance from the other intelligences vast enough to dictate prudence - at least for now'

Spiritual Intelligence to understand and express spiritual issues such as about life, death, and after life.

2. **Left Brain:** *Linguistic, and Logical-Mathematical.*

Linguistic intelligence (Verbal) involves sensitivity to spoken and written language, the ability to learn languages, and the capacity to use language to accomplish certain goals. This intelligence includes the ability to effectively use language to express oneself rhetorically or poetically; and language as a means to remember information. Writers, poets, lawyers and speakers are among those that Howard Gardner sees as having high linguistic intelligence.

Logical-mathematical intelligence consists of the capacity to analyze problems logically, carry out mathematical operations, and investigate issues scientifically. In Howard Gardner's words, in entails the ability to detect patterns, reason deductively and think logically. This intelligence is most often associated with scientific and mathematical thinking.

3. *Stem Brain: Bodily-Kinesthetic and naturalist intelligence/*

Bodily-kinesthetic intelligence entails the potential of using one's whole body or parts of the body to solve problems. It is the ability to use mental abilities to coordinate bodily movements. Howard Gardner sees mental and physical activity as related.

Naturalist intelligence enables human beings to recognize, categorize and draw upon certain features of the environment. It 'combines a description of the core ability with a characterization of the role that many cultures value'.

4. *Mid Brain: Intrapersonal intelligence*

Intrapersonal intelligence or emotional intelligence entails the capacity to understand oneself, to appreciate one's feelings, fears and motivations. In Howard Gardner's view it involves having an effective working model of ourselves, and to be able to use such information to regulate our lives.

Cesar Millan's thoughts about Intellectual, Emotional, Instinctual, and Spiritual; *Jungs typology* of four attitudes and functions, and *Howard Garners* multiple intelligences all discusses the same thought of the four different sub-brains. You can develop all the above intelligences in a balance way by harmonizing your four sub-brains. Your target is to harmonize all four sub-brains with this key, **"TSF-24,"** to unlock your universe of success.

The above and below order is the correct approach to maximizing your brain in creating solutions to challenges but more so creating success for yourself. Again the correct creative process is as follows;

Correct Creative Process

1. The Social/Spiritual Power of Strength/Spirit or Social Intelligence (*Highest* Potential or Aptitude – Right Brain).

2. The Intellectual Power of Thoughts, Mind or Intellectual Intelligence. (*Higher* Potential or Aptitude – Left Brain)

3. The Physical (Instinctual) Power of Doing, Soul/Body or Physiological Intelligence (*Lower* Potential or Aptitude- Stem Brain)

4. The Emotional Power of Results, Heart or Emotional Intelligence. (*Lowest* Potential or Aptitude - Midbrain)

You are working from the highest to the least potential, capability, intelligence, or aptitude. As Paul Scheele, creator of PhotoReading system and Dr. Pawel Lewicki of the University of Tulsa stated that the inner pathway of the preconscious processor or **superconscious (right brain)** processes complex knowledge faster and smarter overall than our ability to think and identify meaning of stimuli **consciously (left brain). Five various form of intelligences are found as activities of the right brain.** So use or develop your right brain first, and then left brain, follow by inviting your senses (**stem brain**) to assist you with inspired actions. Then have passion or emotion (mid brain) to complete your target. This order of the creative process will give you the highest success in whatever you are pursuing – that is TSF!

The **12 Steps Model** that Alcoholic Anonymous follows and many similar programs works because it follows the Correct Creative Process (See Appendix for the 12 Step Model summary as relates to the four sub-brains) *What I mean by this is--what you are working from is-*.

Correct Creative Process

1. Have a Purpose, Intention, Mission, or Strength (Social/Spiritual power). Have a purpose or mission first, then ask for help from Mentors and Role Models.

To

2. Have a Target, Goal, Vision, Ideas (Intellectual power)
Be teachable and coachable . Mentors and Role Models assist you
in clarifying your Ideas (Dreams, Goals, Visions, and Targets) by
developing your mental faculties. When you see your ideas clearly in
your minds-eye, it will be easy to achieve or crystallize.

To

3. Have Actions (Physical power)
Be willing to work hard for it and pay the prize of achieving it. To
accomplish your Ideas (Dreams, Goals, Visions, Targets), you need
to take inspired action. These are the actions your subconscious will
move you to do.

To

4. Results (Heart or Emotional power). Have a burning desire or
passion in what you are doing or pursuing! Your actions above will
attract the results that will come in to your life. Your emotions, feelings,
beliefs dictate the final RESULT!

This will explain the latter statement of "...rather than working from
--..."

Incorrect Creative Process

1. Results... (Emotional)

To

2. Actions... (Physical)

To

3. Target, Goal, Vision, Idea... (Intellectual)

To

4. Purpose, Intention, Mission, Strength... (Social/Spiritual)

...as you have probably done in the past, and which the vast majority
of people continue to do in the future.

That is to say, most people will look at the RESULTS in their life and
then let the RESULTS dictate their ACTIONS, which gives them
IDEAS to build their STRENGTHS. *Put it in a different way, people will
let their EMOTIONS decide what is best for them, which lead to ACTIONS,
which in turn they rationalize or justify it with some IDEAS, that it was the*

best decision at the time. This process of justification and rationalization of their emotional decision gives them STRENGTH, or spiritual empowerment (god like), or rather, self-affirmation that it was them alone who made the decision.

For example, if you are an alcoholic or a drug addict (the ends result):

Incorrect Creative Process

1. **Result** - You are an alcoholic or a drug addict. You looked at what led you to where you are.

To

2. **Actions** - You decide on your own that to stop being an alcoholic or drug addict, you have to stop drinking alcohol or taking drugs. Take or remove the bottle or drugs.

To

3. **Ideas** - The above actions gives you good ideas because the alcohol is killing you and destroying your family. Therefore, it's worth it to quit drinking or taking drugs. You did it.

To

4. **Strength** – The above experience gives you self-empowerment or spiritual empowerment as god-like that you did it on your own– not to drink or take drugs.

Life will show that the above scenario does not solve the problem. As soon as a conflict comes in to your life again, which disturbed your inner peace; you are right back to the alcohol or drug to comfort you. Your solution was external (taking away the alcohol or drug) and was built on RESULTS, not discovering the inner conflicts (Social/Strength) first, which led to you becoming an alcoholic or drug addict. Alcohol or ANY other form of addiction is due to an unresolved internal conflict from the past. **When you discover your inner conflict first, with the help of others, you now begin your journey of healing. When you change your inner-self, your outside will automatically change.**

It's takes humility to resolve any conflicts! Without humility, you are fooling yourself! Humility is the key to unlock the universe and its floodgates of help to come to your assistance or aid.

Let's look at another example of solutions or decisions built on RESULTS of following the **INCORRECT** CREATIVE PROCESS.

In all educational environments or school systems, teachers and administrators battle challenges brought in by their students--**the results.** Most of these challenges unfortunately are inherent in the system they (*the teachers and administrators)* are in, which is then transferred to their students.

The current educational system does not recognize all of the four intelligences which are created by all four areas of the brain; which creates the types or groups (*except two)* of students, sitting in their classroom.

The groups of students, not understanding their own brain's inclination, which contributes to the way they do things, and behave, is penalized by the educational system for not performing to their expectations, which is governed by a *left*-brain curriculum. Students (*even the workplace)* can be categorized by their brain inclination:

1. *Left*-Brains--The intellectuals' minds, or the "Nerds," or "Geeks" as some calls them. Most school curriculum is designed for this group. In fact, third-world and developing countries' educational systems are primarily designed for this group.

2. *Right*-Brains--The creative minds, "day dreamers" or "visionaries."

3. *Stem*-Brains--The athletes, or "the Jocks," and those who enjoy hard labor (blue collars).

4. *Mid*-Brains--The "emos,"' troublemakers" "drama queens and kings" as others name them or high energy students who uses or directed their energy in a destructive way to get attention to themselves.

Depending on which educational system you will attend, the right-, *stem*-, and more so, the *mid*-brain-inclined students are lost in the process. **Teachers and administrators are not trained to recognize these groups and help them accordingly, by training them to**

harmonize ALL four areas of their brains, to create the success they are seeking.

But to help their students, teachers must harmonized their brain first as their classroom atmosphere is a projection of their own personality or what's going on inside themselves – *spiritually, intellectually, physically, and emotionally. The greatest asset they can bring to change their students is changing who they are first to the person they want their students to aspire to be or become.*[63].

To understand the concepts above and why it is so critical for your success, let us examine each power separately, so you will understand "why" and "how" to create your total success.

For teachers, I have designed and created a booklet (at <u>www. AreYouAHuman.Com</u>) for your students to discover themselves. But also benefits you as you get to know your students and "how" their mind works.

The four major or main school of psychology will help you see how your mind works and put your life in perspective.

First, the **Humanist and Sociocultural School** observed and study behavior control and managed by the *Right Brain* (or Superconscious Mind, or Social Intelligence).

Second, the **Cognitive School** observed and study behavior control and managed by observed and study behavior control and managed by *Left Brain* (or Conscious Mind, or Intellectual Intelligence).

Third, the **Behaviorist School** observed and study behavior control and managed by the *Stem Brain* (or Nonconscious Mind, or Physiological Intelligence).

And last, the **Psychodynamic School** observed and study behavior control and managed by the *Mid-brain* (or Subconscious Mind, or Emotional Intelligence).

CHAPTER 5

THE SOCIAL OR SPIRITUAL BRAIN OR THE "INTUITIVE MIND" - YOUR SUPERCONSCIOUS POWER

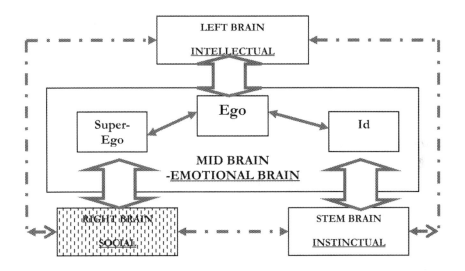

"Your Mind, Body and Internal environment (emotions) is a manifestation of your External environment."

Your right brain or your **intuitive mind** (other writings called this your sixth sense or in religion it is called your "Spirit" or "Strenght") is the most neglected area in personal development and why many of these programs don't work. It is the area of the brain connected to the Super-Ego of the Mid Brain which is composed of the *hippocampus which is responsible for making the unknown, known,* **Cingulate Gyrus** *which coordinates Sensory input with emotions, regulates aggressive behavior and gives emotional responses to pain, and the* **Amygdala** *which is responsible for alerting the body in survival situations..* This area helps you see the "the Big Picture" in any issues or situation intuitively without logically understanding it. It's said, "Its like seeing around the corners." It's the **extravert** attitude of yours and when it's developed connects you to your outside world of mentors and roles models who will guide you to great success.

Brian Tracy in his book, <u>Changing Your Thinking Change Your Life:</u>

Bob Ainuu Afamasaga

How to Unlock Your Full Potential for Success and Achievement,[64] wrote the following excerpt about the "superconscious mind."

Your superconscious mind is your direct connection with the Infinite Intelligence. It contains all knowledge, and can bring you all the ideas and answers you will ever need to achieve any goal or target that you can set for yourself.

This power is the source of all inspiration, imagination, intuitions, and hunches. **It operates 24-hours a day, and will bring you exactly the right answer to your problem or question, exactly when you are ready for it.** It is stimulated by clear goals or target, vivid mental pictures, and clear, positive commands in the form of affirmations.

The reason why activities in the right brain is called **superconscious** because it processes billions of bit of data first and faster , then notify the conscious (left) if notes something important. In other words, your inner **mind or superconscious is aware of at any particular moment, your present perceptions, memories, thoughts, fantasies, and feelings, what have you before you consciously aware of it.**

Psychologist Robert J. Sternberg, in his Triarchic Theory of Intelligence[65] states that creative Intelligence (or superconscious mind) involves *insights, synthesis and the ability to react to novel situations and stimuli.* This he considers the experiential aspect of intelligence and reflects how an individual connects the internal world to external reality.

Sternberg considers the Creative facet to consist of the ability which allows people to think creatively and that which allows people to adjust creatively and effectively to new situations.

Sternberg believes that more intelligent individuals will also move from consciously learning in a novel situation to automating the new learning so that they can attend to other tasks as explained below.

Basic assumption: That there are two broad classes of abilities associated with intelligence: *novelty skills and automatization skills.* A task measures intelligence if it requires the ability to deal with novel demands or the ability to automatize information processing (two ends of a continuum).

Novel tasks or situations are good measures of intellectual ability because they assess an individual's ability to apply existing knowledge to new problems.

Also, note that multiple intelligences expert psychologist Howard Gardner found more types of intelligence activities occurred in this area of your brain than the other three. The intelligences that falls within the domain of the right brain are; *Spatial, Musical, Interpersonal (social), Existential intelligence, and Spiritual intelligence as discussed earlier*

People who are **right brain dominant** have fully developed this area of their brain. This is the beginning or starting point or launching pad of any successful personal development program. Success is not ALL about positive thinking or thought! There is more to it. As you know by now that right brain dominant people are *spatial or visual, musical, interpersonal or social, existential and spiritual intelligence. These intelligences may be used in a positive or a negative way by the right brain dominant person.*

It's being said that *visual or spatial* imagery is the primary source of thought. We think in pictures! When someone says the word "elephant," we don't see the word elephant but a picture of an elephant. Art psychologist Rudolf Arnheim argues that the most important operations of thinking come directly from our perception of the world, with vision serving as the sensory system *par excellence* which undergirds and constitutes our cognitive processes. "[66]

The social brain has the ability to perceive the visual as mentioned above or visual intelligence. These learners tend to think in pictures and need to create vivid mental images to retain information. They enjoy looking at maps, charts, pictures, videos, and movies. Their skills include: puzzle building, reading, writing, understanding charts and graphs, a good sense of direction, sketching, painting, creating visual metaphors and analogies (perhaps through the visual arts), manipulating images, constructing, fixing, designing practical objects, interpreting visual images. Possible career interests are: navigators, sculptors, visual artists, inventors, architects, interior designers, mechanics, and engineers.

The social brain has the ability to produce and appreciate music or music intelligence. These musically inclined learners think in sounds, rhythms and patterns. They immediately respond to music either appreciating or criticizing what they hear. Many of these learners are extremely sensitive to environmental sounds (e.g. crickets, bells, dripping taps). Their skills include: singing, whistling, playing musical instruments, and recognizing tonal patterns, composing music, remembering melodies, understanding the structure and rhythm of music. Possible career paths: musician, disc jockey, singer, and composer.

The social brain has the ability to be sensitive to, or have the capacity for, conceptualizing or tackling deeper or larger questions about human existence, such as the meaning of life, why are we born, why do we die, what is consciousness, or how did we get here or existential intelligence - "wondering smart, cosmic smart, spiritually smart, or metaphysical intelligence". [67]

The possibility of this intelligence has been alluded to by Gardner in several of his works. He has stated that existential intelligence might be manifest in someone who is concerned with fundamental questions about existence, or who questions the intricacies of existence. And while Professor Gardner has offered a preliminary definition as: "Individuals who exhibit the proclivity to pose and ponder questions about life, death, and ultimate realities," he has not fully confirmed, endorsed, or described this intelligence.

Despite this avoidance on Gardner's part to definitively commit to existential intelligence, there are many who have accepted the presence of this intelligence as fact and have attempted to clarify what it might look like if it were part of the MI array. For those who have met children who appear to have "old souls," it is often easy to accept the existence of existential intelligence as something very real and important. **These are the children who appear to have a sixth sense, they may be psychic, or ones who pose, and sometimes even answer, life's larger questions.** Like:

Why am I here? Why are we here? Are there other dimensions and if so what are they like? Can animals understand us, or do animals go to heaven? Are there really ghosts?

Where do we go when we die? Why are some people evils? Is there life on other planets? Where is heaven? Why does God live? These may be those children who can be described as "fully aware" of the cosmos -- of its diversity, complexity, and wonder. Frequently, these are the children who persist in asking those "big" questions that adults cannot answer. *All the above is in the domain of the social or the intuitive brain. Also, spiritual intelligences, the ability to understand and express issues such as issues about life, death and after life* are functions of the social brain.

The social brain has ability to relate and understand others or social intelligence. These learners try to see things from other people's point of view in order to understand how they think and feel. They often have an uncanny ability to sense feelings, intentions and motivations. They are great organizers, although they sometimes resort to manipulation. Generally they try to maintain peace in group settings and encourage co-operation. They use both verbal (e.g. speaking) and non-verbal language (e.g. eye contact, body language) to open communication channels with others.

Their skills include: seeing things from other perspectives (dual-perspective), listening, using empathy, understanding other people's moods and feelings, counseling, co-operating with groups, noticing people's moods, motivations and intentions, communicating both verbally and non-verbally, building trust, peaceful conflict resolution, establishing positive relations with other people. Possible Career Paths: Counselor, salesperson, politician, and business person.

Pioneer psychologist Abraham Maslow and Carl Rogers pioneered the Humanist School of Psychology which unbeknown to them were observing behaviors controlled and managed by the right side of the brain. Both, were right brain scientist as their researched indicated their gravitation towards ideas, concepts, and issues from a "big picture" perspective. As Right Brain dominant psychologist, they were "seeing" the world from a right brain dominant perspective. They were discussing and observing behaviors by the four sub-brains, but from a right brain perspective as you will see below.,

I am fascinated and intrigued by Maslow's **Hierarchy of Needs and the Self-Actualization concepts.** His **Hierarchy of Needs** parallel the four sub-brains that I am purporting throughout this book and Self-Actualization is what we must all strive for by harmonizing all four sub-brains of our head.

Maslow's Hierarchy of Needs is as follows; *the physiological needs, the needs for safety and security, the needs for love and belonging, the needs for esteem, and the need to actualize the self,* in that order. The following write-up was from **Dr. C. George Boeree's website** on Personality Theories.
68

1. The physiological needs. *(Stem Brain Functions – Physical Stability)* These include the needs we have for oxygen, water, protein, salt, sugar, calcium, and other minerals and vitamins. They also include the need to maintain a pH balance (getting too acidic or base will kill you) and temperature (98.6 or near to it). Also, there's the needs to be active, to rest, to sleep, to get rid of wastes (CO_2, sweat, urine, and feces), to avoid pain, and to have sex. Quite a collection!

Maslow believed, and research supports him, that these are in fact individual needs, and that a lack of, say, vitamin C, will lead to a very specific hunger for things which have in the past provided that vitamin C -- e.g. orange juice. I guess the cravings that some pregnant women have, and the way in which babies eat the most foul tasting baby food, support the idea anecdotally.

2. The safety and security needs *(Mid Brain Functions – Emotional Stability).* When the physiological needs are largely taken care of, this second layer of needs comes into play. You will become increasingly interested in finding safe circumstances, stability, and protection. You might develop a need for structure, for order, some limits.

Looking at it negatively, you become concerned, not with needs like hunger and thirst, but with your fears and anxieties. In the ordinary American adult, this set of needs manifest themselves in the form *of our urges* to have a home in a safe neighborhood, a little job security and a nest egg, a good retirement plan and a bit of insurance, and so on.

3. The love and belonging needs *(Right Brain Functions – Social Stability).* When physiological needs and safety needs are, by and large, taken care of, a third layer starts to show up. You begin to feel the need for friends, a sweetheart, children, affectionate relationships in general, even a sense of community. Looked at negatively, you become increasing susceptible to loneliness and social anxieties.

In our day-to-day life, we exhibit these needs in our desires to marry, have a family, be a part of a community, a member of a church, a brother in the fraternity, a part of a gang or a bowling club. It is also a part of what we look for in a career.

4. **The esteem needs** *(Left Brain Functions – Intellectual Stability)*. Next, we begin to look for a little self-esteem. Maslow noted two versions of esteem needs, a lower one and a higher one. The lower one is the need for the respect of others, the need for status, fame, glory, recognition, attention, reputation, appreciation, dignity, even dominance. The higher form involves the need for self-respect, including such feelings as confidence, competence, achievement, mastery, independence, and freedom. Note that this is the "higher" form because, unlike the respect of others, once you have self-respect, it's a lot harder to lose!

Self-actualization

The last level is a bit different. Maslow has used a variety of terms to refer to this level: He has called it **growth motivation** (in contrast to deficit motivation), **being needs** (or **B-needs**, in contrast to D-needs), and **self-actualization**.

These are needs that do not involve balance or homeostasis. Once engaged, they continue to be felt. In fact, they are likely to become stronger as we "feed" them! They involve the continuous desire to fulfill potentials, to "be all that you can be." They are a matter of becoming the most complete, the fullest, "you" -- hence the term, self-actualization.

Now, in keeping with his theory up to this point, if you want to be truly self-actualizing, you need to have your lower needs taken care of, at least to a considerable extent. This makes sense: If you are hungry, you are scrambling to get food; If you are unsafe, you have to be continuously on guard; If you are isolated and unloved, you have to satisfy that need; If you have a low sense of self-esteem, you have to be defensive or compensate. When lower needs are unmet, you can't fully devote yourself to fulfilling your potentials.

It isn't surprising, then, the world being as difficult as it is, that only a small percentage of the world's population is truly, predominantly, self-actualizing. Maslow at one point suggested only about two percent!

The question becomes, of course, what exactly Maslow means by self-actualization. To answer that, we need to look at the kind of people he called self-actualizers. Fortunately, he did this for us, using a qualitative method called **biographical analysis**.

He began by picking out a group of people, some historical figures, some people he knew, whom he felt clearly met the standard of self-actualization. Included in this august group were *Abraham Lincoln, Thomas Jefferson, Albert Einstein, Eleanor Roosevelt, Jane Adams, William James, Albert Schweitzer, Benedict Spinoza, and Alduous Huxley, plus 12 unnamed people* who were alive at the time Maslow did his research. He then looked at their biographies, writings, the acts and words of those he knew personally, and so on. From these sources, he developed a list of qualities that seemed characteristic of these people, as opposed to the great mass of us.

These people were **reality-centered**, which means they could differentiate what is fake and dishonest from what is real and genuine. They were **problem-centered**, meaning they treated life's difficulties as problems demanding solutions, not as personal troubles to be railed at or surrendered to. And they had a **different perception of means and ends**. They felt that the ends don't necessarily justify the means, that the means could be ends themselves, and that the means -- the journey -- was often more important than the ends.

The self-actualizers also had a different way of relating to others. First, they enjoyed **solitude**, and were comfortable being alone. And they enjoyed deeper **personal relations** with a few close friends and family members, rather than more shallow relationships with many people.

They enjoyed **autonomy**, a relative independence from physical and social needs. And they **resisted enculturation**, that is, they were not susceptible to social pressure to be "well adjusted" or to "fit in" -- they were, in fact, nonconformists in the best sense.

They had an **unhostile sense of humor** -- preferring to joke at their own expense, or at the human condition, and never directing their humor at others. They had a quality he called **acceptance of self and others**, by which he meant that these people would be more likely to take you as you are than try to change you into what they thought you should be. This same acceptance applied to their attitudes towards themselves: If some quality of theirs wasn't harmful, they let it be, even enjoying it as a personal quirk. On the other hand, they were often strongly motivated to change negative qualities in themselves that could be changed. Along with this comes **spontaneity and simplicity**: They preferred being themselves rather than being pretentious or artificial. In fact, for all their nonconformity, he found that they tended to be conventional on the surface, just where less self-actualizing nonconformists tend to be the most dramatic.

Further, they had a sense of **humility and respect** towards others -- something Maslow also called democratic values -- meaning that they were open to ethnic and individual variety, even treasuring it. They had a quality Maslow called **human kinship** or *Gemeinschaftsgefühl* -- social interest, compassion, humanity. And this was accompanied by a **strong ethics**, which was spiritual but seldom conventionally religious in nature.

And these people had a certain **freshness of appreciation**, an ability to see things, even ordinary things, with wonder. Along with this comes their ability to be **creative**, inventive, and original. And, finally, these people tended to have more **peak experiences** than the average person. A peak experience is one that takes you out of yourself, that makes you feel very tiny, or very large, to some extent one with life or nature or God. It gives you a feeling of being a part of the infinite and the eternal. These experiences tend to leave their mark on a person, change them for the better, and many people actively seek them out. They are also called mystical experiences, and are an important part of many religious and philosophical traditions.

Maslow doesn't think that self-actualizers are perfect, of course. There were several flaws or **imperfections** he discovered along the way as well: First, they often suffered considerable anxiety and guilt -- but realistic anxiety and guilt, rather than misplaced or neurotic versions. Some of them were absentminded and overly kind. And finally, some of them had unexpected moments of ruthlessness, surgical coldness, and loss of humor.

Two other points he makes about these self-actualizers: Their values were "natural" and seemed to flow effortlessly from their personalities. And they appeared to transcend many of the dichotomies others accept as being undeniable, such as the differences between the spiritual and the physical, the selfish and the unselfish, and the masculine and the feminine.

I agree with Dr. Maslow's conclusion that we must pursue a life of self-actualization or become "successfully intelligent"[69]. But, 3 (Belonging Needs) and 4 (Esteem Needs) should be reversed in Maslow's model. Our Esteem Needs dictates our Belonging Needs, not the other way around if it were to be a healthy process towards "true" self-actualizations. If we have a sense of self-worth, we will seek similar people and if we have less self-worth, those are the kind of people we will be attracted to. Having a balance Esteem Needs will lead to a balance Belonging Needs.

So in conclusion, according to Maslow's Model (revised) – first, your physiological needs (stem brain), safety needs (mid brain), esteem need (left brain) and then belonging needs (right). How we accomplish this is by harmonizing or balancing all four areas of our brain.

CHAPTER 6

THE INTELLECTUAL BRAIN OR THE *"THINKING MIND"*: YOUR CONSCIOUS POWER

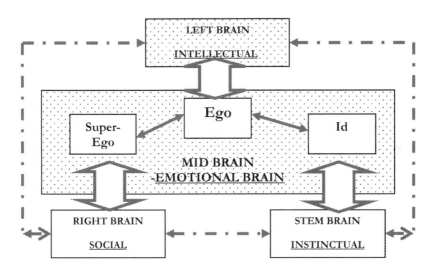

"Your Body, Internal (emotional), and External (physical, information, people) environment is a manifestation of your Mind."

Now, that you understand that your Superconscious Mind (or Social Intelligence) connects you to others automatically, whether you are aware of it or not; this connectivity allows others to mold you to the person they want you to be. **The good news is that there are checks and balances in your brain to stop this from happening or filter this process to your likings. But the choice is yours to use or not. This is where your "conscious mind," or intellectual (analytical) intelligence or the left side of you brain comes in (or as known in religion as "Mind").**

Your "conscious mind" is connected to the Ego or Conscience of the Mid brain (Super-Ego, Ego, and id) which the Hypothalamus (*regulates your body's internal environment and balances your systems with the external world*) **and Basal Ganglia** (*which integrate thoughts and feelings with physical actions*) **are part of. <u>You can change your internal environment with thought through the Hypothalmus and</u>**

Basal Ganglia using your "six mental faculties."

It's your introverted attitude. Your state of or tendency toward being wholly or predominantly concerned with and interested in your own mental life".[70] Introverts tend to be quiet, low-key, deliberate, and relatively non-engaged in social situations. You take pleasure in solitary activities such as reading, writing, drawing, watching movies, listening to music, inventing, and designing. An introverted, you likely to enjoy time spent alone and find less reward in time spent with large groups of people (although you may enjoy one-to-one or one-to-few interactions with close friends). You prefer to concentrate on a single activity at a time and like to observe situations before you participate. [71]

Introversion should not be confused with shyness, although introverts may also be shy. Introverts choose solitary over social activities by preference, whereas shy people avoid social encounters out of fear. [72]

As an introvert, you are energized when alone. **You tend to "fade" when with people and can easily become over stimulated with too many others around.** An introvert tends to think or analyzes things before speaking. When given the chance, an introvert will sit alone and think or analyzes things rather than talk with someone else. In other words, introverts are analytically intelligent.

Psychologist Robert J. Sternberg, in his Triarchic Theory of Intelligence states that "Analytical Intelligence" similar to the standard psychometric definition of intelligence e.g. as measured by Academic problem solving: analogies and puzzles, and corresponds to his earlier componential intelligence. Sternberg considers this reflects how an individual relates to his internal world.[73]

Sternberg believes that Analytical Intelligence (Academic problem-solving skills) is based on the joint operations of metacomponents and performance components and knowledge acquisition components of intelligence as explained below.

Metacomponents: control, monitor and evaluate cognitive processing. These are the *executive* functions to order and organize performance and knowledge acquisition components. They are the **higher-order processes** that order and organize the performance components. Used to analyze problems and pick a strategy for solving them. They decide what to do and the performance components actually do it.

Performance Components: execute strategies assembled by the metacomponents. They are the basic operations involved in any cognitive act. They are the cognitive processes that enable us to encode stimuli, hold information in short-term memory, make calculations, perform mental calculations, mentally compare different stimuli, and retrieve information from long-term memory.

Knowledge acquisition components: are the processes used in gaining and storing new knowledge - i.e. capacity for learning. The strategies you use to help memorize things exemplify the processes that fall into this category.

Sternberg feels that IDs in intelligence are related to IDs in the use of these cognitive processes. He feels that people with better reasoning ability generally spend more time understanding the problem but reach their solution faster than those who are less skilled at the task. This intelligence falls in the domain of the left brain hemisphere.

Multiple intelligences expert psychologist Howard Gardner found the following intelligences that I classify as activities within the left brain hemisphere are; *Linguistic, and Logical-Mathematical*

Verbal/Linguistic Intelligence is the ability to use words and language. These learners have highly developed auditory skills and are generally elegant speakers. They think in words rather than pictures. Their skills include: listening, speaking, writing, story telling, explaining, teaching, using humor, understanding the syntax and meaning of words, remembering information, convincing someone of their point of view, analyzing language usage. Possible career interests are Poet, journalist, writer, teacher, lawyer, politician, and translator

Logical/Mathematical Intelligence is the ability to use reason, logic and numbers. These learners think conceptually in logical and numerical patterns making connections between pieces of information. Always curious about the world around them, these learners ask lots of questions and like to do experiments. Their skills include: problem solving, classifying and categorizing information, working with abstract concepts to figure out the relationship of each to the other, handling long chains of reason to make local progressions, doing controlled experiments, questioning and wondering about natural events, performing complex mathematical calculations, working with geometric shapes. Possible career paths are scientists, engineers, computer programmers, researchers, accountants, and mathematicians

As mentioned earlier that *Linguistic intelligence* involves sensitivity to spoken and written language, the ability to learn languages, and the capacity to use language to accomplish certain goals. *Logical-mathematical* intelligence in Howard Gardner's words entails the ability to detect patterns, reason deductively and think logically. This intelligence is most often associated with scientific and mathematical thinking and parallels Sternberg's analytical intelligence definition.

It's this academic problem-solving skill that you use to consciously manufacture or create your DREAM, GOAL, IDEA, TARGET, and VISION.

It's here where you create whatever you desire, needs, inspires and interest--**consciously** by using your **six mental faculties** of *knowledge, reasoning (thinking abilities), understanding, judgment, discernment and wisdom* within the framework of the above mentioned intelligences. The six mental faculties can be organized under the three components of Dr. Sternbergs's model. The **Metacomponents** are *wisdom and discernment*; **Performance** Components are *judgments and thinking abilities*; and **Knowledge** Components are *knowledge and understanding.* You can transform or morph yourself in to whatever you inspire, want, need, and desire by using your six mental faculties.

Wisdom (Successful intelligence)[74] is your ability to put **knowledge, understanding, , reasoning or thinking abilities discernment, and judgment** to work, or to use it, the intelligent application of learning. A person might have considerable knowledge but not know how to use it because of lacking wisdom.

Discernment (Creative and Practical intelligence) involves seeing or recognizing things, but it emphasizes distinguishing the parts, weighing or evaluating one in the light of the others. You consciously go beyond the given and tapped in to your right brain to see the big picture of the matter or situation and weigh, evaluate against another through your five senses. [75]

Reasoning or thinking abilities (Analytical intelligence) is the mind and thoughts directing to an admirable, upright end, or just the opposite.[76] It's your ability to solve and judge ideas. Yale's Robert Sternberg suggested six steps to better thinking abilities (analytical) or reasoning.

I. Recognize that there is a problem.

II. Define the problem

III. Represent information about the problem accurately.

IV. Invest resources

V. Allocate resource wisely.

VI. Track your progress during the problem-solving process.

Judgment (Practical intelligence) is the cognitive process of reaching a decision or drawing conclusions or the mental ability to understand and discriminate between relations[77]. It's your ability to use your ideas and implement them effectively. In other words, it is your ability to translate theory into practice and abstract ideas into practical accomplishments. You accomplish this by recognizing your pattern of strengths and weaknesses. Strengthen those skills in which you excel and find a way around those skills in which you don't do well. And last, believe in yourself.

Knowledge (Analytical and Practical intelligence) essentially, means familiarity with facts acquired by personal experience, observation, or study[78]. You consciously directed your mental process to access information or data within itself, your left lobes or from the right lobes, mid and stem brain area. So therefore, your acquisition of knowledge in whatever area your want to pursue to create your target is vital. Your target or goals will not be clear unless your have enough knowledge on the subject.

Understanding (Analytical Intelligence) is the ability to see how the parts or aspects of something relate to one another, **to see the entire**

matter and not just isolated facts. [79] It's your ability formulate new or clever solutions to problems by putting yourself in someone else shoe. You actively seek out and plan to become a role model. You understand a matter when you serve as role model. You allow others and yourself to make mistakes. You take sensible risk and encourage others to do the same.[80]

It's the application of your six mental faculties above that you will create the **cause** that will bring the **effects** that you desire, need, inspires, and interest. Take time to study and understand each of your mental faculties above so you can create your dream and target clearly or with clarity. It's not developing or understanding your six mental faculties why so many of us do not have clear goals, vision, ideas or target.

Looking to Change Your Life?

If you want to make changes in your life, you must look to the cause, and the cause is the way you are using the conscious mind or your analytical intelligences--the way you are thinking and using your six mental faculties. You cannot think both negative and positive thoughts at the same time. One or the other must dominate. The mind is a creature of habit, so it becomes your responsibility to make sure that positive emotions and thoughts constitute the dominating influence in your mind.

In order to change external conditions, you must first change the internal. Most people try to change external conditions by working directly on those conditions as the previous example about alcoholics or drug addicts. *It is like standing in front a mirror and trying to change the image in the mirror. This always proves futile, or at best temporary, unless it is accompanied by a change of thoughts and beliefs.*

Awakening to this truth, the way to a "better," "more successful life," becomes crystal clear. Train your conscious mind or your six mental fculties to think thoughts of success, happiness, health, prosperity, and to weed out fear and worry.

Keep your conscious mind or intellectual or analytical intelligence busy with the expectation of the best, and make sure the thoughts you habitually think are based upon what you want to see happen in your life.

WHAT IS IT THAT MAKES A PERSON A WINNER?

"It's all in the mind," says Arnold Schwarzenegger, Governor of California, multimillionaire, successful real estate tycoon, movie star, bodybuilder, and five-time winner of the Mr. Universe title. Arnold has it made. *But it wasn't always so.* Arnold can remember when he had nothing except a belief that his mind was the key to where he wanted to go.

"When I was very young, I visualized myself being and having what it was I wanted. Mentally, I never had any doubts about it. The mind is really so incredible. Before I won my first Mr. Universe, I walked around the tournament like I owned it. The title was already mine. I had won it so many times in my mind, that there was no doubt I would win it. Then, when I moved on to the movies, the same thing. I visualized myself being a successful actor and earning big money. I could feel and taste success. I just knew it would all happen."

The technique Arnold is talking about, the technique that brought him so much success is called "visualization," or *a better term is "imaginary experiences" as coined by Mr. Stuart Lichtman.* **A visualization or imaginary experience is using your imagination to see yourself in a situation that hasn't yet happened, picturing yourself having or doing the thing you want, or successfully achieving the results you desire.** This process is done through the right side of you brain but it's your conscious decision (left) to see or activate the process of visualization.

The reason why this works is because imaginary experiences or visualizations activate ALL four areas of your brain; superconscious, conscious, nonconscious, and subconscious--to work harmoniously to make it happen. *Experiences whether real or imaginary are the language the brain understands.*

Dr. Robert Anthony called this technique "Pre-Play." Instead of *continue playing--*"Instant Re-play,"*--the replaying of past experiences,* he suggested; creating your future through "Pre-Play."

Let's say you want to be more confident. Using visualization or imaginary experience, you picture yourself working, talking to people, all with great confidence. You imagine yourself in situations that normally give you difficulty, and you see yourself in these situations as confident, at ease, and performing well.

You might picture your friends and associates complimenting you on your newfound confidence. You feel the pride and satisfaction of being a confident person, and in your mind you enjoy the things that happen to you as a result of your confidence. You visualize everything that would or could happen to you, and live as if it really is happening to you.

With the help of Mentors and Role Models, any thought put into your mind and nourished regularly will produce results in your life.

What is it that you want in your life? Better health? *Then get health consciousness.* Greater prosperity? *Get prosperity consciousness.* More spirituality? *Get spiritually consciousness.*

Everything exists in the universe, and exists as a possibility. All that is required is for you to feed in the necessary energy until your objective becomes your own.

How reassuring it is to think that no matter what a person's past or present situation, no matter how many times he or she has previously failed, if that person would regularly feed his or her consciousness with the right information (spiritual, intellectually, physical, and emotional), his or her situation would change!

This remarkable ability has been given to each and every one of us to use or to ignore. **It costs no money**. **It takes no special talent. It takes only the decision and action on your part to take the time and put forth the necessary effort to develop the appropriate consciousness.** That's all! Everything else will automatically fall into place.

Vic Johnson in his Sunday, February 12th, 2006, eMeditation Series titled, Good Health Begins in the Mind, said the following:

> "Disease and health, like circumstances, are rooted in thought. Sickly thoughts will express themselves through a sickly body." - **Path to Prosperity**

Almost 100 years ago James Allen wrote these words in his book, **Path to Prosperity**: "in the near future, the fact that all disease has its origin in the mind will become common knowledge."

He would be honored to know that a June, 1997 story in the Wall Street Journal said that HMOs were reporting that as much as 70% of all visits to a primary care physician were for a psychosomatic illness — a disorder that involves both mind and body.

According to Dr. David Sobel, a primary care physician and author of the highly respected *Mind-Body Health Newsletter,* only 16% of people who visit their physician for common maladies like nausea, headache, and stomach upset, are diagnosed with a physical, organic cause. That means that a whopping 84% are suffering from an illness that originated in THOUGHT!

The evidence suggests that in most cases today we are thinking and talking our way to sickness and disease or as <u>Bob Proctor</u> puts it: "dis — ease."

Jeff Keller, writing in **Attitude is Everything**, says, "it makes absolutely no sense to keep repeating that you have "chronic back pain that will never go away" or that you get "three or four bad colds every year." By uttering these statements, you are actually instructing your body to manifest pain and disease."

In his book <u>A Clear Path to Healing</u>, Dr. Barry Weinberg writes, "The creation of health, as in all creations, must first start in the mind. Once the mind is made up and the commitment and unwavering determination to heal has been made, healing is inevitable."

Cognitive Psychologists were very interested in this area of the mind. They study your ability to acquire, organize, remember, and use knowledge to guide your behavior. They argued that what goes on inside your head is of critical importance. How you feel (mid), what you do (stem), what inspires (right) you starts with what you're thinking (left), not with some impersonal stimulus from the environment.

Although Cognitive psychologist focuses on the mind or brain, they don't rely on intuitions (right), observing rats or cats (stem), view behaviors as driven by powerful mental conflict within the subconscious (mid), but study human behavior and then make inferences about the mind from those observations. For example, Swiss psychologist Jean Piaget gave children a series of problems to solve and then documented the mistakes they made and their reasons for their answers. After testing many children at varying ages, he formed his theory about how children develop their ability to reason.[81]

The influence of cognitive psychology is everywhere. You see it in the numerous self-help books that proclaim the power of self-talk, and in the concept of attitude adjustments. If you hear someone say, "When life gives you lemons, make lemonade," he or she is speaking from cognitive perspective.[82]

CHAPTER 7

THE INSTINCTUAL BRAIN OR THE SENSING MIND: YOUR NONCONSCIOUS POWER

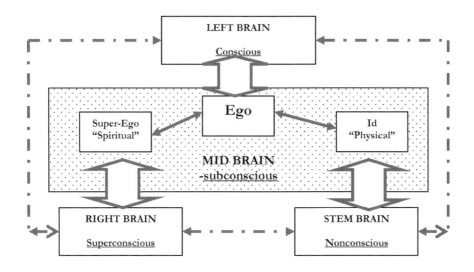

"Your Mind, Internal, and External environment is a manifestation of your Body."

So far you have learned that your superconscious mind or right brain connects you to "Original Source Energy" and other people (Mentors and Roles Models) who will help you create your success if you choose. You learned that your *conscious* mind or left brain will filter your *superconscious* mind's connectivity to others on what you will use to create your Dream, Goal, Idea, Target and Vision. Now, the combining activities of both the *right*- and *left*-brain (or *superconscious* mind and *conscious* mind) will move the body (or *nonconscious* mind) into action or motion or vice versa. The nonconscious mind is a reservoir of your heritage in your DNA whether good or bad. Your Left and Right Brain can trigger or evoke information from this reservoir.

The Thalamus, Pineal and Pituitary glands or id in the Mid Brain is access by the Instinctual Brain. The body is the manifestation of activities of the *Superconscious*, *Conscious*, and *Subconscious* mind and has its own intelligence – **practical or physiological intelligence.** This area of the brain controls and manages what is known in religion as the "Soul" or "Body." This should not be again, confused with "Spirit" or "Strength" which is control and manage by the Right brain.

Psychologist Sternberg believes that Practical Intelligence involves the ability to grasp, understand and deal with everyday tasks. This is the Contextual aspect of intelligence and reflects how you relate to the external world about yourself.[83]

Sternberg states that Intelligence is: "Purposive adaptation to, shaping of, and selection of real-world environments relevant to one's life"

Purposive means that intelligence is directed towards goals, however vague or subconscious they may be. This means that intelligence is indicated by one's attempts to adapt to one's environment.

Practical Intelligence can be said to be intelligence that operates in the real world. People with this type of intelligence can adapt to, or shape their environment. It might also be called **"Street-smarts"** or instinctual intelligence as Cesar Milans calls it. In measuring this facet, not only mental skills but attitudes and emotional <u>factors that can influence intelligence</u> are measured.

So this practical intelligence is a combination of:

(a) adaptation to the environment in order to have goals met

(b) changing the environment in order to have goals met

(c) or, if (a) and (b) don't work moving to a new environment in which goals can be met.

Sternberg believes that individuals considered intelligent in one culture may be looked on as unintelligent in another.

An important asset of this theory is to avoid defining intelligence in terms of intelligence tests rather than performance in the everyday world (which is, after all, what intelligence tests try to predict!).

Multiple intelligences expert psychologist Howard Gardner found the following intelligences that I classify as activities within the *Stem Brain: Bodily-Kinesthetic and naturalist intelligence.*

Bodily-kinesthetic intelligence entails the potential of using one's whole body or parts of the body to solve problems. This problem solving process is impacted by what's in your DNA. It is the ability to use mental abilities to coordinate bodily movements. Howard Gardner sees mental and physical activity as related.

Naturalist intelligence enables human beings to recognize, categorize and draw upon certain features of the environment. It 'combines a description of the core ability with a characterization of the role that many cultures value'.

Anthony Robbins, in his book, Unlimited Power, Chapter 9, titled, "Physiology: The Avenue of Excellence" discussed and explained the *nonconscious* power or mind. Mr. Robbins uses the term "Physiology" to describe what I called the "Nonconscious" mind. It is the same thing.

So, following, is an explanation of what the nonconscious mind or practical or instinctual intelligence is. Just substitute the word "Physiology" with the word "nonconscious." **All italic words are my insertions**.

"Physiology is the most powerful tool we have for instantly changing states (*Being*), for instantly producing dynamic result. There's an old saying: "If you would be powerful, pretend to be powerful." Truer words were never spoken. I expect people to get powerful results from my seminars, results that will change their lives. To do that, they have to be in the most resourceful physiology possible, for there's no powerful action without powerful physiology.[84]

If you adopt a vital, dynamic, excited physiology, you automatically adopt the same kind of state (Being). The biggest leverage we have in any situation is physiology-because it works so fast, and it works without fail. Physiology and internal representations are totally linked. If you change one, you instantly change the other. I like to say, "There is no mind, there is only body," and "there is no body, there is only mind." If you change your physiology--that is, your posture, your breathing patterns, your muscle tension, and your tonality--you instantly change your internal representations and your state (Being).[85]

Can you ever remember a time when you felt totally rundown? How did you perceive the world? When you feel physically tired or your muscles are weak or you have pain somewhere, you perceive the world quite differently from when you feel rested, alive, and vital. Physiological manipulation is a powerful tool for controlling your own brain. So it's extremely important that we realize how strongly it affects us, that it's not some extraneous variable, but an absolutely crucial part of a cybernetic loop that's always in action.[86]

When your physiology runs down, the positive energy of your state (*Being*) runs down. When your physiology brightens and intensifies, your state does the same thing. So physiology is the lever to emotional change. In fact, you can't have an emotion without a corresponding change in physiology. And you can't have a change in physiology without a corresponding change in state (*Being*). There are two ways to change state (*Being*), by changing internal representations (*subconscious*) or by changing physiology (*nonconscious*). So if you want to change your state (being) in an instant-what do you do? *Zap!* You change your physiology--that is, your breathing, your posture, facial expression, the quality of your movement, and so on.[87]

If you start to grow tired, there are certain specific things you can do with your physiology to continue to communicate this yourself: a slump in shoulder position, relaxation of many major muscle groups, and the like. You can become tired simply by changing your internal representations so that they give your nervous system a message that you are tired. If you change your physiology to the way it is when you feel strong, it will change your internal representations and how you feel at that moment. If you keep telling yourself that you're tired, you're forming the internal representation that keeps you tired. If you say you have the resources to be alert and on top of things, if you consciously adopt that physiology, your body will make it so. Change your physiology and you change your state.[88]

...Everything that scientists are finding today emphasizes one thing; sickness, and health, vitality and depression are often decisions. They're things we can decide to do with our physiology. They are usually not conscious decisions, but they are decisions nonetheless.[89]

No one consciously says, "I'd rather be depressed than happy." We think of depression as a mental state, but it has very clear, identifiable physiology. It's not hard to visualize a person who is depressed. Depressed people often walk around with their eyes down. They drop their shoulders. They take weak, shallow breaths. They do all things that put their body in a depressed physiology. Are they deciding to be depressed? They sure are. Depression is a result, and it requires very specific body images to create it.[90]

The exciting thing is that you can just as easily create the result called ecstasy by changing your physiology in certain specific ways. After all, what are emotions? They are complex association, a complex configuration of physiological states (*Being*). Without changing any of his internal representations, I can change the state of any depressed person in seconds. You don't have to look and see what pictures a depressed person is making in his mind. Just change his physiology, and zap, you change his state (Being).[91]

If you stand up straight, if you throw your shoulders back, if you breathe deeply from your chest, if you look upward-if you put yourself in a resourceful physiology – you can't be depressed. Try it yourself[92].

Think of something you imagine you can't do but would like to be able to do. Now how would you stand if you knew you could do it? How would you talk? How would you breathe? Right now, put yourself congruently as possible in the physiology you would be in if you knew you could do it. Make your whole body give the same message. Make your stance; breathing and face reflect the physiology you'd have if you knew you could do it. Now note the difference between this state (*Being*) and the one you were in. If you are congruently maintaining the right physiology, you will feel "as if" you can handle what you didn't think you could before.[93]

...Try this for yourself; if you are upset or crying and want to stop, look up. Put your shoulders back and get into a visual state (Being.) Your feelings will change instantly. You can do this for your kids. When they get hurt, have them look up. The crying and pain will be stopped, or at least decreased tremendously, in a moment.[94]

The same technique can be practiced whenever we feel we can't do something--we can't approach that woman or man, we can't talk to the boss, and so on. We can change our states and empower ourselves to take action either by changing the pictures and dialogues in our minds or by changing how we are standing, how we are breathing, and the tone of voice we are using. The ideal is to change both physiology and tone. Having done this, we can immediately feel resourceful and be able to follow through with the actions necessary to produce the results we desire.[95]

The same is true with exercise. If you work out hard and you're short of breath and you keep saying to yourself how tired you are or how far you've run, you will indulge in a physiology-like sitting down or panting-that supports that communication. If, however, even though you're out of breath, you consciously stand upright and direct your breathing into a normal rate, you will feel recovered in a matter of moments.[96]

The following account demonstrates the power of the nonconscious mind. It's Norman Cousins's story. In his <u>Anatomy of an Illness</u>, he described how he made a miraculous recovery from a long, debilitating illness by laughing his way to health. Laughter was one tool Cousins used in a conscious effort to mobilize his will to live and to prosper. A major part of his regimen was spending a good deal of his day immersed in films, television programs, and books that made him laugh. This obviously changed the consistent internal representations he was making, and the laughter radically changed his physiology--and thus the messages to his nervous system of how to respond. He found that immediate, positive physical changes ensued. He slept better, his pain was lessened, his entire physical presence improved.[97]

Eventually, he recovered completely, even though one of his doctors initially said he had a "one-in-five-hundred chance" of making a full recovery. Cousins concluded: "I have learned never to underestimate the capacity of the human mind and body to regenerate--even when prospects seem most wretched. The life force may be the least understood force on earth."[98]

Some fascinating research that is beginning to surface may shed some light on Cousins's experience and others like it. The studies look at the way our facial expressions affects the way we feel and conclude it' not so much just that we smile when we feel good or laugh when we're in good spirits. Rather, smiling and laughing set off biological a process that, in fact, makes us feel good. They increase the flow of blood to the brain and change the level of oxygen, the level of stimulation of the neurotransmitters. The same thing happens with other expressions. Put your facial expression in the physiology of fear or anger or disgust or surprise, and that's what you'll feel.[99]

An important corollary of physiology is congruency. If I'm giving you what I think is a positive message, but my voice is weak and tentative and my body language is disjointed and unfocused, I'm incongruent. Incongruity keeps me from being all I can be, from doing all I can do, and from creating my strongest State (Being). Giving oneself contradictory messages is a subliminal way of pulling a punch.[100]

You may have experienced times when you didn't believe a person, but you weren't sure why. What the person said made sense, but you somehow came away not really believing him. Your subconscious mind picked up what your conscious mind didn't. For example, when you asked a question, the person may have said, "Yes," but at the time his head may have been slowly shaking no. Or he may have said, "I can handle it," but you noted his shoulders were hunched over, his eyes were down, and his breathing was shallow-all of which told your unconscious that he was really saying, "I can't handle it." Part of him wanted to do what you were asking, and part of him didn't. Part of him was confident, and part of him wasn't. Incongruency worked against him. He was trying to go into two directions at once. He was representing one thing with his words and quite another with his physiology.[101]

We've all experienced the price of incongruence when part of us really wants something but another part within seems to stop us. Congruency is power. People who consistently succeed are those who can commit all of their resources, mental and physical, to work together toward achieving a task. Stop a moment now and think of the three most congruent people You know. Now think of the three most incongruent people You know. What's the difference between them? How do congruent people affect you personally versus people who are incongruent?[102]

Developing congruity is a major key to personal power. When I'm communicating, I'm emphatic in my words, my voice, my breathing, and my entire physiology. When my body and my words match, I'm giving clear signals to my brain that this is what I want to produce. And my mind responds accordingly.[103]

If you say to yourself, "Well, yeah, I guess this is what I ought to be doing," and your physiology is weak and indecisive, what sort of a message does the brain get? It's like trying to view a television with a flickering tube. You can barely make out the picture. The same is true for your brain: if the signals your body provides are weak or conflicting, the brain doesn't have a clear sense of what to do. It's like a soldier going into battle' with a general who says, "Well, maybe we ought to try this. I'm not sure if it will work, but let's go out and see what happens." What kind of a state does that put the soldier in?[104]

If you say, "I absolutely will do that," and your physiology is unified, your posture, your facial expression, your breathing pattern, the quality of your gestures and movements, and your words and your tonality match you absolutely will do it. Congruent states are what we all want to move toward, and the biggest step you can take is to be sure you're in a firm, decisive, congruent physiology. If your words and your body don't match up, you're not going to be totally effective.[105]

One way to develop congruency is to model the physiologies of people who are congruent. The essence of modeling is to discover which part of the brain an effective person uses in a given situation. If you want to be effective, you want to use your brain in the same way. If you mirror someone's physiology exactly, you will tap the same part of your brain. Are you in congruent state now? If not, shift into one. What percentage of the time are you in incongruent states? Can you be congruent more often? Start to do so today. Stop and Identify five people who have powerful physiologies that you would like to mirror. How do these physiologies differ from yours? How do the people sit? Stand? Move? What are some of their key facial expressions and gestures? Take a moment and sit in the way one of these people sits. Make similar facial expressions and gestures. Notice how you feel. [106]

Some recent research gives scientific support to this. According to a story in *Omni* magazine, two researchers have found that words have a characteristic electrical pattern in the brain. Neurophysiologist Donald York of the University of Missouri Medical Center and Chicago speech pathologist Tom Jenson found that the same patterns hold true from person to person. In one experiment, they were even able to find the same brain wave pattern in people who spoke different languages. They've already taught computers to recognize those brain wave patterns so they can interpret the words in a person's mind even before they're spoken! The computers can literally read minds, much the way we can when we precisely mirror physiology.[107]

Some unique aspects of physiology--special looks or tonalities, or physical gestures-can be found in people of great power, like John F. Kennedy, Martin Luther King, Jr., or Franklin Roosevelt. If you can model their specific physiologies, you'll tap into the same resourceful parts of the brain and start to process information the way they do. You will literally feel the way they felt. Obviously, since breathing, movement, and tonality are critical factors in creating state, photos of these people do not provide as specific an amount of information as would be desirable. A movie or video of them would be ideal. For a moment mirror just their postures, facial expressions, and gestures as accurately as you can. You will begin to feel similar feelings. If you remember how that person's voice sounds, YOU might say something in that tone of voice.[108]

Being attentive to physiology creates choices. Why do people take drugs, drink alcohol, smoke cigarettes, and overeat? Aren't these all indirect attempts to change state by changing physiology? This *section* has provided you with the direct approach to quickly changing states (Being). By breathing or moving body or facial muscles in a new pattern, you immediately change your state. It will produce the same results as food, alcohol, or drugs without harmful side effects to either your body or your psyche.[109]

Remember, in any cybernetic loop, the individual who has the most choice is in control. In any device, the most critical aspect is flexibility. All other things being equal, the system with the most flexibility has more choices and more ability to direct other aspects of the system. It's the same with people. The people with the most choices are the ones most in charge. Modeling is about creating possibility. And there's no faster, more dynamic way than through physiology.

The next time you see someone who is extremely successful someone you admire and respect, copy their gestures. Feel the difference and enjoy the change in thought patterns. Play. Experience it. New choices await you!

Now let's take a look at another aspect of physiology--the foods we eat, the way we breathe, and the nutrients we supply to ourselves.

You can change your internal representations all day long, but if your biochemical is messed up, it's going to make the brain create distorted representations. It's going to throw off the whole system. In fact, it's highly unlikely you'll even feel like using what you've learned. You could have the most beautiful race car in the world, but if you try to run it on beer, it's not going to work. You have the right car and the right fuel, but if the spark plugs are not firing right, you won't get peak performance.[110]

Your target with a workout or fitness program is to increase your energy level. The higher your energy level, the more efficient your body will be. The more efficient your body, the better you feel and the more you will use your talent to produce outstanding results.

Create the best physiological intelligence for your body by owning and controlling it.

Biological, Behavioral and Evolutionist psychology have a lot to say about your nonconscious or physiological intelligences.

The Biological psychologists look to the body to explain the mind. They believed that we were born this way and look to see the influence of hormones, genes, the brain, and the central nervous system on the way we intend, think, act and feel. They were instrumental in the development of medications to treat mental disorder.

The Behavioral psychologist contents that we are just rats caught in a maze. The rat's behavior can be changed by just changing where it had found the food from the previous trails. John Watson believed that psychology should seek to understand people by studying what happens to them and how they respond. He believed that behavior usually started as a respond to an environmental event. From this he went on to reason that the consequences of that response would determine whether that behavior would increase over time or become less frequent.

The Evolutionist psychologists' contents that creatures whose inherited characteristics were best adapted to the environment were the ones that survived and reproduced. This principle of natural selection was applied to human behavior. They believed that a key to understanding human nature is in the behavior of our ancestors. We can reconstruct the problems our ancestors dealt with, and then understand the problem solving tendencies that helped then to survive and thus became a genetic part of human being.

Whether you are observing the manifestation of the mind through the body, or through behavior or survival characteristics', it's the Stem Brain or nonconscious that is in control. It's you responsibility to manage and control this part of your brain – stem brain.

CHAPTER 8

THE <u>EMOTIONAL</u> BRAIN OR THE *FEELING MIND*: YOUR SUBCONSCIOUS POWER

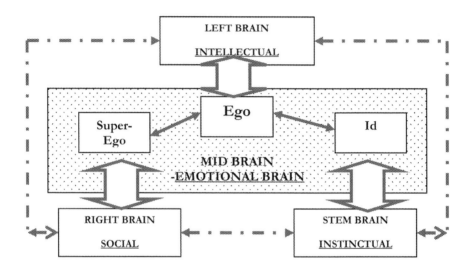

"Your Mind, Body and External environment is a manifestation of your Internal environment."

Your superconscious mind or right brain is social and spiritual. Your conscious or left brain or analytical mind filters activities from your superconscious mind or right brain and creates your life by choice or default. This information or data activates the nonconscious or stem brain or instinctual mind which moves the whole body into action or motion. ALL of these activities of the right, left and stem brain is stored in the subconscious for future references or usages **if** emotions are attached to it whether positive or negative. The Subconscious dictates what will be attracted to you. **The "Law of Attraction" is governed by the Subconscious or Mid Brain. In religion, what is known or discussed as the figurative Heart is the Subconscious or Mid Brain.**

In order to understand how your superconscious (Spirit), conscious(Mind), nonconscious(Soul) and subconscious(Heart) minds work together as a team to create your reality, let me again use an analogy.

Your subconscious mind (figurative Heart) is like fertile soil that accepts any seed - *thoughts from the conscious mind, senses from the nonconscious mind and images from the superconscious mind that you plant within it.* **Your habitual thoughts, images, senses and beliefs with emotions are the seeds** which are being constantly sown within, and they produce in your life what is planted just as surely as corn kernels produce corn. You will "reap what you sow." **This is the law of attraction.**

Your subconscious will not discriminate. It will allow, create, invite and attract failure, ill health and misfortune just as easily as success and abundance. *It is treacherous if not properly trained and guided.* It works to reproduce in your life according to the seeds you have nurtured within. Your subconscious accepts what is impressed upon it with feeling and emotion whether these thoughts are positive or negative. It does not evaluate things like your conscious mind does, and it does not argue with you to see if this is facts, truth or lies.

Once you grasp the fact that your subconscious will bring to you whatever you need, and you begin working, daily projecting thoughts with emotions through your conscious mind by utilizing your six mental faculties and images of what you want through your superconscious, seemingly chance and fortuitous events will begin to happen to you.

Your powerful inner collaborator, working with your instructions from your superconscious, conscious, and nonconscious, will bring to you the people and circumstances you require to meet your goals.

"A thousand unseen hands," as Joseph Campbell[111] describes them, "...will come to your aid." **Synchronicity appears to the uninitiated to be coincidence or luck, but it is neither.** *It is simply the operation of natural laws which you have set in motion with your thoughts through your superconscious (Right Brain), conscious(Left Brain) and nonconscious(Stem Brain).*

Let me explain how it works. Modern physics now sees the universe as a vast, inseparable web of dynamic energy activity. Not only is the universe alive and constantly changing, but everything in the universe affects everything else.

At its most primary level, the universe seems to be whole and undifferentiated, a fathomless sea of energy that permeates every object and every act. It is all one.

In short, scientists are now confirming what mystics, and seers have been telling us for thousands of years--we are not separate but part of one giant whole, part of the third dimension as Quantum physicist discovered. Our one whole giant Universe exist within the fourth dimension as a backdrop. Time and space exist in the fifth dimension and can not be explained by Einstein's theory of Relativity. Energy only exist in the third (physical) and fourth (spiritual) dimension.

We now know that everything in the universe is made up of energy. Einstein demonstrated this with his $E=MC^2$ (energy) is the same as $M=E/C^2$ (mass/physical matters) but in different sub-atomic structure.

The chair that you're sitting on is energy in a different molecular structure - mass. The walls of the room that you are now in, your computer, the events that happen to you are all made up of vibrations of energy at different speeds.

And our thoughts, too, are vibrations of energy. Our thoughts are of the same substance as the building blocks of the universe. Once we become aware of this remarkable fact, we can use it to our great advantage.

When, for example, you begin imprinting success upon your subconscious mind (figurative heart or mid brain) from information or data from your superconscious, conscious, and nonconscious mind, it sets up a continuous vibration of energy that resonates upon the whole. The subconscious works day and night with this success vibration, attracting to you the people and circumstances necessary for your success. And remember that the subconscious will work equally hard to attract to you the circumstances necessary for your failure if that is how you habitually think.

We are fortunate that the laws of physical reality and the laws of the mind are now beginning to be understood.

In years past, it might have seemed incredible that we could create our reality through this process, yet now, with these new insights, we are beginning to understand how it works.

Our thoughts being energy, it only makes sense that our repeated images, affirmations, *imagined experiences,* and visualizations from the conscious, superconscious, and nonconscious mind, when impressed on to the subconscious will create deeply held beliefs, fears and desires, vibrating within the larger web of reality, would have an affect upon that reality.

In fact, when you stop and really think about it, since we are all connected, how could it be otherwise?

The brain with four minds or intelligence power gives you the tools to create a happy, successful, and abundant life. Your destiny is yours for the making.

The Brain: SELF-ACTUALIZATION			
Superconscious or *Social Intelligence*	Conscious or *Intellectual Intelligence*	Nonconscious or *Physiological Intelligence*	Subconscious or *Emotional Intelligence*
Creative Intelligence	Analytical Intelligence	Practical Intelligence	Successful Intelligence
we/us	I	myself	Me
Super-Ego	Ego	id	√Self-Worth
Higher Self	Ego	Created Self	√ Self-Worth
Self Two	Self-Image	Self One	√ Self-Worth
Spiritual	Conscience	Physical	√ True-Self

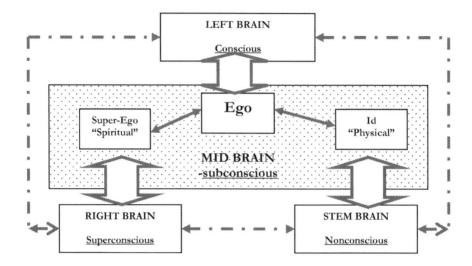

It is interesting to note that our subconscious is said to be made up of two components.

One subconscious posed for public display (spiritual), the other secretly connived for selfish advantage (physical). This two-faced, double-hearted posture is described in other writings as Higher Self , Created Self[112], or Super-Ego, and id[113] or Self Two and Self One. [114]

The above discussions missed one more concept which Dr. Sigmund Freud[115] discovered – **the Ego.**

Dr. Sigmund Freud, founder of the **Psychodynamic School** theorized that the subconscious (figurative heart or Mid Brain) is composed of three parts-**the Id, Ego, and Super-Ego.**   Freud believed that the Id is based on our pleasure *(or pain)* principle. The Id wants whatever feels good *(or painful)* at the time, with no consideration for the reality of the situation. [116]

*The **id** is composed of the **Thalamus** which is the meeting point for almost all nerves that connect one part of the brain to another part of the brain, the body to the brain, and brain to the body; the **Pituitary Gland** which secrets chemicals that activates your body's hormones; and the **Pineal Gland** which chemically regulates your cycles of sleep and wakefulness. The activities of the id can be monitored through these mid brain parts.*

The **Ego or "Conscience"** is based on the reality principle. The Ego understands that other people have needs and desires and that sometimes being impulsive or selfish can hurt us in the long run. It's the Ego's or Conscience's job to meet the needs of the Id, while taking into consideration the reality of the situation. [117] Therefore, the Ego or conscience must be trained to help both the id and Super-Ego make right choices.

*The **Ego or Conscience** is composed of the **Hypothalamus** which is the chemical factory that regulates your body's internal environment and balances your systems with the external world and the **Basal Ganglia** which integrate your thoughts and feelings with actions. The activities of Ego or Conscience can be observed through these mid brain parts.*

The **Super-Ego** is the moral part of us and develops due to the moral and ethical restraints placed on us by our caregivers or society. Many equate the **Super-Ego** with the **Conscience** as it dictates our belief of right and wrong. [118] For the purpose of this writing, *the Conscience is the Ego, not the Super-Ego as many have suggested.* The properties of the Conscience change as it depends on what it learns using its six mental faculties. The Super-Ego does not change because its properties are innate. That is, the belief of **what is right** is built in to the Super-Ego.

*The **Super-Ego** is composed of the **Hypocampus** which makes long term memeories and closely related to our search for novelty; the **Amydala** which is responsible for alerting the body in survival situations; and **Cingulate Gyrus** which coordinates Sensory input with emotions, regulates aggressive behavior and gives emotional responses to pain. The activities of the **Super-Ego** can be monitor or observe through these brain parts.*

In short, as illustrated in the diagram above, what Dr. Freud was discussing in his writings is that the **id (or Created Self & Self One or Physical Person) is wired to your nonconscious mind (stem and cerebellum brain) and is the one that wants to control you.** All forms of addiction, whether sex or drugs and so forth is your id taking over your Ego and Super-Ego. People who are of this personality type are *masochistic* and see themselves as "I am not worth anything" self-esteem. They see and treat everyone else this way because that's how they see their reality. They project this inner-self to their surroundings.

The **Super-Ego (or Higher Self & Self Two or Spiritual Person)** is your inner master within you that is connected to your Superconscious (Right Brain) and is the moral judge. All forms of self-righteousness are when your Super-Ego takes over your Ego or Conscience and Id. People of this personality type are *narcissistic* and view themselves as "I am holy." They project this inner-self to others and their surrounding and treat them that way.

Your **Ego or Conscience, (or Self-Worth or True Self)** or what other writings calls your **"Self-Image,"** keeps the balanced between your id and Super-Ego. Your Ego or Self-Image or Conscience is wired to your Conscious Mind. Your Ego connecting to your Conscious Mind filters reality through its six mental faculties of; *wisdom, knowledge, thinking abilities, understanding, discernment, and judgment, to create a balance and healthy you!*

In a healthy person, the Ego or Self-Image or Conscience is the strongest, so that it can satisfy the needs of the id, not upset the Super-Ego, and still take into consideration the reality of every situation. It is not an easy job by any means, but if the id gets too strong, *impulses and self-gratification take over your life.* If the Super-Ego becomes too strong, the person *would be driven by rigid morals*, would be judgmental and unbending in his or her interactions with the world, as mentioned earlier.

We stated earlier that the Ego's or Conscience's job was to satisfy the id's impulses, not offend the moralistic character of the Super-Ego, while still taking into consideration the reality of the situation. Think of the id (fleshly desires of the body) as the 'devil on your shoulder' and the Super-Ego (spiritual desires of the body) as the 'angel on your shoulder and Ego or Conscience as "YOU." YOU, have the free will to try to keep your id and Super-Ego in balance by using your six mental faculties **to avoid using its defense mechanism**. You don't want either one to get too strong so you talk to both of them, hear their perspective, and then make a decision. This decision is the Ego or Conscience talking, the one looking for that healthy balance if it's trained properly.

It is this mental dialogue within the subconscious (figurative Heart or Mid Brain) that some people hear and become afraid. But instead of being frightening by it, understand, control, and manage it. We ALL have this inner dialogue or voices. It's just those others' inner subconscious dialogues are more audible than others. The more we have internal conflicts within ourselves, the more we hear these conversations and they become louder and louder! We ALL sense this inner voice (Conscience or Ego) or conversation within ourselves. Interestingly, other people carry this conversation with themselves without understanding this process.

When you converse with yourself and settle differences between your id and the Super-Ego using your six mental faculties, you created a balanced self-love or "sense of self-worth" that is neither narcissistic nor masochistic.

The Ego or Conscience, as I stated earlier, is wired to the "Conscious Mind," the seat of "Intellectual or Analytical Intelligence." It has its challenges in satisfying both the id and the Superego. But it has tools it can use in its job as the mediator and facilitator; tools that help defend the Ego or the "You." *An Ego or Conscience not using its six mental faculties will resort to defend and protect itself.* These tools are called the defense mechanism of the "Ego" in the subconscious mind – **denial, displacement, projection, reaction formation, regression, sublimation, and repressions.**[119]

1.   Denial – the refusal to acknowledge thoughts, feelings, or memories that present a threat. Example. An abuse woman repeatedly brags to her friends about how much her partner loves her.

2.   Displacement – applying negative feelings to "safe" target rather than the source of the feelings. Example. After a day filled with criticism from his supervisor, a man goes home and yells at his dog.

3.   Projection – placing your thoughts, feelings, or behavior on to someone else. Example. The brother of a successful business woman tells his parents that his sister is jealous of him.

4.   Reaction Formation – espousing the opposite of an unacceptable feelings or thoughts. The adolescent who says, "I don't like him, you know I think boys are gross," actually has a crush on the boy.

5.   Regression - reverting to a behavior that is associated with an

earlier period development. Example. A healthy seven year old starts wetting his bed.

6. Sublimation – a type of displacement channeling unacceptable thoughts in to an appropriate area, often associate with art. Many artists will say that there is expression of their painful past experience.

7. Repression – pushing unacceptable thoughts deep in to the unconscious where they are inaccessible. Example. Twenty years after honorable discharge from the military, a former prisoner of war is unable to recount any of his experience in captivity.

Your Ego or Conscience working together with your six mental faculties of your Conscious Mind will reduced its stresses from having to defend itself. In fact, a properly trained ego or conscience does not have to defend itself. The above defenses are ALL internal conflicts that must be resolved or they are the contributing factor to many ailments.

As an **emotiovert,** your emotions or feelings dictates your decision making process. Your creative, analytical and practical intelligences that Robert Steinberg discusses are stored in the subconscious with emotions attached to it. When all three are balanced, it will create **"Successful intelligence"** as noted by Robert Sternberg, **"Intrapersonal intelligence"** as labeled by Howard Gardner or as Daniel Golemans calls it, **"Emotional intelligences. "**

Your ability to perceive, identify, and manage your emotion provides the basis for the kinds of social and emotional competencies that are important for your success in almost any job or environment. Emotionally intelligent people, Goleman says, have the ability to marshal their emotional impulses (or, at least, more so than those who are not emotionally intelligent); they have the self-awareness to know what they are feeling, and are able to think about and express those things; they have empathy for the feelings of others and insight into how others think; they can do things like delay gratification; they are optimistic and generally positive; they understand easily the dynamics of a given group, and, most important, where they fit inside that group.[120]

The key to your emotional intelligence is loving yourself first before you can love anyone else. You can't give something you don't possess or have.

Why do you need to understand the above concept about your subconscious and emotional intelligences? Because it is said that the subconscious (or figurative heart) is treacherous and can be very deceptive.

It is frightening how skillful your id or Created Self is at rationalizing with your Conscience or Ego wrongs that attracts to your body or nonconscious. Your DNA or genes contains numerous information that wants to control you. While it may deceive us and hide our real motives from us, the Universe, Infinite Intelligence, Source, or Dynamic Energy, or whatever you call it, sees it for what it is through its numerous laws in place in the Universe. We cannot fool the Universe! We ONLY fool and hurt ourselves. Whatever we cause, there's an effect! No exception!

To acquire a complete subconscious (a balanced Super-Ego, Ego and Id), you must be prepared emotionally to set aside preconceived opinions, willing to let Source Energy, Infinite Intelligence, be found true, even if it does demolish some of our pet ideas or cherished views.

Selfish motives must be purged to make our subconscious receptive to the Universe's will and ways.

Why? When you use the Ego's seven's defense mechanism listed above to rationalize the desires of id or the Super-Ego, and they are in conflict with one another or with information or habits/patterns stored in subconscious, **you experience signs of conflicts, or a tug of war within your subconscious.**

When you experience signs of conflict, you are using up energy that could go toward producing your success. [121] These signs or manifestation of conflicts within your subconscious is what Dr. Freud and his disciples have been observing and studying all these years. The field of Psychodynamic is the study of the **mid brain.**

Before you can achieve any success, you need to resolve these conflicts within your subconscious, and get all four areas of your brain to harmonize. These conflicts between the Created Self or id and Higher Self or Super-Ego, or with the Ego within your subconscious, are so frequent that you simply consider these "signals" from them to be simply *health problems or stress issues.* These signals of conflicts within your subconscious are:[122]

> ➢ Headaches, body pains, acid stomach

> ➢ Insomnia, oversleeping

> ➢ Fatigue, sluggishness, drowsiness

> ➢ Anger, fear, upset

> ➢ Confusion, difficulty understanding

> ➢ Difficulty concentrating, difficulty focusing

> ➢ Boredom, loss of energy

> ➢ Nagging feelings that something is wrong.

The various challenges listed under each of the four AXIS of the Psychiatric and Psychology Manual (DSM-IV) are all inner conflicts. **The truth is, the above signals are from your Ego or Conscience in your subconscious, telling you of a conflict within you—between your id and Super-Ego.[123] or within all three.**

When your Created Self or id experiences a conflict with your Higher Self or Super-Ego within your subconscious, your Ego or Conscience send messages to you through your Conscious Mind or intellectual intelligence. This is to make you aware of the conflict and to resolve it by choosing an alternative solution. Unfortunately, the conscious mind or intellectual intelligence is constantly engaging in other activities, so that it sends back a busy signal to your Ego or Conscience in your subconscious. Since your subconscious can't get through to get your attention, *it sends you non-verbal signals through your body by means of "body feelings" or "physiological intelligence."* These non-verbal signals manifest itself by many physical ailments that we experiences.

Your **subconscious mind or mid brain** resorts to indirect signals to you, by modifying various things in your body that it controls, such as:

➢ **The flow of blood** (that we consciously note as feelings of hot or cold, depending on whether it dilates the blood vessels or constrict them)

➢ **Muscle tension** (that we conscious note as stress pain or a feeling of relaxation depending on whether it tenses or relaxes your muscles)

➢ **Headaches** (when it severely constricts blood flow to parts of the brain)

➢ **The flow of bile and enzymes** into your stomach (that we consciously note as stomach pain, and the pressure of bloating, when too much enzyme flows, and congestion when too little flows).

It's the above non-verbal or physiological communication signals that Lie Detectors picks up during those sessions, unless the person is a sociopath (Charles Manson) Sensopath (Jeffrey Darmer) or psychopath (Theodore John Kaczynski -The **Unibomer**) and Emotiopaths (Suicide Bombers). The Lie Detectors do not work with the above paths. These people have managed to consciously switch back and forth between the id, ego, Super-Ego and all three components to satisfy their personal purpose. Their Ego or Conscience is numb or insensitive to the outside world and themselves.

People who live double lives, or split (or multiple) personalities, are able to consciously switch back and forth between the Ego, Super-Ego, id and all three simultaneously, depending on which personality or self-image or conscience they want to present or project to others.

At their psychological evaluations or discussions, they easily fool mental health professionals. At church, or other environments, which requires their spiritual Being be exhibited, they live through the Super-Ego or the "Spiritual" Being of the subconscious and fooled their church members. In private, or places where people don't know them, they live through their id (instant gratification), which is their "Physical"

Being, by engaging in activities that is in conflict with the laws of the universe. Sociopaths, psychopaths, sensopaths and emotiopaths loves mental and spiritual health professionals. Professionals are easily manipulated because of their pride and ego.

But, when there is cooperation within your subconscious; between your id or Created Self and Higher Self, or Super-Ego, you experience these familiar signs which you may simply identify as 'good days" for you. These signs of cooperation or self-worth are:[124]

> ➢ Feeling of well being, contentment

> ➢ Eagerness, enthusiasm, alertness

> ➢ High energy

> ➢ Joy, loving, happiness, *mildness, peace, self control, kindness*

> ➢ Clarity, understanding

You have a clean conscience or ego. You sleep well with pleasant or beautiful dreams. Nightmares are pictorial representations of conflicts within your subconscious! Do you see the importance of knowing your subconscious or figurative heart? If the literal heart needs a checkup from time to time, is it at regular intervals receiving good nourishment in sufficient amounts? Does it beat steady and strong, or sluggish and weak? Does it maintain the proper blood pressure? Is it receiving the exercise it needs?

(To be healthy, the heart needs to pump vigorously for long periods of time.) Does its pacemaker vary its speed to meet the changing needs? Is it being subjected to an emotional environment that puts it under heavy stress?

If the physical heart needs checkups, how much more so does the figurative heart or your subconscious need one! Give your subconscious a check up, and then you are safeguarding it. Why so?

Your subconscious mind attracts whatever is familiar to itself. The frightened subconscious attracts frightening experiences. A confused subconscious attracts more confusion.

The subconscious mind, which is the "proover," will always prove you are right. If you believe that you can't be right, you will create the circumstances and find the people to prove that you can't.

For example, thinking and believing that you are a fat person will keep you fat. This information will be impressed into your subconscious, stored as habit patterns (in Id) for future reference and core belief system. You may lose weight and override the belief, but as soon as you relax and are off guard, your subconscious will take over and automatically support your belief that you are a fat person again. Likewise, if you think you are a skinny person, the same process is involved.

Remember, the job of the subconscious is to prove that your belief is correct.

It functions like the automatic pilot of an airplane. If the autopilot is set to go east, you can manually override the controls and go north. But as soon as you let go, the automatic pilot, which has been programmed to go east, will control the plane and you will fly east.

Your subconscious does not change the reality of the world around you. It just filters the information that you present to it in order to support your beliefs or the picture that you hold in your mind.

Your success can never exceed the Self-Image or Ego or Conscience of you have of yourself in your subconscious!! Science and psychology have isolated this truth. This image controls your mind (Superconscious, Conscious, and Nonconscious), just like it controls your heartbeat. To remake your hidden self image for success and fulfillment is to remake your entire life. Other writings identify it as putting on a new personality.

If you are wondering what kind of Self-Image or Conscience you have, it is not difficult to figure out. All that is required is for you to take a look at the various aspects of your life. Take a look at the results you're getting. Possibly your relationships, your income, and the position you hold at work, or the type of business you are operating. Take a look at your own personal appearance. These are all the results; they are the outer expression of your inner image. As we alter this inner image, everything else begins to change.[125] Remember, the way we see the outside world is a mirror of who we are inside.

One of the great errors that almost everyone makes is either--they are attempting to change their income, they are attempting to change their position or job, they are attempting to change their business, *they are attempting to change their spouses, they are attempting to change their children, or* they are attempting to change something outside of themselves, without changing what's going on inside. *I mentioned this earlier in the book.* For me to try and change the results in my life, in other words, what's going on outside of me, without changing what's going on inside, would be just about as foolish for me to try to change the reflection in a mirror without changing my physical appearance. It's never going to happen. But that's what people are doing, they're trying to change something outside without changing what's going on inside.[126] PAY CONSTANT ATTENTION TO YOURSELF FIRST!

You attracted into your life every image that is stored in your subconscious! You attracted who you are; spouse, friends, money... etc.

Remember this; **no person and no circumstances on earth can prevent you from improving your self image. The degree to which you improve the image of yourself will be in exact proportion to the amount of truth that you can honestly accept and amount of positive change you put in to engineering your new Self-Image[127]** *or new personality or conscience.*

If you believe that business is bad, or that there are no new opportunities for your business, your subconscious will not point out new opportunities or direct you in ways to improve your present business.

This would be a violation of the principle of subconscious; it will only point out problems that support your belief that things are bad, or that there are no new opportunities.

Your subconscious cannot think for itself. It will draw to you only those things that are consistent with your deepest inner beliefs, nothing more, and nothing less. If you do not know this as a truth, and do not realize that you create habit patterns in your subconscious or emotional intelligence out of your ideas (conscious mind connecting with Ego/Conscience), you will feel powerless to affect change. You will feel that you are the victim of people, circumstances, and conditions.

If you accept yourself as powerless, you will imagine that the only way to get what you want is to get it from another person, panhandling, or through an organization. You will look to something or someone outside of yourself to fulfill your desires as I stated earlier.

When you come to the understanding that everything that you want can be created through your subconscious (heart) or emotional intelligence, nonconscious (body) or physiological intelligence, superconscious (spirit) or social intelligence, and conscious (mind) or intellectual intelligence, by applying the **TSF-24** to control, manage, and own your four power sources or intelligence, you come to the realization that only you can give yourself what you desire, need, intent, and interest. When you apply TSF-24 to your life, you will finally achieve what psychologist Abraham Maslow called "Self-Actualization."

Do you know your temperament, and interaction style? Why do you need to know it? It's is because all of this is the beginning of your journey of self-actualization and self discovery. Find out in the next Chapter.

CHAPTER 9

YOUR TEMPERAMENT!

"Your four Sub-Brains is YOU. Your dominant sub-brain is your main Temperament and is YOU."

What's your temperament? You should know it by now as it was determined by the "Do you know who you are survey" at the beginning of the book or your Blood Type. It's your dominant sub-brain or brain inclination. For example, if your survey result was LSRM, then your dominant sub-brain is Left Brain or Rationals Temperament. If your survey result was SMLR, then your dominant sub-brain is Stem Brain or Guardian Temperament. If your survey result was MSLR, then your dominant sub-brain is Mid brain or Artisan Temperament and so forth.

Below is a list of some famous individuals within each Temperament.[128]

RIGHT BRAIN – *IDEALIST:*

Oprah Winfrey, Jane Fonda, Shirley MacLaine, Pearl S. Buck, Charlotte Bronte, Emily Bronte, Emily Dickenson, Herman Hesse, Albert Camus, James Joyce, Leo Tolstoy, Ann Morrow Lindbergh, Oliver Stone, Erica Jong, Mohandas Gandhi, Eleanor Roosevelt, Leon Trotsky, Vladimir Lenin, Mikhail Gorbachev, Thomas Paine, Alexander Hamilton, Molly Brown "The Unsinkable," Princess Diana, Lord Alfred Russel Wallace, Siddhartha [Buddha], Albert Schweitzer, Carl Rogers, Abraham Maslow, Isabel Myers, Carl Jung, Soren Kierkegaard, and Plato

LEFT BRAIN- *RATIONALS:*

Steve Allen, Isaac Asimov, William F. Buckley, Ayn Rand, George Bernard Shaw, Walt Disney, Mark Twain, Gregory Peck, Thomas Jefferson, Abraham Lincoln, Dwight D. Eisenhower, Ulysses S. Grant, Douglas MacArthur, George Marshall, Peter the Great, Margaret Thatcher ,Fredrick Douglass, Napoleon Bonaparte, William Tecumsah Sherman, Albert Einstein, Richard Feynman, Ludwig Boltzmann,

Nikola Tesla, Lise Meitner, Charles Darwin, David Hume, Friedrich Nietzsche, Adam Smith, Marie Curie, Booker T. Washington, Aristotle, Bill Gates, Buckminster Fuller, Steve Wozniak, and George Soros

STEM BRAIN- GUARDIAN:

Louis B. Mayer, Jimmy Stewart, Fred McMurray, Ed Sullivan, Kareem Abul-Jabbar, Barbara Walters, Larry King, Dan Rather, Mike Wallace, Thomas Hardy, Andy Rooney, Oscar Levant, President George Washington, President Harry S., Truman, President Jimmy Carter, President Gerald Ford, President George HW Bush, President Leonid Brezhnev, Queen Elizabeth I, Queen Elizabeth II, Queen Victoria, Justice Sandra Day O'Connor, Justice Oliver Wendell Holmes, Justice Thurgood Marshall, General Omar Bradley, General Benard Montgomery, Warren Buffet, Sam Walton, Ray Kroc, John D. Rockefeller, Armond Hammer, J C Penny, F W Woolworth, William K Kellogg, Charles Post, Andrew Mellon, Brigham Young, Thomas Hobbes, and Mother Teresa,

MID BRAIN – ARTISAN[129]-

Elvis Presley, Elizabeth Taylor , Pablo Picasso , "Magic" Johnson, Madonna, Ernest Hemingway F. Scott Fitzgerald, Norman Mailer, Hugh Hefner, Neil Simon Wolfgang Amadeus Mozart , Paul Gauguin , Johnny Carson, Mel Brooks, Jonathan Winters, Barbra Streisand, Clint Eastwood, Michael Jordan, Franklin D. Roosevelt, Theodore Roosevelt, Winston Churchill , George S. Patton, Erwin Rommel , Charles XII of Sweden, Nikita Khrushchev, Boris Yeltsin, John Paul Getty, Donald Trump, Charles Lindbergh, and Jean-Jacques Rousseau.

TEMPERAMENTS

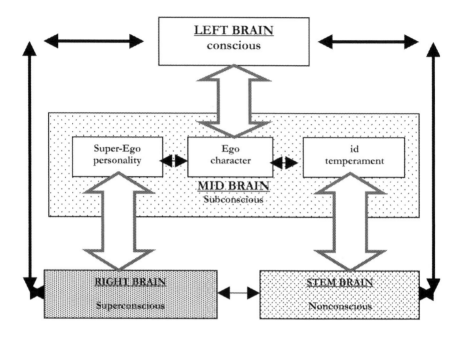

Knowing your temperament and interaction style is important to your implementation of TSF-24. It will help you customized TSF-24 to how your own brain specifically operates.

Temperament Theory explains the reasons for behavior and sources of deep psychological stress. **It demonstrate your' core needs and values as well as the talents you are more drawn to develop.**[130] **It is what is called that part of your personalities or characters that is built-in to us genetically.** These genes contained information that falls within the four domain of our sub-brains–*social, spiritual, spatial, visual, existential; logical, mathematically; kinesthetically-bodily, naturalist, and emotional.* All information passed down in our genes can be change or rewire by choices we make with the exception of physical characteristics, traits and attributes. The neuroplasticity of our brain enable us to accomplish this. Also, our attitude whether positive or negative and our diets affects our genes as shown by the field of epigenetic.

In life, we ONLY have two choices or outlooks – blessing or maledictions or positive or negative. To make those choices, you **MUST** acquire knowledge before making those choices. The lobes of you brain were designed for this. You acquire knowledge by learning, observation or experience. Said it in another way, you MUST be solution oriented, instead of being a problem oriented. Your choice of either one will dictate the final outcome in your life. Your temperament will constantly make those two choices. Although there is always a degree of flexibility allowed (Neuroplasticity of the brain), to a large extent we "are" our temperaments for our whole lives. *Psychologist Carl Jung pioneer this field and Eysenck made it more scientifically acceptable, and the Big Five made it official.*[131]

Historical Development

Dr. David Keirsey introduced the Temperament Sorter after being introduced to MBTI (MBTI is based on Carl Jung's work) by a friend. Keirsey traces the idea of temperament back to the ancient Greeks. Hippocrates, a Greek physician who lived from 460-377 B.C., who proposed the **four humors**, which are related to the four temperaments.[132]

These **four humors** named and promoted by Galen as: **sanguine, choleric, phlegmatic, and melancholic.** Keirsey developed a modern temperament theory in his books **"Please Understand Me (1978)" and "Please Understand Me II (1998)".** By reading Isabel Myers' very brief portraits of sixteen types, Keirsey found that by combining Sensing with the perceiving functions, **(SP and SJ)**, and intuition with the judging functions, **(NF and NT)**, he had descriptions similar to his four temperaments. Keirsey originally named the temperaments after Greek gods **Dionysius, Apollo, Prometheus**, and **Epimetheus.** Recognizing the temperaments from Ernst Kretchmer's descriptions of four forms of madness, he developed the positive aspects and named the temperaments after the mythological gods, but later renamed them, for clarity, **as Artisan, Idealist, Rational, and Guardian** in his book **"Portraits of Temperament (1987)."**[133]

Keirsey's labeling or observations of these four temperaments unbeknownst to him, represents the four sub-brains – **right, left, stem, mid.** When we discussed the **Artisan, Idealist, Rationales, and Guardian temperaments**, we are really discussing the functions of each sub-brain that managed and controls it. His labeling will be used throughout the book to represent each specific area of the brain. Thanks to Dr. Keirsey's for fine tuning this theory.

The chart below compares modern and ancient aspects of the theory:

	LEFT BRAIN	RIGHT BRAIN	STEM BRAIN	MID BRAIN
Hippocrates's four humors	phlegm	yellow bile	black bile	blood
Organ:	brain/lungs	spleen	gall bladder	liver
Characteristics:	calm, unemotional	easily angered	despondent, sleepless	courageous, amorous
Aristotle's four sources of happiness	dialogike (logical investigation)	ethikos (moral virtue)	propraitari (acquiring assets)	hedone (sensuous pleasure)
Galen's four temperaments	phlegmatic	choleric	melancholic	sanguine
Paracelsus's four totem spirits	curious sylphs	inspired nymphs	industrious gnomes	changeable salamanders
Adicke's four world views	skeptical	doctrinaire	traditional	innovative
Dreikurs' four mistaken goals	Power	Recognition	Service	Retaliation
Spränger's four value attitudes	Theoretic	religious	economic	Artistic
Kretchmer's four character styles	Anesthetic	hyperesthetic	depressive	Hypomanic
Erich Fromm's four orientations	Marketing	receptive	hoarding	Exploitative

Myers's Jungian aspects of sixteen types	NT - intuitive thinking	NF - intuitive feeling	SJ - sensory judgment	SP - sensory perception
Keirsey/ Bates four temperaments (old)	Promethean	Apollonian	Epimethean	Dionysian
Keirsey's four temperaments	Rational	Idealist	Guardian	Artisan
TSF-24 Whole Brain Model	Left Brain	Right Brain	Stem Brain	Mid Brain
TSF-24 Whole Brain Model	Nitrogen	Hydrogen	Carbon	Oxygen
TSF-24' Whole Brain Model	Introvert	Extrovert	Sensovert	Emotiovert
Dr. D'Adamo's Blood Type	Type A	Type B	Type O	Type AB
Dr. D'Adamo's GenoType	Nomad, Teacher and Explorer	Warrior, Gatherer and Explorer	Hunter	Explorer

The following four (4) main temperaments are what everyone inherits. But there expression is dependent on each individual and their sub-brain dominant. Your dominant sub-brain determines your main temperament, personality and Blood Type. Below is a detail explanation of each temperament. You have ALL of them inside you but in the order of how your mind works as you will learn in the Personality Chapter.

Linda V. Beren[134], the founder of Interstrength® Associates expands on the above concept of psychologist David Keirsey with her version of the four temperaments patterns as follow:

- People of the Catalyst™ Temperament . . .(Diplomatic Skill Set)-*Right Brain or Idealist.*

- People of the Theorist™ Temperament . . .(Strategic Skill Set)-

Left Brain or Rationals.

- People of the Stabilizer™ Temperament . . (Logistical Skill Set-*Stem Brain or Guardian.*

- People of the Improviser™ Temperament . . .(Tactical Skill Set)-*Mid Brain or Artisan*

1. For the **Right Brain** temperaments which are labeled as NF - "**The Idealists,**" Keirsey describes the NF group's primary objective as *"Identity Seeking"*. The NF grouping includes the types: ENFJ - "The Teachers" INFJ - "The Counselors" ENFP - "The Champions" and INFP - "The Healers"[135]

All **Idealists™** (NFs) share the following core characteristics:[136]

- Idealists are enthusiastic, they trust their intuition, yearn for romance, seek their true self, prize meaningful relationships, and dream of attaining wisdom.

- Idealists pride themselves on being loving, kindhearted, and authentic.

- Idealists tend to be giving, trusting, spiritual, and they are focused on personal journeys and human potentials.

- Idealists make intense mates, nurturing parents, and inspirational leaders.

Idealists™, as a temperament, is passionately concerned with personal growth and development. Idealists strive to discover who they are and how they can become their best possible self--always this quest for self-knowledge and self-improvement drives their imagination. And they want to help others make the journey. Idealists are naturally drawn to working with people, and whether in education or counseling, in social services or personnel work, in journalism or the ministry, they are gifted at helping others find their way in life, often inspiring them to grow as individuals and to fulfill their potentials.

Idealists are sure that friendly cooperation is the best way for people to achieve their goals. Conflict and confrontation upset them because they seem to put up angry barriers between people. Idealists dream of creating harmonious, even caring personal relations, and they have a unique talent for helping people get along with each other and work together for the good of all. Such interpersonal harmony might be a romantic ideal, but then Idealists are incurable romantics who prefer to focus on what might be, rather than what is. The real, practical world is only a starting place for Idealists; they believe that life is filled with possibilities waiting to be realized, rich with meanings calling out to be understood. This idea of a mystical or spiritual dimension to life, the "not visible" or the "not yet" that can only be known through intuition or by a leap of faith, is far more important to Idealists than the world of material things.

Highly ethical in their actions, Idealists hold themselves to a strict standard of personal integrity. They must be true to themselves and to others, and they can be quite hard on themselves when they are dishonest, or when they are false or insincere. More often, however, Idealists are the very soul of kindness *or principle love.* Particularly in their personal relationships, Idealists are without question filled with love and good will. They believe in giving of themselves to help others; they cherish a few warm, sensitive friendships; they strive for a special rapport with their children; and in marriage they wish to find a "soulmate," someone with whom they can bond emotionally and spiritually, sharing their deepest feelings and their complex inner worlds.

Idealists make up 14 percent[137] of the population. But their ability to inspire people with their enthusiasm and their idealism has given them influence far beyond their numbers.

They are people of **the Catalyst™** Temperament . . .(**Diplomatic Skill Set):** Want to be authentic, benevolent, and empathic. Search for identity, meaning, and significance. Are relationship oriented, particularly valuing meaningful relationships. Tend to be idealistic and visionary, wanting to make the world a better place. Look to the future. Trust their intuition, imagination, and impressions. Focus on developing potential, fostering and facilitating growth through coaching, teaching, counseling, and communicating. Generally are enthusiastic. Think in terms of integration and similarities and look for universals. Often are gifted in the use of metaphors to bridge different perspectives. Usually are diplomatic. Frequently are drawn to work that inspires and develops people and relationships.[138]

2. **For the Left Brain** temperaments which are labeled as NT - "**The Rationals,**" Keirsey describes the NT group's primary objective as "**Knowledge Seeking**". The NT grouping includes the types: ENTJ - "The Fieldmarshals," INTJ - "The Masterminds," ENTP - "The Inventors," and INTP - "The Architects.[139]

All **Rationals**™ (NTs) share the following core characteristics:[140]

- Rationals tend to be pragmatic, skeptical, self-contained, and focused on problem-solving and systems analysis.

- Rationals pride themselves on being ingenious, independent, and strong willed.

- Rationals make reasonable mates, individualizing parents, and strategic leaders.

- Rationals are even-tempered, they trust logic, yearn for achievement, seek knowledge, prize technology, and dream of understanding how the world works.

Rationals™ are the problem solving temperament, particularly if the problem has to do with the many complex systems that make up the world around us. Rationals might tackle problems in organic systems such as plants and animals, or in mechanical systems such as railroads and computers, or in social systems such as families and companies and governments. But whatever systems fire their curiosity, Rationals will analyze them to understand how they work, so they can figure out how to make them work better.

In working with problems, Rationals try to find solutions that have application in the real world, but they are even more interested in the abstract concepts involved, the fundamental principles or natural laws that underlie the particular case. And they are completely pragmatic about their ways and means of achieving their ends. Rationals don't care about being politically correct. They are interested in the most efficient solutions possible, and will listen to anyone who has something useful to teach them, while disregarding any authority or customary procedure that wastes time and resources.

Rationals have an insatiable hunger to accomplish their goals and will work tirelessly on any project they have set their mind to. They are rigorously logical and fiercely independent in their thinking--are indeed skeptical of all ideas, even their own--and they believe they can overcome any obstacle with their will power. Often they are seen as cold and distant, but this is really the absorbed concentration they give to whatever problem they're working on. Whether designing a skyscraper or an experiment, developing a theory or a prototype technology, building an aircraft, a corporation, or a strategic alliance, Rationals value intelligence, in themselves and others, and they pride themselves on the ingenuity they bring to their problem solving.

Rationals comprise 35 percent[141] of the population. But because of their drive to unlock the secrets of nature, and to develop new technologies, they have done much to shape our world.

They are people of the **Theorist™ Temperament** . . .(**Strategic Skill Set**): Want knowledge and to be competent, to achieve mastery. Seek expertise to understand how the world and things in it work. Are theories oriented. See everything as conditional and relative. Are oriented to the infinite. Trust logic and reason. Want to have a rationale for everything. Are skeptical. Think in terms of differences, delineating categories, definitions, structures, and functions. Hunger for precision, especially in thought and language. Usually are skilled at long-range planning, inventing, designing, and defining. Generally are calm. Foster individualism. Frequently gravitate toward technology and the sciences. Tend to be well suited for engineering and devising strategy, whether in the social sciences or physical sciences.[142]

3. For the **Stem Brain** temperaments which are labeled as **SJ - "The Guardians,"** Keirsey describes the SJ group's primary objective as **"Security Seeking"**. The SJ grouping includes the types: ESTJ - "The Supervisors," ISTJ - "The Inspectors," ESFJ - "The Providers," and ISFJ - "The Protectors." [143]

All **Guardians™** (SJs) share the following core characteristics:[144]

  * Guardians pride themselves on being dependable, helpful, and hard-working.

  * Guardians make loyal mates, responsible parents, and stabilizing leaders.

- Guardians tend to be dutiful, cautious, humble, and focused on credentials and traditions.

- Guardians are concerned citizens who trust authority, join groups, seek security, prize gratitude, and dream of meting out justice.

Guardians™ are the cornerstone of society, for they are the temperament given to serving and preserving our most important social institutions. Guardians have natural talent in managing goods and services--from supervision to maintenance and supply--and they use all their skills to keep things running smoothly in their families, communities, schools, churches, hospitals, and businesses.

Guardians can have a lot of fun with their friends, but they are quite serious about their duties and responsibilities. Guardians take pride in being dependable and trustworthy; if there's a job to be done, they can be counted on to put their shoulder to the wheel. A guardian also believe in law and order, and sometimes worry that respect for authority, even a fundamental sense of right and wrong, is being lost. Perhaps this is why Guardians honor customs and traditions so strongly--they are familiar patterns that help bring stability to our modern, fast-paced world.

Practical and down-to-earth, Guardians believe in following the rules and cooperating with others. They are not very comfortable winging it or blazing new trails; working steadily within the system is the Guardian way, for in the long run loyalty, discipline, and teamwork gets the job done right. Guardians are meticulous about schedules and have a sharp eye for proper procedures. They are cautious about change, even though they know that change can be healthy for an institution. Better to go slowly, they say, and look before you leap.

Guardians make up as much as 44 percent[145] of the population, and a good thing, because they usually end up doing all the indispensable but thankless jobs the rest of us take for granted.

They are people of the Stabilizer™ Temperament ... (Logistical Skill Set): Want to fit in, to have membership. Hunger for responsibility, accountability, and predictability. Tend to be generous, to serve, and to do their duty. Establish and maintain institutions and standard operating procedures. Tend to protect and preserve, to stand guard and warn. Look to the past and tradition. Foster enculturation with ceremonies and rules. Trust contracts and authority. Want security and stability. Think in terms of what are conventional, comparisons, associations, and discrete elements. Generally are serious, concerned, and fatalistic. Usually are skilled at ensuring that things, information, and people are in the right place, in the right amounts, in the right quality, at the right time. Frequently gravitate toward business and commerce.[146]

4. For the **Mid Brain** temperaments which are labeled as **SP - "The Artisans,"** Keirsey describes the SP group's primary objective as **"Sensation Seeking".** The SP grouping includes the types: ESTP - "The Promoters," ISTP - "The Crafters," ESFP - "The Performers," and ISFP - "The Composers.[147]

All **Artisans**™ (SPs) share the following core characteristics:

* Artisans tend to be fun-loving, optimistic, realistic, and focused on the here and now

* Artisans pride themselves on being unconventional, bold, and spontaneous.

* Artisans make playful mates, creative parents, and troubleshooting leaders.

* Artisans are excitable, trust their impulses, want to make a splash, seek stimulation, prize freedom, and dream of mastering action skills.

Artisans™ are the temperament with a natural ability to excel in any of the arts, not only the fine arts such as painting and sculpting, or the performing arts such as music, theater, and dance, but also the athletic, military, political, mechanical, and industrial arts, as well as the "art of the deal" in business.

Artisans are most at home in the real world of solid objects that can be made and manipulated, and of real-life events that can be experienced in the here and now. Artisans have exceptionally keen senses, and love working with their hands. They seem right at home with tools, instruments, and vehicles of all kinds, and their actions are usually aimed at getting them where they want to go, and as quickly as possible. Thus Artisans will strike off boldly down roads that others might consider risky or impossible, doing whatever it takes, rules or no rules, to accomplish their goals. This devil-may-care attitude also gives the Artisans a winning way with people, and they are often irresistibly charming with family, friends, and co-workers.

Artisans want to be where the action is; they seek out adventure and show a constant hunger for pleasure and stimulation. They believe that variety is the spice of life, and that doing things that aren't fun or exciting is a waste of time. Artisans are impulsive, adaptable, competitive, and believe the next throw of the dice will be the lucky one. They can also be generous to a fault, always ready to share with their friends from the bounty of life. Above all, Artisans need to be free to do what they wish, when they wish. They resist being tied or bound or confined or obligated; they would rather not wait, or save, or store, or live for tomorrow. In the Artisan view, today must be enjoyed, for tomorrow never comes.

There are not as many Artisans, perhaps 7[148] percent of the population, and they create much of the beauty, grace, fun, and excitement the rest of us enjoy in life.

They are people of the Improviser™ Temperament . . .(Tactical Skill Set): Want the freedom to choose the next act. Seek to have impact, to get results. Want to be graceful, bold, and impressive. Generally are excited and optimistic. Are absorbed in the action of the moment. Are oriented toward the present. Seek adventure and stimulation. Hunger for spontaneity. Trust impulses, luck, and their ability to solve any problem they run into. Think in terms of variation. Have a talent for noticing and describing rich detail, constantly seeking relevant information. Like freedom to move, festivities, and games. Tend to be natural negotiators. Seize opportunities. Usually are gifted tacticians, deciding the best move to make in the moment, the expedient action to take. Are frequently drawn to all kinds of work that requires variation on a theme.[149]

Now that you know that part of your personalities or characters that is built-in to you genetically, how do you interact with other temperaments or people? Knowing your interaction style helps you locate interpersonal conflicts and situational energy drains. It gives you a map for greater flexibility in your interactions with others.[150]

All interaction styles and temperaments have either an optimistic or pessimistic approach or solution or problem oriented approach. You have either choice! You will learn in the next chapter how you have an optimistic and pessimistic self or approach.

interactions styles

Linda V. Beren, identified **four interactions styles** which are how each sub-brain operates and is as follow:

The Right Brain - In-Charge™ *(Drive to get an achievable result)* - The theme is getting things accomplished through people. People of this style are focused on results, often taking action quickly. They often have a driving energy with an intention to lead a group to the goal. They make decisions quickly to keep themselves and others on task, on target, and on time. They hate wasting time and having to back track. Mentoring, executing actions, supervising, and mobilizing resources are all ways they get things accomplished. They notice right away what is not working in a situation and become painfully aware of what needs to be fixed, healed, or corrected.

The Left Brain - Chart-the-Course™ *(Drive to get a desired result)* : The theme is having a course of action to follow. People of this style focus on knowing what to do and keeping themselves, the group, or the project on track. They prefer to enter a situation having an idea of what is to happen. They identify a process to accomplish a goal and have a somewhat contained tension as they work to create and monitor a plan. The aim is not the plan itself, but to use it as a guide to move things along toward the goal. Their informed and deliberate decisions are based on analyzing, outlining, conceptualizing or foreseeing what needs to be done.

The Stem Brain - Behind-the-Scenes™*(Drive to get an integrated result)* - The theme is getting the best result possible. People of this style focus on understanding and working with the process to create a positive outcome. They see value in many contributions and consult outside inputs to make an informed decision. They aim to integrate various information sources and accommodate differing points of view. They approach others with a quiet, calm style that may not show their strong convictions. Producing, sustaining, defining, and clarifying are all ways they support a group's process. They typically have more patience than most with the time it takes to gain support through consensus for a project or to refine the result.

The Mid Brain -Get-Things-Going™ *(Drive to get an embraced result)* - The theme is persuading and involving others. They thrive in facilitator or catalyst roles and aim to inspire others to move to action, facilitating the process. Their focus is on interaction, often with an expressive style. They Get-Things-Going with upbeat energy, enthusiasm, or excitement, which can be contagious. Exploring options and possibilities, making preparations, discovering new ideas, and sharing insights are all ways they get people moving along. They want decisions to be participative and enthusiastic, with everyone involved and engaged.

Okay, now that you know your temperaments and how you interact with others, how does it fit in with your personality type? See you in the next Chapter.

CHAPTER 10

YOUR PERSONALITY!

"Your dominant Temperament is you main personality that managed the other three temperaments. Your dominant temperament is your dominant attitude. <u>You are ALL four</u> but the order of you sub-brains dictates your preferences to create YOU and your Personality."

As you already learned by now that your four sub-brain – right, left, stem, and mid controlled and managed all activities of your brain. You learned your temperaments and interaction styles are governed by it. How about your personality? How is your personality formed?

Personality typing is a tool with many uses. It's especially notable for it's helpfulness in the areas of **growth and self-development.**.

Learning and applying the theories of personality type can be a powerful and rewarding experience, if it is used as a tool for discovery, rather than as a method for putting people into boxes, or as an excuse for behavior. [151] *It is a tool to discover your strengths and weaknesses. It is a tool to discover why you do things in certain ways. It is a tool not to make excuses for your behavior but to improve your behavior to achieve all the success you inspire, want, need and desire.*

The sixteen personality types that are use in many Personality Type programs such as **Socionics, Myers-Briggs and many others** are based on the well-known research of Carl Jung, Katharine C. Briggs, and Isabel Briggs Myers. Dr. Carl Jung first developed the theory that individuals each had a psychological type. He believed that there were **two basic kinds of "functions"** which humans used in their lives: *how we take in information* , and *how we make decisions.* He believed that within these two categories, there were two opposite ways of functioning. *We can perceive information via 1) our senses (stem), or 2) our intuition (right). We can make decisions based on 1) objective logic (Left), or 2) subjective feelings (mid).* Jung believed that we all use these four functions in our lives, but that each individual uses the different functions with a varying amount of success and frequency. [152]

He believed that we could identify an order of **preference** for these functions within individuals. The function which someone uses most frequently is their **"dominant"** function. The dominant function is supported by an **auxiliary** (2nd) function, **tertiary** (3rd) function, and **inferior** (4th) function.

He asserted that individuals either "extraverted" or "introverted" as their dominant function. (*For extraverted or introverted functions that Dr. Jung asserted and for the purpose of this writing, he was identifying the natural human inclination outlook to be either optimistic or pessimistic, positive or negative approach as dictated by either the dominant or inferior temperament or sub-brain. Extroverted, introverted, sensovert, and emotiovert are* **attitudes** *for each temperament, not functions.* **Functions** *are dominant, auxiliary, tertiary and inferior arrangement of the sub-brains. Choices in life is either positive or negative which will lead to either blessings or maledictions. Preferences are either intuitive, thinking, sensing and feeling*)

Dr. Jung felt that the dominant **function** was so important, that it overshadowed all of the other functions in terms of defining personality type. (*Under the "TSF-24 Approach," your dominant function is your dominant sub-brain inclination, temperament, and interaction styles. This is your optimistic or your positive natural self. You should know your dominant sub-brain from the Survey before Chapter One. The auxiliary sub-brain supports the dominant sub-brain which is your main attitude. The auxillary sub-brain is that you use to take in information. Your inferior sub-brain is your weakness and supported by your tertiary sub-brain. Your inferior sub-brain is your pessimistic or negative self. Your inferior sub-rain is how your deal with things of the day by day. Your tertiary is how you make decision.*) Therefore, Jung defined eight personality types:

Extraverted Intuition – *Right Right*

Extraverted Thinking– *Right Left*

Extraverted Sensing– *Right Stem*

Extraverted Feeling – *Right Mid*

Introverted Thinking– *Left Left*

Introverted Intuition– *Left Right*

Introverted Sensing – *Left Stem*

Introverted Feeling – *Left Mid*

Katharine Briggs expounded upon Jung's work, quietly working in silence and developing his theories further. But it was Katharine's daughter Isabel who was really responsible for making the work on Personality Types visible. Isabel, using her mother's work and Jung's work, **asserted the importance of the auxiliary function working with the dominant function in defining** Personality Type. While incorporating the auxiliary function into the picture, it became apparent that there was another distinctive preference which hadn't been defined by Jung: **Judging (Sensovert or Stem Brain) and Perceiving (Emotiovert or Mid Brain).** Below is the addition to Dr. Jung's Model, thus creating 16 personality profiles.

Sensovert Intuition– Stem *Right*

Sensovert Thinking– Stem *Left*

Sensovert Sensing – Stem *Stem*

Sensovert Feeling – Stem *Mid*

Emotiovert Thinking– Mid *Left*

Emotiovert Intuition– Mid *Right*

Emotiovert Sensing – Mid *Stem*

Emotiovert Feeling– Mid *Mid*

The entire discovery by Jung, Katherine and Isabel were on track as they represent personalities and preferences control and managed by each of the four sub-brains that I have discussed throughout the book. The developed theory today is that every individual has a primary mode of operation or attitude *(extravert, introvert, sensovert, and emotiovert)* based on his/her dominant brain inclination and four functions*(dominant, auxiliary, tertiary and inferior)* which is either *(2 choices)* optimistic or pessimistic. The four catergories or positions below is the core or foundations of personalities and how the mind works:

1. Your flow of energy or attitude.

2. How you take in information

3. How you prefer to make decisions

4. The basic day-to-day lifestyle that you prefer

Within each of these categories, your main "preference" to be :

1. Your flow of energy or attitude -**Extraverted, Introverted, Sensovert, or Emotiovert** optimistic or pessimistic approach.

2. How you take in information - **Intuition, Analytical, Senses or Emotion** optimistic or pessimistic approach.

3. How you prefer to make decisions - **Creating, Thinking, Sensing, or Feeling optimistic or pessimistic approach.**

4. The basic day-to-day lifestyle that you prefer - **Inspiring, Analyzing, Judging (sensing) or Perceiving (emotions) optimistic or pessimistic approach.**

We all naturally use one mode of operation within each category more easily and more frequently than we use the other mode of operation depending on your brain dominancy. So, we are said to "prefer" one function over the other. **The combination of your four "sub-brains" with the four functions defines your personality type.** More so, the order of your DNA sequence determines your personality.

Although everybody operates across the entire spectrum of the preferences (*intuitive, thinking, senses, and feelings*), each individual has a natural attitude (*extravert, introvert, Sensovert and emotiovert*)which leans in one direction or the other within the four sub-brains – right, left, stem, and mid. Your *choice to be either optimistic (blessing) or pessimistic (maledictions) is determined by your dominant* **sub-brains** *(dominant and auxiliary) or* **inferior sub-brains** *(tertiary and inferior).*

Dominant Sub-Brain	Auxiliary Sub-brain	Tertiary Sub-brain	Inferior Sub-brain
ALL your positive or Optimist Attitude is naturally created by the above sub-brains!		ALL your Negative or Pessimistic Attitude is naturally created by the above two sub-brains!	
Good GENES- These genes must be turned ON to create the healthy YOU!		BAD GENES- These genes must be turned OFF or CONTROLLED because they are killing you!	
DA (Dominant and Auxiliary) is your OPTIMISTIC SELF!		TI (Tertiary and Inferior) is your PESSIMISTIC SELF! CHANGE YOUR INFERIOR SUB-BRAINS AND CHANGE YOUR LIFE!	

First, our Flow of Energy or Attitude defines **how we receive the essential part of our stimulation.** Do we receive it from within ourselves (Introverted) or from external sources (Extraverted)? or from our senses (Sensovert)? or from our emotions (Emotiovert)? Is our dominant function focused externally, internally? senses? emotion? Your brain inclination or dominancy will determined which energy source for your supported auxiliary. The tertiary and inferior are you weakness. For example, if you are a Right Brain dominant, then your preferences throughout each temperament or sub-brain is extraverted. *Your energy flow will be extraverted. Below, you take information and make decision through your intuition.*

Second, the topic of "How You **Take in Information**" deals with our preferred method of taking in and absorbing information. Do you trust your five senses (Sensing) to take in information, or do you rely on our instincts (Intuition)? Do you analyze information first before you take it in (Analyses)? Do you take it in by how you feel (feeling)?

The third type of preference, "How you prefer to **Make Decisions,**" refers to whether you are prone to decide things based on logic and objective consideration (Thinking), or based on your personal, subjective value systems (Feeling), or based on your intuitions (intuition), or based on your five senses (senses).

These first three preferences above were the basis of Jung's theory of Personality Types. Isabel Briggs Myers developed the theory

125

of the **fourth preference**, which is concerned with how you deal with the external world on a **Day-to-day Basis.** Are you organized and purposeful, and more comfortable with scheduled, structured environments (Judging), or are you flexible and diverse, and more comfortable with open, casual environments (Perceiving)? *or are you creative about things you do? or are you analytical in things you do?* From a theoretical perspective, you know that if your highest Extraverted function is a Decision Making function, we prefer Judging(stem brain). If our highest Extraverted function is an Information Gathering function, we prefer Perceiving(mid brain). The above assumptions are based on the Myers-Briggs Model.

Judging (Sensing) and Perceiving (Emotions) functions is performed by stem and mid brain respectively under the "TSF-24 Personality Model." Its frequency usage is dependent on which sub-brain is dominant and so forth. All four functions are activities of each specific area of the brain – right, left, stem, and mid.

1. **Your dominant controls and managed "How you draw your energy or attitude."**

2. **Your auxiliary controls and managed "How you take in formation."**

3. **Your tertiary controls and managed "How you make decisions."**

4. **Your inferior controls and managed "How you deal with day by day activities."**

Personality Types Today

The theory of Personality Types, as it stand today based on the "TSF-24 Personality Model" is we have a choice of either pessimistic or optimistic or choosing to use our inferior sub-brains instead of our dominant and contends that:

1st Base	2nd Base				3rd Base
Sub-Brains	Functions				Temperaments
	Dominant	Auxiliary	Tertiary	Inferior	
Right	Extrovert	Extrovert	Extrovert	Extrovert	Idealist
Left	Introvert	Introvert	Introvert	Introvert	Rationals
Stem	Sensovert	Sensovert	Sensovert	Sensovert	Guardian
Mid	Emotiovert	Emotiovert	Emotiovert	Emotiovert	Artisan
Right	Intuition	Intuition	Intuition	Intuition	Idealist
Left	Analyzing	Analyzing	Analyzing	Analyzing	Rationals
Stem	Senses	Senses	Senses	Senses	Guardian
Mid	Emotion	Emotion	Emotion	Emotion	Artisan
Right	Intuiting	Intuiting	Intuiting	Intuiting	Idealist
Left	Thinking	Thinking	Thinking	Thinking	Rationals
Stem	Sensing	Sensing	Sensing	Sensing	Guardian
Mid	Feeling	Feeling	Feeling	Feeling	Artisan
Right	Creative	Creative	Creative	Creative	Idealist
Left	Analytical	Analytical	Analytical	Analytical	Rationals
Stem	Judging	Judging	Judging	Judging	Guardian
Mid	Perceiving	Perceiving	Perceiving	Perceiving	Artisan

Your optimistic (+) or pessimistic (-) choices, traits and temperaments which all formed your personality is controlled and managed by your brain dominance or inferior which was determined at infancy (or as a fetus) by some significant (survival) event (s) and environment in your life.

The major recombination's of the **four sub-brains** (or DNA's G, C, A, T) create **24 different Personalities (24 Codons)** which are completely different from the **16 personality** of the Myers-Briggs Model and all other Personality Models. We all function in all of these realms on a daily basis but in the order of your sub-brain dominancy and functions within each sub-brain. This order of your sub-brain is determined by your DNA sequence which was a survival mechanism chosen by the fetus to protect itself from the mother's environment, lifestyle and diet.

The example below illustrates it. You may insert your Personality Type that you discovered at the beginning of the book.

Whole Brain Personality Model[153]
Example: LMRS or Left, Mid, Right, and Stem

1st Base	2nd Base				3rd Base
Sub Brains	Functions				Temperaments
	Dominant Personality		Inferior Personality		
	Dominant	Auxiliary	Tertiary	Inferior	
	Your flow of energy is either	Your flow of energy is either	Your flow of energy is either	Your flow of energy is either	
Right	Extrovert	Extrovert	Extrovert	Extrovert	Idealist
Left	Introvert	Introvert	Introvert	Introvert	Rationals
Stem	Sensovert	Sensovert	Sensovert	Sensovert	Guardian
Mid	Emotiovert	Emotiovert	Emotiovert	Emotiovert	Artisan
	How you take in information	How you take in information	How you take in information	How you take in information	
Right	Intuition	Intuition	Intuition	Intuition	Idealist
Left	Analyzing	Analyzing	Analyzing	Analyzing	Rationals
Stem	Senses	Senses	Senses	Senses	Guardian
Mid	Emotion	Emotion	Emotion	Emotion	Artisan
	How you prefer to make decisions	How you prefer to make decisions	How you prefer to make decisions	How you prefer to make decisions	
Right	Intuiting	Intuiting	Intuiting	Intuiting	Idealist
Left	Thinking	Thinking	Thinking	Thinking	Rationals
Stem	Sensing	Sensing	Sensing	Sensing	Guardian
Mid	Feeling	Feeling	Feeling	Feeling	Artisan
	Day-by-day lifestyle that your prefer is	Day-by-day lifestyle that your prefer is	Day-by-day lifestyle that your prefer is	Day-by-day lifestyle that your prefer is	
Right	Creative	Creative	Creative	Creative	Idealist
Left	Analytical	Analytical	Analytical	Analytical	Rationals
Stem	Judging	Judging	Judging	Judging	Guardian
Mid	Perceiving	Perceiving	Perceiving	Perceiving	Artisan

As I stated earlier that we **have ALL four temperaments within us** because we have four sub-brains that managed and controls each one. A significant life changing event and environment rearrange the order how our brain works and therefore determines the **dominant sub-**

brain, dominant temperaments, and functions which will determine our main personality.

For example, Jane Doe above is LMRS (See Chart Above) or *Left, Mid, Right, and Stem* Personality Type. She grew up in an abusive family environment. She decided that she will become a better person than her parents. She chooses an optimistic approach to life!

Jane is **LEFT (**Base 1**) brain** dominant (Base 2) which is a Rationals (Base 3) or **"Knowledge Seeking"** temperament with an optimistic approach to life. Therefore, her dominant Temperament and attitude is an **Introvert Rational,** auxiliary is an **Introvert Artisan,** and tertiary is **Introvert Idealist** and inferior **Introvert Guardian**. [Note: The Idealist and Guardian are Inferior and therefore is taken over by the introvert, not the extrovert and sensovert respectively) Since her dominant temperament is **Rational** and attitude is **Introverted,** her personality combinations will be as follow: *Optimistic Introvert Rational (dominant), Optimistic Introverted Artisan (Auxiliary), pessimistic Introverted Idealist (tertiary) and pessimistic Introverted Guardian (Inferior). Her personality conflicts or battle on a daily basis occurs at the last two sub-brains. Recall that tertiary controls and managed "how you make decisions" and inferior "how you deal with life on a day to day basis."*

As a Left brain dominant, Jane is an optimistic **introvert** that draws energy from within herself (Optimistic *Introverted Rational*). She primarily is "knowledge seeking" or Rationals. Her auxiliary personality is the **Artisan** which primary objective is **"Sensation Seeking."**. As an auxiliary optimist Intro-emotiovert, Jane's "takes in information or data" by her feeling or emotions about it *(Introverted feelings).*

Jane's dominant and auxiliary is her main personality. These are two temperaments that she has control over. She is *knowledge seeking* (Left) and at the same time *sensation seeking (Mid)*. She is an introvert who derives her energy from within and through her emotions. She takes in information by analyzing it first and with emotions takes it in.

Jane's **tertiary** personality is an **Idealist** which tertiary function is **Identity Seeking.** Jane battles within herself to be around people *(introverted Idealist).* She can choose to have a positive outlook by being around people or hates the thought of it. She battles making decision intuitively (introverted intuiting) and privately a creative person (*Introverted creating*) on a day to day lifestyle which is stressful or no stressful choice.

Jane's **Inferior** personality is the **Guardian** which primary objective is **"Security Seeking."** As an Optimist or a Pessimist Sensovert daily, Janes battle to use her instincts or street smart to make positive or negative decisions (optimist or pessimist *introverted senses*). She battles privately (introspections) judging things on a day-to-day lifestyle (positive or negative *Introverted judging).*

Jane knows her tertiary and inferior sub-brains. Therefore, she chooses to focus on changing and harmonizing it with the rest of her brain. If she doesn't want to make an effort to change this, she can hire people whose strength is her weakness to balance herself. Successful people always hired their weakness.

The above example is "How personalities are formed! Your sub-brain order is based on your "Survey" results (at the beginning). The survey is just a tool which demonstrates the order how your mind operates. But to get your precise sub-brain dominant, get a Blood Type Test. Your Survey result represents your MIND and Blood result represents your BODY. You will learn more about this in the next Chapter. The result order of your sub-brains determines your brain dominant inclination – right, left, stem, or mid. You have ALL temperaments as part of your personality. Again, your dominant temperament is determined by your dominant brain inclination as shown by the example above. ALL functions, attitudes that Jung and Myers-Briggs discovered are active within each temperaments which is control by your main brain dominant.

Above all, you choose daily or when ever you face a challenge to take an optimistic or pessimistic approach to your problem. You have free will! This battle is fought at the Tertiary and Inferior sub-brains!

As we grow, learn, and in the trials and tribulations of life, we develop some areas of ourselves more thoroughly than other areas. With this in mind, it becomes clear that you must harmonize all areas of your brain. However, *you can identify your natural preferences or choices, and learn about your natural strengths and weaknesses within that context of the "TSF-24 Personality Model" approach as shown above.* This is the greatest accomplishment of the *"TSF-24 Model"* is that you can learn about your weakness and strength ahead in advance. You can even find out about your children's personalities before they are actually formed or developed by understanding their DNA sequence. I have developed and designed a Booklet specifically to help and assist you. It's available at www.AreYouAHuman.Com .

It would be injustice for me not to discuss other Personality Models. In fact as I discovered, all other Personality Types Models fit in to the *"TSF-24 Personality Model"*. For example the "Big Five "Approach;

Psychologist Gordon Allports and Raymond Cattel organized our trait and behaviors in five categories which became know as the "Big Five" with the acronym **OCEAN, another Personality Model differ from the Myers-Brigg Model.** This Model is based on what I called "Two Choices" Model in life – **DA** (Dominant/Auxiliary) versus **TI** (Tertiary/Inferior)!

1. **Openness to experience.** At one end would be individuals who are creative, intellectual, and open-minded versus people who are shallow, simple, and less intelligent (**Stem Brain Approach**)

2. **Conscientiousness.** Here would be organized, responsible, and cautious persons versus those who are irresponsible, careless, and frivolous. (**Left Brain Approach**)

3. **Extroversion.** These people are assertive, outgoing, and energetic versus the quiet, reserve, and shy. (**Right Brain Approach**)

4. **Agreeableness.** Here individuals who are sympathetic, kind, and affectionate versus those who are cold, argumentative, and cruel. (**Right Brain Approach**)

5. **Neuroticism.** Here we contrast an anxious, unstable, and moody personality versus one that is emotional stable, calm, and content. (**Mid Brain Approach**)[154]

The Five categories above can be summarized in to the four sub-brain models. The Extraversion and Agreeableness choice discusses functions of the Right Brain. I therefore included it under the appropriate sub-brain.

Below is another example using the Big Five Model within the context of the TSF-24 Personality Model?

1st Base	2nd Base				3rd Base
	Whole Brain Personality Model Big Five Revised Model				
Sub-Brains	Functions				Temperaments
	Dominant	Auxiliary	Tertiary	Inferior	
Right	Extro version Agree ableness	Extro version Agree ableness	Extro version Agree ableness	Extro version Agree ableness	Idealist
Left	Openness to experience	Openness to experience	Openness to experience	Openness to experience	Rationals
Stem	Conscient iousness.	Conscient iousness.	Conscient iousness.	Conscient iousness.	Guardian
Mid	Neuroticism.	Neuroticism.	Neuroticism.	Neuroticism.	Artisan

The above Model will be interpreted as follow (using example LMRS) - Left Brain Dominant, and **conscientiousness (DA VS TI)** on all four temperaments (Introverted Rational, Artisan, Idealist, and Guardian - **16** functions control and managed by Introvert). Next, auxiliary is *neuroticism* **(DA VS TI)** on three temperaments (Introverted Artisan, Idealist, and Guardian – **12** functions). Next, Tertiary is *extraversion and agreeableness* **(DA VS TI)** on two temperament (Introverted Idealist, and Guardian – **8** functions). And last, Inferior is *openness to experience (DA VS TI)* on one temperaments (Introverted Guardian – **4** functions).

The above measure of personality should be called the "Big Four" instead of "Big Five" as all five categories falls within the four areas of the brain, just as the Myers-Briggs Personality Model did.

Another Personality Model is by Psychologist, Professor Hans Eysenck of the University of London, used some different numbers to measure personality. On the basis of his research, he came to believe that there were 21 personality traits that were consistent with three major dimensions of personality. If you take his personality assessment, the

Eysenck Personality Profiler, your scores will fit into three categories:

I.   **Extraversion.** Measures traits including actual level, sociability, expressiveness, assertiveness, ambition, dogmatism, and aggressiveness. **(Right Brain Approach)**

II.   **Neuroticism.** Measures traits like inferiority, unhappiness, anxiety, dependence, hypochondria, guilt, and obsessiveness. **(Mid Brain Approach)**

III.   **Psychoticism.** Measures traits such as risk-taking, impulsivity, irresponsibility, manipulativeness, and practicality. **(Left Brain Approach)**

IV.   *Somaticism. Measures traits which physical symptoms arise from psychological problems. (Stem Brain Approach). I have included this category in Professor Hans Eysenck's research to complete his Personality Model and hope that this will add to his research and model. This is the missing part of his model which will bring his total personality traits to 24, instead of 21.*

You have probably notice that all personality theories discussed above all overlapped and fall within the four sub-brains which I have discussed throughout the book. I have labeled it according to which area of the brain they are discussing.

TSF-24 Personality Model Eysenck Personality Profiler					
1ˢᵗ Base Sub-Brains	**2ⁿᵈ Base** Functions				**3ʳᵈ Base** Temperaments
	Dominant	Auxiliary	Tertiary	Inferior	
Right	Extraversion	Extraversion	Extraversion	Extraversion	Idealist
Left	Psychoticism..	Psychoticism..	Psychoticism..	Psychoticism..	Rationals
Stem	Somaticism.	Somaticism.	Somaticism.	Somaticism.	Guardian
Mid	Neuroticism	Neuroticism	Neuroticism	Neuroticism	Artisan

The above Model can be interpreted using the process applied at the Myers-Briggs and Big Five Models.

Last *Personality Model* is the **MMPI-2 or the Minnesota Multiphasic Personality Inventory** which has **10** *clinical scales*, each designed to tell the difference between a special group (like people suffering from major depression) and a normal group. These scales measure problems like paranoia, schizophrenia, depression, and antisocial personality traits. The higher a persons scores on a clinical scale, the more likely it is that he or she belongs in the clinical group.

It also contains *15 content scales.* These measures various mental health problems that aren't, in and of themselves, diagnosable psychiatric disorders. The job of the content scales is to pinpoint specific problems that either contribute to or put someone at risk for, a full blown psychological disorder.

The MMPI-2 or the Minnesota Multiphasic Personality Inventory should be organized under the *""TSF-24 Personality Model""* as ALL its scales falls within the four area of the brain that I have discussed throughout the book. It will make this Model objective, instead of being subjective and easy to use and follow. The "Suggestion Solution/Secret" Chapter discusses the application of the *"TSF-24 Personality Model"* which will simplify the MMPI-2.

These theories of Personality Types contends that each of us has a natural preference which falls into one category or the other in each of these four areas, and that our native Personality Type indicates how we are likely to deal with different situations that life presents, and in which environments we are most comfortable.

Therefore, learning about your Personality Type helps you to understand why certain areas in your life come easily to you, and others are more of a struggle. Learning about other people's Personality Types help you to understand the most effective way to communicate with them, and how they function best.

Our Personality Type is formed by the various combination **(Right, Left, Stem, Mid)** of how your mind operates whether its base on functions (Jung), five basic characteristics (Big Five), or three categories (Eyssenck). The dominant brain is supported by the auxiliary and inferior is supported by tertiary brain. Your Temperaments, interaction styles and Personality Type are governed by the specific dominant sub-brains and the combinations of functions within each temperament. **Your weakness or personality flaw is governed by your last two sub-brains. That's your pessimistic life outlook and where your life battles are fought!**

The truth of the matter is that our DNA sequence determines our personality from birth. There are ONLY 24 DNA sequences that the fetus chooses from to create and protect itself from mom's environment, lifestyle and diet.

Below is the list of the **24 Sub-Brain Combination Personality Types** based on the *"TSF-24 Personality Model"*. **DA (Dominant/Auxiliary) is your positive life outlook temperaments and TI (Tertiary/Inferior) is your negative outlook personality. You have FREE WILL to choose either one to dictate your life or work to balance all four!!**

The 24 Sub-Brain Personality Recombination's creates 6^{155} genetic clusters (6 Genotypes) as shown by the Table below. You will learn more about how each cluster came in to existence in the Blood and Body Type Chapters and how this is related to your success. I should rephrase the above statement by saying that the 4 sub-brains (or DNA Base) create 6 genotypes which creates 12 phenotypes which creates the 24 personalities of the *"TSF-24 Personality Model"* **or "The Human Genetic Code Periodic Table."**

The shaded area in each Table shows your dominant personality combination (DA- Positive Self) and no shaded displayed your weak or inferior personality (TI – Negative Self) combination. You can rewire or retag genes that make up your inferior sub-brain and harmonize your four sub-brains. Again, the choice is yours. You can continue to live the current life or you can decide to live a different life from now onwards!

The 16 Personalities that Dr. Jung, Katherine and Isabel Briggs Meyer discovered also explained the sub-brain recombination's of the "TSF-24 Approach" below. Dr. Keirsey discussed this in many of his works. The information below was from the BSM Consulting website www. personalitypage.com . You can visit it for more details and explanation of the below discussions. I have rearranged the various personalities to matched the 24 personalities of the "The Human Genetic Code Periodic Table."

The Myers-Briggs Model covers 16 out of 24 personalities of the "The Human Genetic Code Periodic Table" below. You will notice your sub-brain combination and the parallel name or label under Myers-Briggs Model to the right. The 24 personalities are "universal" or "global" in that no matter what race or country you live in, your Blood Type or DNA sequence has the same personality. **You will learn more about this Table below in more details in the Blood and Body Type Chapters and how they are all related to your personality and success.**

In short, each of the 24 DNA sequence or sub-brain (MIND) combination or sequencehas its own unique, two or more personality profiles and DSM-V predisposition. Every person has two personality profiles (one from mother and other from dad), except those of the MID brain or AB Blood groups which have three or four personality profiles. Your ACTUAL profile is determined by your actual Blood Type test result and which Column the result is noted. For example, if your Survey result is LSRM and Blood Type result is A+, then your profile is INTJ. If your Survey result is MLRS and Blood Type result A+, then your profiles are ESFP and ENTJ. One profile or persoanlity is dominant over the other. Each of the personality is summarized below.[156]

24 MIND Seq.	24 BLOOD TYPES		DSM-V	24 UNIVERSAL PERSONALITY PROFILES.	
	M	B			
RLMS	B+	A+	Axis IV-III	INFJ Counselor	*ENTP Visionary*
RLSM	B+	A+	Axis IV-II	INFP Idealist ,	*ENTJ Executive*
RSLM	B+	O+	Axis IV-II	ENFP Inspirer	*ESTJ Guardian*
RSML	B+	O+	Axis IV-I	ENFJ Teacher	*ESFJ Provider*
RMSL	B+-	AB- O+-	Axis IV-I	ENFJ Teacher ,	*ESTP Promote* *ESTJ Guardian*
RMLS	B+-	AB- A+-	Axis IV-III	INFJ Counselor,	*ESFP Performer* *ENTJ Executive*
LRSM	A+	B+	Axis I-II	ENTJ Executive	*INFP Idealist*
LRMS	A+	B+	Axis I-III	ENTP Visionary	*INFJ Counselor*
LSRM	A+	O+	Axis I-II	INTJ Scientist	*ISFJ Protector*
LSMR	A+	O+	Axis I-IV	INTP Architect	*ISTJ Inspector*

LMRS	A+-	AB- B+-	Axis I-III	**ENTJ** Executive,	***ISFP*** *Composer,* ***INFP*** *Idealist*
LMSR	A+-	AB- O+-	Axis I-IV	**INTJ** Scientist	***ISTP*** *Mechanic* ***ISFJ*** *Protector* ,
SLRM	O+	A+	Axis III-II	**ISFJ** Protector	***INTJ*** *Scientist*
SLMR	O+	A+	Axis III-IV	**ISTJ** Inspector	***INTP*** *Architect*
SRLM	O+	B+	Axis III-II	**ESTJ** Guardian	***ENFP*** *Inspirer*
SRML	O+	B+	Axis III-I	**1ESFJ** Provider	***ENFJ*** *Teacher*
SMLR	O+-	AB- A+-	Axis III-IV	**ISTJ** Inspector	**ISTP** Mechanic, **INTP** Architect,
SMRL	O+-	AB- B+-	AxisIII-I	**ESFJ** Provider	**ESTP** *Promoter* ***ENFJ*** *Teacher* ,
MSLR	AB- O+-	A+-	Axis II-IV	**ISTP** Mechanic, ISFJ Protector,	*INTJ Scientist*
MSRL	AB- O+-	B+-	Axis II-I	**ESTP** Promoter **ESTJ** Guardian	***ENFJ Teacher***
MLSR	AB- A+-	O+-	Axis II-IV	**ISTP** Mechanic, **INTP** Architect,	*ISTJ Inspector*
MLRS	AB- A+-	B+-	Axis II-III	**ESFP** Performer **ENTJ** Executive,	*INFJ Counselor*
MRSL	AB- B+-	O+-	Axis II-I	**ESTP** *Promoter* ***ENFJ*** *Teacher* ,	**ESFJ** Provider
MRLS	AB- B+-	A+-	Axis II-III	***ISFP*** *Composer* ***INFP*** *Idealist*	**ENTJ** Executive,

1. ENFJ (Extroverted feeling with intuiting): These people are easy speakers. They tend to idealize their friends. They make good parents, but have a tendency to allow themselves to be used. They make good therapists, teachers, executives, and salespeople.

2. ENFP (Extroverted intuiting with feeling): These people love novelty and surprises. They are big on emotions and expression. They are susceptible to muscle tension and tend to be hyperalert. they tend to feel self-conscious. They are good at sales, advertising, politics, and acting.

3. ENTJ (Extroverted thinking with intuiting): In charge at home, they expect a lot from spouses and kids. They like organization and structure and tend to make good executives and administrators.

4. ENTP (Extroverted intuiting with thinking): These are lively people, not humdrum or orderly. As mates, they are a little dangerous, especially economically. They are good at analysis and make good entrepreneurs. They do tend to play at oneupmanship.

5. ESFJ (Extroverted feeling with sensing): These people like harmony. They tend to have strong shoulds and should-nots. They may be dependent, first on parents and later on spouses. They wear their hearts on their sleeves and excel in service occupations involving personal contact.

6. ESFP (Extroverted sensing with feeling): Very generous and impulsive, they have a low tolerance for anxiety. They make good performers, they like public relations, and they love the phone. They should avoid scholarly pursuits, especially science.

7. ESTJ (Extroverted thinking with sensing): These are responsible mates and parents and are loyal to the workplace. They are realistic, down-to-earth, orderly, and love tradition. They often find themselves joining civic clubs!

8. ESTP (Extroverted sensing with thinking): These are action-oriented people, often sophisticated, sometimes ruthless -- our "James Bonds." As mates, they are exciting and charming, but they have trouble with commitment. They make good promoters, entrepreneurs, and con artists.

9. INFJ (Introverted intuiting with feeling): These are serious students and workers who really want to contribute. They are private and easily hurt. They make good spouses, but tend to be physically reserved. People often think they are psychic. They make good therapists, general practitioners, ministers, and so on.

10. INFP (Introverted feeling with intuiting): These people are idealistic, self-sacrificing, and somewhat cool or reserved. They are very family and home oriented, but don't relax well. You find them in psychology, architecture, and religion, but never in business.

11. INTJ (Introverted intuiting with thinking): These are the most independent of all types. They love logic and ideas and are drawn to scientific research. They can be rather single-minded, though.

12. INTP (Introverted thinking with intuiting): Faithful, preoccupied, and forgetful, these are the bookworms. They tend to be very precise in their use of language. They are good at logic and math and make good philosophers and theoretical scientists, but not writers or salespeople.

13. ISFJ (Introverted sensing with feeling): These people are service and work oriented. They may suffer from fatigue and tend to be attracted to troublemakers. They are good nurses, teachers, secretaries, general practitioners, librarians, middle managers, and housekeepers.

14. ISFP (Introverted feeling with sensing): They are shy and retiring, are not talkative, but like sensuous action. They like painting, drawing, sculpting, composing, dancing -- the arts generally -- and they like nature. They are not big on commitment.

15. ISTJ (Introverted sensing with thinking): These are dependable pillars of strength. They often try to reform their mates and other people. They make good bank examiners, auditors, accountants, tax examiners, supervisors in libraries and hospitals, business, home ec., and phys. ed. teachers, and boy or girl scouts!

16. ISTP (Introverted thinking with sensing): These people are action-oriented and fearless, and crave excitement. They are impulsive and dangerous to stop. They often like tools, instruments, and weapons, and often become technical experts. They are not interested in communications and are often incorrectly diagnosed as dyslexic or hyperactive. They tend to do badly in school.

For Careers, Personal Relationships and Growth of all the above 24 personalities, visit www.personalitypage.com *or* www.keirsey.com *or* www.advisorteam.org *or* www.interstrength.com.

It is important that you know your personality type based the "TSF-24 Personality Model" Approach. There are many **practical applications for Personality Types. Knowing you Personality Type will help you in the following areas aside from going to the specific psychologist who specialized in how your mind operates for help or assistance.** See Chapter 13- Suggested Solutions to Challenges.

One of the dilemmas in the current mental heath professionals system is there's no treatment model that directs them to treat people within their field of expertise. For example, clients who are inferior mid brain must see psychotherapist, inferior stem brain clients must see behaviorist psychologist...etc. The DSM-IV-TR (Diagnostic and Statistical Manual of Mental Disorder)[157] Catalog listed more that 200 mental illnesses, grouped under 16 diagnostics categories which all falls within the four sub-brains. **Everyone's (all of us including ALL in the helping professionals) inferior and tertiary sub-brains incline them to some form of disorder, whether mild, moderate, or severe.** The "TSF-24 Personality Model" will help you seek the right professional help. The "TSF-24 Personality Model" will help mental health professionals treat or help individually quickly. The "TSF-24 Personality Model" is based on the "Human Genetic Code Periodic Table."

Other areas that the "TSF-24 Personality Model" can help are as follow:

□ Career **Guidance** what types of tasks are you most suited to perform? Where are you naturally most happy? The intelligence survey that you took at the beginning should help you in this area.

□ Managing **Employees** How can you best understand an employee's natural capabilities, and where they will find the most satisfaction?

□ **Inter-personal Relationships** How can you improve your awareness of another individual's Personality Type, and therefore increase your understanding of their reactions to situations, and know how to best communicate with them on a level which they will understand?

□ **Education** How can you develop different teaching methods to effectively educate different types of people? How to help students improve their inferior temperament? Which area of education should pursue?

□ **Counseling** How can you help individuals understand themselves better, and become better able to deal with their strengths and weaknesses? Can you tell when a client is lying or telling the truth? Can their personality show what type or kind of lying style is your client is more prone to?

The purpose of your temperaments are

1. To create your experience (Stem)

2. To connect you to a higher source (Right)

3. To create your True Self (Left)

4. To experience joy, happiness, enthusiasm...etc (Mid).

The combinations of the above is dictated by the 24 DNA sequences.

CHAPTER 11

YOUR BLOOD TYPE AND DIET

"Your Blood Type is who you are, your Being! Your Blood Type tells the story of your life while growing up as a fetus and who you became. It tells the story about your environment, diet and mother's lifestyle. Your Blood Type contains many genetic expressions you have control over to create the person you want to become. Your blood is YOU!"

You have already learned by now that your personality is the combination of your four temperaments or sub-brains. Your main temperament (Rationals, Idealist, Guardian, Artisan) dictates your main personality. My discussion throughout the book is that your temperaments or brain dominance is determined by an event(s) that happened while as a fetus, or embryo (or between age 12-14 for females) is a factor of your environment, diet and lifestyle of your mother. This event and environment influences your *Blood Type which is also your Temperament but more so the DNA sequence that the fetus chooses to protect itself!.*

Just as you were born with all four sub-brains, temperaments, likewise <u>you were born with all four blood types.</u> ALL of these were <u>predetermined</u> by your DNA sequence. What differentiate one from another or dominance over other types is survival events that happened earlier in your life and your environment, diet as I mentioned earlier. It can change also by those same factors later or during your life time from the father to mother's Blood Type or vice versa, whichever was dominant. Every person has two Blood Types. One from the mother and one from father. The fetus will use one for the MIND and one for the BODY which ever will maximized its protection for each area. Your Survey result demonstrates the MIND Blood Type and the actual Blood Type test demonstrate the BODY Blood Type. Both results are confirmed by your DNA sequence on the "Human Genetic Code Perodic Table."

The four (4) Blood Types that everyone is born with expressed itself in six different ways, creating the natural six genotype of the 24 DNA sequence. This is how the 6 Genotype (from the 24 [6x4] Personalities or 6 Groupings.) is related to the 6 Blood Type Genotypes. There are actually 48 Blood Types as you will discover in this Chapter. 24 represent the MIND and 24 reresent the BODY as you notice on both Tables below. How are blood types related to the six genotypes again?[158]

TSF-24 BLOOD TYPES			
Blood type and Tissue type	6 Possible **Genotypes**	12 Possible **Phenotypes**	24 Expanded Possible **Phenotypes**
A **(Ectoderm)**	AA AO	A(ABO) AO **AB**	A-+ or AB-+ A+ or O+ **A+ or B+**
B **(Endoderm)**	BB BO	B(ABO) BO **BA**	B-+ or AB-+ B+ or O+ **B+ or A+**
O **(Mesoderm)**	OO	O(ABO) OA OB	O- +or AB -+ O+ or A+ O+ or B+
ABO (Ectoendoderm)	AB	(ABO)O **(ABO)A** **(ABO)B**	AB+- or O+- **AB+- or A+-** **AB+- or B+-**

First what is a genotype or a phenotype? *Genotype is the "internally coded, inheritable information" carried by all living organisms. This stored information is used as a "blueprint" or set of instructions for building and maintaining a living creature. These instructions are found within almost all cells (the "internal" part), they are written in a coded language (the genetic code), they are copied at the time of cell division or reproduction and are passed from one generation to the next ("inheritable"). These instructions are intimately involved with all aspects of the life of a cell or an organism. They control everything from the formation of protein macromolecules, to the regulation of metabolism and synthesis*[159]

Phenotype is the "outward, physical manifestation" of the organism. These are the physical parts, the sum of the atoms, molecules, macromolecules, cells, structures, metabolism, energy utilization, tissues, organs, reflexes and behaviors; anything that is part of the observable structure, function or behavior of a living organism. [160]

A blood test is used to determine whether the A and/or B characteristics are present in a blood sample (Phenotype). It is not possible to determine the exact genotype from a blood test result of either type A or type B. **But with the "Survey," and Human Genetic Code Periodic Table, yes you can determined the exact genotype! You will know exactly which of the 24 Blood Type (MIND/BODY or Genotype/Phenotype) is yours. The current Blood Type testing identifies the six Blood Types which is the foundation of the 24 phenotypes Blood Types and the Survey identify the 24 genotype Blood Types of each of the 24 DNA Sequence. Each DNA sequence has 2 Blood Type – one for the MIND or GENOTYPE and one for the BODY or PHENOTYPE.**

If someone has blood type A, they must have at least one copy of the A allele, but they could have two copies. One from each parent. Their genotype is A and phenotype is either AA or AO or AB. Similarly, someone who is genotype blood type B could have a phenotype of either BB or BO or BA. The Table below summarized "how" the Blood Types are related to the four sub-brains but more so the 24 DNA sequences. Blood Typing follows the rule that DNA formation or combination is adhered to - ONLY three letters of the four will combine at one time to create a codon (for DNA) or blood type. The information contained in this chapter is not found in any literature but conclusions that the author discovered from the 24 DNA sequences that belongs to the Human species. You have already seen the credibility of this discovery from your own Survey and Blood Test results. How was I able to create those Survey and Table, Blood Type results of the MIND and BODY? You know the answer!

Table One

1 Psychology (related Fields)			4 Medicine (related Fields) and Law Enforcements				
4 Sub-Brain: Right, Left, Stem, Mid			4 Blood Types: A, B, O, ABO 24 Blood Types(MIND+BODY=48) and Body Types				
24 Sub-Brains and Personalities						Genotype	Phenotype
R	L	RLMS – RLM	B	A	BA(ABO)O – BA(ABO)	*B+*	A+
		RLSM – RLS			BAO(ABO) – BAO	*B+*	A+
	S	RSLM – RSL		O	BOA(ABO)- BO	*B+*	O+
		RSML – RSM			BO(ABO)A – BO(ABO)	*B+*	O+
	M	RMSL – RMS		ABO	B(ABO)OA – B(ABO)O	*B*	ABO-O
		RMLS – RML			B(ABO)AO – B(ABO)A	*B*	ABO-A

L	R	LRSM – LRS			ABO(ABO) – ABO	A+	B+
		LRMS – LRM	A	B	AB(ABO)O – AB(ABO)	A+	B+
	S	LSRM – LSR	A		AOB(ABO) – AOB	A+	O+
		LSMR – LSM		O	AO(ABO) – AO(ABO)	A+	O+
	M	LMRS – LMR		ABO	A(ABO)BO – A(ABO)B	A	ABO-B
		LMSR – LMS			A(ABO)OB – A(ABO)O	A	ABO-O
S	L	SLRM – SLR		A	OAB(ABO) – OAB	O+	A+
		SLMR – SLM			OA(ABO)B – AO(ABO)	O+	A+
	R	SRLM – SRL	O	B	OBA(ABO) – OBA	O+	B+
		SRML – SRM			OB(ABO)A – OB(ABO)	O+	B+
	M	SMLR – SML		ABO	O(ABO)AB – O(ABO)A	O	ABO-A
		SMRL – SMR			O(ABO)BA – O(ABO)B	O	ABO-B
M	S	MSLR – MSL		O	(ABO)OAB – (ABO)OA	ABO-O	A
		MSRL – MSR			(ABO)OBA – (ABO)OB	ABO-O	B
	L	MLSR – MLSR		A	(ABO)AOB – (ABO)AO	ABO-A	O
		MLRS – MLR	ABO		(ABO)ABO – (ABO)AB	ABO-A	B
	R	MRSL – MRS		B	(ABO)BOA – (ABO)BO	ABO-B	O
		MRLS – MRL			(ABO)BAO – (ABO)BA	ABO-B	A

A blood test which will show of either type AB or type O phenotype is more informative. Someone with blood type genotype AB must have he A, O and B alleles. The genotype must be AB. Someone with genotype blood type O has either the A nor the B allele as shown on the Table above. Therefore, the phenotype is A or B and genotype must be OO.

The Table above explains how someone can go from an A+ to O- or vice versa; or A+ to B+ or vice versa; or O- or A- or vice versa; A- to B- or vice versa; or O- to O+ like the girl in Australia after her liver transplant[161]. There's nothing unusual about these occurrences. Those of the Artisan Temperament or Mid Brain dominant is very natural for them to change their Blood Type from a positive to a negative.

A person's phenotype Blood Type can change within its own Blood Type genotype. For example, a person who is Right Brain or Genotype A+ and Blood Type B+, can later changed to O+ Blood Type depending on environment, diet and lifestyle. It's just the way the body is designed to care for itself! It has 24 recombination to protect itself.

There are four versions (or alleles) of the blood type genes (genotype): A, B, O, ABO. These four versions is how the fetus reacts to the mother's diets, lifestyle and environment as you will learn in the next chapter. Since everyone has two copies of these genes, there are **six possible combinations or genotypes as shown above**. A person 6 genotypes creates 24 (2x12) phenotypes or outward expression of the Blood Type. There are **24 possible NATURAL Blood Types expressions** which are shown above and in the "Human Genetic Code Periodic Table." Twelve's of the above Blood phenotypes are what scientist called Chimeras (Blood Chimeras).

In medicine, a Chimera is a person composed of two genetically distinct types of cells. Human chimeras were first discovered with the advent of blood typing when it was found that some people had more than one blood type.

Those in the Table below that Dr. D'Adamo labeled as the NORMAD, WARRIOR, and EXPLOERER are natural blood type Chimeras. They have two Blood Types that may express itself as positive or negative. You will identify this in the Six (6) Phenotype Table below.

Table Two

1 **4 Sub-Brain:** Right, Left, Stem, Mid 24 Sub-Brains and Personalities			3 **4 Blood Types:** A, B, O, ABO **48 Blood Types (24 MIND/24 BODY) and 24 Body Types**			4 DSM-IV Treatment Model	5 6 Genotype Dr. D'Adamo 6 Groups
			MIND Genotype	**BODY** Phenotyp	24 **DNA**		
R	L	RLMS	*B+*	A+	GCA	Axis IV--III	Gatherer
		RLSM	*B+*	A+	GCT	Axis IV-II	Gatherer
	S	RSLM	*B+*	O+	GAC	Axis IV-II	Gatherer
		RSML	*B+*	O+	GAT	Axis IV-I	Gatherer
	M	RMSL	*B*	ABO-O	GTA	Axis IV-I	Warrior
		RMLS	*B*	ABO-A	GTC	Axis IV-III	Warrior
L	R	LRSM	*A+*	B+	CGA	Axis I-II	Teacher
		LRMS	*A+*	B+	CGT	Axis I-III	Teacher
	S	LSRM	*A+*	O+	CAG	Axis I-II	Teacher
		LSMR	*A+*	O+	CAT	Axis I-IV	Teacher
	M	LMRS	*A*	ABO-B	CTG	Axis I-III	Nomad
		LMSR	*A*	ABO-O	CTA	Axis I-IV	Nomad
S	L	SLRM	*O+*	A+	ACG	Axis III-II	Hunter
		SLMR	*O+*	A+	ACT	Axis III-IV	Hunter
	R	SRLM	*O+*	B+	AGC	Axis III-IV	Hunter
		SRML	*O+*	B+	AGT	Axis III-I	Hunter
	M	SMLR	*O*	ABO-A	ATC	**Axis III-IV**	Explorer
		SMRL	*O*	ABO-B	ATG	AxisIII-I	Explorer
M	S	MSLR	ABO-O	A	TAC	Axis II-IV	Nomad
		MSRL	ABO-O	B	TAG	Axis II-I	Warrior
	L	MLSR	ABO-A	O	TCA	Axis II-IV	Explorer
		MLRS	ABO-A	B	TCG	Axis II-III	Warrior
	R	MRSL	ABO-B	O	TGA	Axis II-I	Explorer
		MRLS	ABO-B	A	TGC	Axis II-III	Nomad

Dr. D'Adamo in his Blood Type Diet below initially discussed the four Blood Types (A, B, O, AB), or Genotypes in this writing, then later expanded to the 6 Genotypes Diet or Phenotypes for this writing, which is just an explantion of diet based on GENOTYPE or PHENOTYPE.

As you see from the Table 1 and Table 2 above , the six genotypes are from the four Blood Types or sub-brains (Genotypes) and expanded further to 24 more blood types. You have probably figured out by now that the four sub-brains controls and managed the four Blood Types just like the four Temperaments.

It was not surprising to see from Dr. D'Adamo's researched that Western Europeans and many Japanese tend to be **GENOTYPE** Blood **Type A or Left Brain or Intellectual intelligences** communities. Their culture, diet and environment are conducive or foster such Blood Type like the following countries. Eastern Europeans, East Indians, northern Chinese, Koreans and a smaller portion of Japanese tend toward GENOTYPE **Type B or Right Brain or Creative intelligences,** as do Ashkenazic and Sephardic Jews. GENOTYPE **Type O or Stem Brain or Practical (instinctual/survival) intelligence,** predominates among Africans and American Indians, but is also the most common, crossing many races and geographic regions. GENOTYPE Type AB or **Mid Brain or Emotional intelligence** is the baby/fetus's respond to the new diverse world environment that we are living - a sociopathic, psychopathic, sensopathic and emotiopathic.

All various PHENOTYPE Blood Types (and Body Types) are the fetus/ embryo's respond to its environment to protect itself and survive. The fetus has 24 combinations (or condons which are words of the DNA.) to pick from to protect itself.

It is interesting to note that the rise of autism and many other child mental disorders are related to their Blood and Body Types and brain inclinations. If you are Phenotype Blood Type A, but more so ectomorph, you have a higher probability of getting autism as an infant, follow by the Phenotype Blood B and least the Phenotype Blood Type O.

Dr. D'Adamo, author of the best selling books **"Eat Right for Your Type"** and **"Live Right for Your Type,"** believes that your personality is influence by your Blood Type. *You Genotype Blood Type is your main Temperament and provide information about your personality! Your Phenotype Blood Types provides your physical characteristics.*

The above Table listed 6 sub-brain combinations that are of the Genotype Blood Type B group under the TSF-24 Mind Approach. The sub-brains controls the DNA activities and expressions, not the other way as currently understood. *The Blood Types phenotypes under this group are A+, O+ AB- and BA+(AB+).* Below is Dr. D'Adamo's discovery which explains the Genotype Blood Type B group.

In an independent study, Dr. D'Adamo found that most Blood Type B's often described themselves in ways related to the following characteristics: *subjective, easygoing, creative, original and flexible.* In another study, Type B's scored significantly higher on "intuiting," indicating a preference *or sixth sense* information; and they scored high on the "intuiting/feeling" combination, indicating that they tend to be insightful, mystical, idealistic, creative, globally-oriented, people-oriented and good at imagining. They also reported that they learned best through listening, then reflecting on and interpreting what they had observed.

4 Sub-Brain:			MIND	BODY	24 Universal Personalities	
					MIND	BODY
R	L	RLMS	B+	A+	INFJ Counselor	ENTP Visionary
		RLSM	B+	A+	INFP Idealist	ENTJ Executive
	S	RSLM	B+	O+	ENFP Inspirer	ESTJ Guardian
		RSML	B+	O+	ENFJ Teacher	ESFJ Provider
	M	RMSL	B+-	AB-+ O+-	ENFJ Teacher	ESTP Promote ESTJ Guardian
		RMLS	B+-	ABO- A+-	INFJ Counselor	ESFP Performer ENTJ Executive

What Makes Type B - **Right Brain or Idealis**t *Unique* - As a Type B, you carry the genetic potential for great malleability and the ability to thrive in changeable conditions *(extraverted or sociable).* Unlike blood types A and O, which are at opposite ends of every spectrum, your position is fluid, rather than stationary, with the ability to move in either direction along the continuum. It's easy to see how this flexibility served the interests of early Type B's who needed to balance the twin forces of the animal and vegetable kingdoms. At the same time, it can be extremely challenging to balance two poles and Type B's tend to be highly sensitive to the effects of slipping out of balance.

The primary challenges that can get in the way of optimum health for Type B include a tendency to produce higher than normal cortisol levels in situations to stress; sensitivity to the B specific lectins in select foods, resulting in inflammation and greater risk for developing Syndrome

X; susceptibility to slow growing, lingering viruses – such as those for MS, CFS, and lupus; and a vulnerability to autoimmune diseases. "If I were to generalize," says Dr. D'Adamo, "I would say that a healthy Type B, living right for his or her own type, tends to have fewer risk factors for disease and tends to be more physically fit and mentally balanced than any of the other blood types." Type B's tended to have a greater ability to adapt to altitude and interestingly, are statistically the tallest of the blood types.

Type B or *Right Brain or Idealist* Diet - For Type Bs the biggest factors in **weight gain are corn, wheat, buckwheat, lentils, tomatoes, peanuts and sesame seeds**. Each of these foods affect the efficiency of your metabolic process, resulting in fatigue, fluid retention, and hypoglycemia – a severe drop in blood sugar after eating a meal. When you eliminate these foods and begin eating a diet that is right for your type, you blood sugar levels should remain normal after meals. Another very common food that Type Bs should **avoid is chicken**. Chicken contains a Blood Type B agglutinating lectin in its muscle tissue. Although chicken is a lean meat, the issue is the power of an agglutinating lectin attacking your bloodstream and the potential for it to lead to strokes and immune disorders. Dr. D'Adamo suggests that you wean yourself away from chicken and replace them with highly beneficial foods such as goat, lamb, mutton, rabbit and venison. Other foods that encourage weight loss are green vegetables, eggs beneficial meats and low fat dairy. When the toxic foods are avoided and replaced with beneficial foods, Blood Type Bs are very successful in controlling their weight.

Exercise for *Right Brain or Idealist* - To maintain the mind/body balance that is unique to Type B's, Dr. D'Adamo recommends that you choose physical exercise that challenges your mind as well as your body. Type Bs need to balance meditative activities with more intense physical exercise. "You tend to do best with activities that are not too aerobically intense, have an element of mental challenge and involve other people." Says Dr. D'Adamo. Excellent forms of exercise for Type B's include **tennis, cycling, hiking and golf.**

Live Right for *Right Brain or Idealist*:! - Here are Dr. D'Adamo's key lifestyle strategies for Type Bs:

- Visualization is a powerful technique for Type Bs. If you can visualize it, you can achieve it.

- Find healthy ways to express your nonconformist side.

- Spend at least twenty minutes a day involved in some creative task that requires your complete attention.

- Go to bed no later than 11:00PM and sleep for eight hours or more. It is essential for B's to maintain their circadian rhythm.

- Use mediation to relax during breaks

- Engage in a community, neighborhood or other group activity that gives you a meaningful connection to a group. **Type Bs are natural born networkers.**

- Be spontaneous.

As they age, Type Bs have a tendency to suffer memory loss and have decreased mental acuity. Stay sharp by doing tasks that require concentration, such as crossword puzzles or learn a new skill or language.

4 Sub-Brain:		MIND	BODY	24 Universal Personalities	
				MIND	BODY
0.0877	LRSM	A+	B+	**ENTJ** Executive	**INFP** Idealist
	LRMS	A+	B+	**ENTP** Visionary	**INFJ** Counselor
S	LSRM	A+	O+	**INTJ** Scientist	**ISFJ** Protector
	LSMR	A+	O+	**INTP** Architect	**ISTJ** Inspector
M	LMRS	A+-	AB+-B+-	**ENTJ** Executive,	**ISFP** Composer, **INFP** Idealist
	LMSR	A+-	AB+-O+-	**INTJ** Scientist	**ISTP** Mechanic **ISFJ** Protector ,

The above six combinations are of phenotype Blood Type A. The phenotypes Blood Types under this group are O+, B+, and AB-+. In a study conducted by Dr. D'Adamo in 1999, he found some interesting connections between blood type and personality. Type As most often described themselves in ways related to the following characteristics: sensitive to the needs of others, good listeners, detail oriented, analytical, creative and inventive.

What Makes Type A or Left Brain or Rationals Unique - Many neurochemical factors in the Type A genetic disposition favor a structured, rhythmic, harmonious life, surrounded by a positive, supportive community *(introverted)*. The harried pace and increased senses of isolation experienced by so many in today's society often make these needs difficult to achieve. Type A best exemplifies the powerful interconnections between mind and body. However, Type A's more internalized *(introverted)* relationship to stress, which served your ancestors well, can be a challenge for the modern Type A. The Blood Type Diet's proactive mix of lifestyle strategies, hormonal equalizers, gentle exercise and specialized dietary guidelines will maximize your overall health; decrease your natural risk factors for cancer, diabetes and cardiovascular disease. The result: high performance, mental clarity, greater vitality and increased longevity.

Type A or Left Brain or Rationals Diet - "When we discuss 'diet,' we are not talking necessarily about a weight loss plan, that's a side benefit to following this plan. We are actually discussing diet in the more traditional sense, meaning a way to eat," explains, Dr. D'Adamo. **Type As flourish on a vegetarian diet** - if you are accustomed to eating meat, you will lose weight and have more energy once you eliminate the toxic foods from your diet. Many people find it difficult to move away from the typical meat and potato fare to **soy proteins, grains and vegetables.** But it is particularly important for sensitive Type As to eat their foods in as natural a state as possible: **pure, fresh and organic.** "I can't emphasize enough how this critical dietary adjustment can be to the sensitive immune system of Type A. With this diet you can supercharge your immune system and potentially short circuit the development of life threatening diseases."

Exercise for the *Left Brain or Rationals* - Heightened cortisol levels make it harder for Type As to recover from stress. Research has demonstrated that overall cortisol levels can be lowered through a regular program of exercises that provide focus and calming effects. Make these activities a regular - and life saving - part of your lifestyle. Dr. D'Adamo recommends, Meditation and Deep Breathing Exercises. Meditation has been studied for its effects on stress hormones. It was found that after meditation, serum cortisol levels were significantly reduced. Writes Dr. D'Adamo, "While it's fine for Type As to participate in more intense physical activity when healthy and in good condition, be aware that these forms of exercise do not act as safety valves for stress in your blood type. I have seen Type As excel at weight lifting and aerobic activities, but you have to be careful about not overtraining, as that will actually raise cortisol levels."

Live Right for *Left Brain or Rationals!* - In addition to exercise, stress management and eating the right foods, here are some key lifestyle strategies for Type A individuals.

- Cultivate creativity and expression in your life

- Establish a consistent daily schedule

- Go to bed no later than 11:00 PM and sleep for eight hours or more. Don't linger in bed, as soon as you get up, get going!

- Take at least two breaks of twenty minutes each during the work day. Stretch, take a walk, do deep breathing exercises or meditate.

- Don't skip meals

- Eat more protein at the start of the day, less at the end

- Don't eat when you are anxious

- Eat smaller, more frequent meals.

- Engage in thirty to forty five minutes of calming exercise at least three times a week.

- Plan regular screening for heart disease and cancer prevention.

- Always chew food thoroughly to enhance digestion. Low stomach acid makes digestion more difficult

4 Sub-Brain:	MIND	BODY	24 Universal Personalities	
			MIND	BODY
SLRM	O+	A+	ISFJ Protector	INTJ Scientist
SLMR	O+	A+	ISTJ Inspector	INTP Architect
SRLM	O+	B+	ESTJ Guardian	ENFP Inspirer

SRML	O+	B+	ESFJ Provider	ENFJ Teacher
SMLR	O+-	AB-+ A+-	ISTJ Inspector	ISTP Mechanic, INTP Architect,
SMRL	O+-	AB-+ B+-	ESFJ Provider	ESTP Promoter ENFJ Teacher ,

The above six combinations are for the Blood Type O.The phenotype Blood Types under this group are AB-, or A+ and B+. In an independent study of 45 MBA students, Type O's most often described themselves in ways related to the following characteristics; responsible, decisive, organized, objective, rule-conscious, and practical. Both male and female Type O's reported a higher percentage of the mesomorphic body type when compared to controls. Interestingly, Type O's also scored significantly higher than the rest in "sensing" (*Sensovert*) – using the 5 senses to gather information, and in the sensing-thinking combination, indicating that they are more detail and fact oriented, logical, precise and orderly. "I believe that the tendency to sense and get facts right stems from the inbred hunter-gatherer need to observe and accurately assess the environment in order to insure survival." Says D'Adamo.

<u>What Makes Stem Brain or Guardian</u> Unique - As a Blood Type O you may be predisposed to certain illnesses, such as **ulcers and thyroid disorders.** In the 1950's it was discovered that Type O's had about twice the instances of ulcers of all kinds than the other blood types. These findings have been replicated many times since then. Type O's tend to have low levels of thyroid hormone and often exhibit insufficient levels of iodine, a chemical element whose sole purpose is thyroid hormone regulation. This causes many side effects such as weight gain, fluid retention and fatigue. Dr. D'Adamo does not recommend iodine supplements, rather a diet rich in saltwater fish and kelp to help regulate the thyroid gland. Bladder Wrack is also an excellent nutrient for type O's. This herb, actually a seaweed, is very effective as an aid to weight control for Type O's. "The fucose in bladder wrack seems to help normalize the sluggish metabolic rate and produce weight loss in Type O's," says Dr. D'Adamo.

Type O's also have a higher level of stomach acid than the other blood types, which often results in stomach irritation and ulcers. Dr. D'Adamo recommends a licorice preparation called DGL (de glycyrrhizinated licorice) which can reduce discomfort and aid healing. DGL protects the stomach lining in addition to protecting it from stomach acids.

Avoid crude licorice preparations as they contain a component of the plant which can cause elevated blood pressure. This component has been removed in DGL. Dr. D'Adamo also recommends Mastic Gum and Bismuth to soothe Type O's common and even frequent tummy troubles.

Diet for **Stem Brain or Guardian - Type Os thrive on intense physical exercise and animal protein.** Unlike the other blood types, Type Os muscle tissue should be slightly on the acid side. Type Os can efficiently digest and metabolize meat because they tend to have high stomach-acid content. The success of the Type O Diet depends on the use of **lean, chemical-free meats, poultry, and fish.** Type Os don't find dairy products and grains quite as user friendly as do most of the other blood types.

The initial weight loss on the Type O Diet is by **restricting consumption of grains, breads, legumes, and beans**. The leading factor in weight gain for Type Os is the gluten found in wheat germ and whole wheat products, which interferes with insulin efficiency and slow down metabolic rate. Another factor that contribute to weight gain is certain beans and legumes (lentils and kidney beans) contain lectins that deposit in the muscle tissues making them less "charged" for physical activity. The third factor in Type O weight gain is that Type Os have a tendency to have low levels of thyroid hormone or unstable thyroid functions, which also cause metabolic problems. Therefore it is good to **avoid food that inhibits thyroid hormone (cabbage, brussels sprouts, cauliflower, mustard green)** but increase hormone production (kelp, seafood, iodized salt).

Several classes of vegetables can cause big problems for Type Os, such as the Brassica family (cabbage, cauliflower, etc.) can inhibit the thyroid function. Eat more vegetables that are high in Vitamin K, which helps the clotting factor which is weak in Type Os. The nightshade vegetables can cause lectin deposit in the tissue surrounding the joints.

Because of the high acidity stomach, Type Os should eat fruits of alkaline nature such as berries and plums. Type Os should severely restrict the use of dairy products. Their system is not designed for the proper metabolism.

Exercise for *Stem Brain or Guardian* **- Type** O's benefit tremendously from brisk regular exercise that taxes the cardiovascular and muscular skeletal system. But the benefit derived surpasses the goal of physical fitness. Type O also derives the benefit of a well timed chemical release system. The act of physical exercise releases a swarm of neurotransmitter activity that acts as a tonic for the entire system. **The Type O who exercises regularly also has a better emotional response.** You are more emotionally balanced as a result of well regulated, efficient chemical transport system. More than any other blood type, O's rely on physical exercise to maintain physical health and emotional balance. **Dr. D'Adamo suggests that Type O's engage in regular physical activity three to four times per week.** For best results, engage in aerobic activity for thirty to forty five minutes at least four times per week. If you are easily bored, choose two or three different exercises and vary your routine.

__Live Right Stem Brain or Guardian!__ - In addition to exercising and eating foods that are Right For Your Type, here are a few key lifestyle strategies for Type O individuals:

- Develop clear plans for goals and tasks – annual, monthly, weekly, daily to avoid impulsivity.

- Make lifestyle changes gradually, rather than trying to tackle everything at once.

- Eat all meals, even snacks, seated at a table.

- Chew slowly and put your fork down between bites of food.

- Avoid making big decisions or spending money when stressed.

- Do something physical when you feel anxious.

- Engage in thirty to forty five minutes of aerobic exercise at least four times per week.

- When you crave a pleasure releasing-substance (alcohol, tobacco, sugar), do something physical.

Dr. D'Adamo recommends that Type O, "Approach this program as a long term strategy. This is not a short term goal, rather a lifestyle that you adapt for a lifetime of health and well being. There is no doubt that there is a connection between the mind and the body. The knowledge that we can do something to change our genetic destiny is powerful

BODY			24 Universal Personalities	
			MIND	BODY
MSLR	AB+- O+-	A+-	ISTP Mechanic, ISFJ Protector,	INTJ Scientist
MSRL	AB+- O+-	B+-	ESTP Promoter ESTJ Guardian	ENFJ Teacher
MLSR	AB+- A+-	O+-	ISTP Mechanic, INTP Architect,	ISTJ Inspector
MLRS	AB+- A+-	B+-	ESFP Performer ENTJ Executive,	INFJ Counselor
MRSL	AB+- B+-	O+-	ESTP Promoter ENFJ Teacher ,	ESFJ Provider
MRLS	AB+- B+-	A+-	ISFP Composer INFP Idealist	ENTJ Executive,

*The above six combinations are of the Blood Type AB. The phenotype Blood Types under this group are O-+, A+-, and B+-.*Type AB often receives mixed messages about emotional health. While you tend to be drawn to other people and are friendly and trusting, there is a side of you that feels alienated from the larger community. At your best, you are intuitive and spiritual, with an ability to look beyond the rigid confines of society. You are passionate in your beliefs, but you also want to be liked by others and this can create conflicts. In an independent study, Type ABs described themselves as **emotional, passionate, friendly, trusting and empathetic.** Type ABs are considered some of the most interesting of the blood types, both John F. Kennedy and Marilyn Monroe were Type ABs and although both are long gone, they hold a place in our national psyche to this day.

Type *AB* *Mid Brain or Artisan Diets* - Type AB reflects the mixed inheritance of their A and B genes. According to Dr. D'Adamo, "**Type AB has Type A's low stomach acid, however, they also have Type B's adaptation to meats.** Therefore, you lack enough stomach acid to metabolize them efficiently and the meat you eat tends to get stored as fat. Your Type B propensities cause the same insulin reaction as Type B when you eat lima beans, corn, buckwheat, or sesame seeds." Inhibited insulin production results in hypoglycemia, a lowering of blood sugar after meals and leads to less efficient metabolism of foods.

Type AB should avoid caffeine and alcohol, especially when you're in stressful situations. Dr. D'Adamo recommends that Type AB focus on foods such as tofu, seafood, dairy and green vegetables if you are trying to lose weight. "Avoid all smoked or cured meats. These foods can cause stomach cancer in people with low levels of stomach acid," recommends Dr. D'Adamo. There is a wide variety of seafood for Type AB, and it is an excellent source of protein for Type AB. A few highly beneficial fish are mahi-mahi, red snapper, salmon, sardines, and tuna.. Some dairy is also beneficial for Type AB – especially cultured dairy such as Yogurt and kefir.

Dr. D'Adamo also recommends smaller, more frequent meals, as they will counteract digestive problems caused by inadequate stomach acid and peptic enzymes. "Your stomach initiates the digestive process with a combination of digestive secretions, and the muscular contractions that mix food with them. When you have low levels of digestive secretions, food tends to stay in the stomach longer." Explains D'Adamo. He also suggests that Type AB pay attention to combining certain foods. For example, you'll digest and metabolize foods more efficiently if you avoid eating starches and proteins in the same meal.

Exercise for Mid Brain or Artisan - Even though people have different capabilities for accommodating stress, we ultimately all have a breaking point. Given enough stressors of a high enough intensity for a long enough period of time, anyone will maladapt. For a Type AB, when it comes to stress hormones, you most resemble Type O in your tendency to overproduce catecholamines like adrenaline. Yet you also have the additional complexity of Type B's rapid clearing of nitrous oxide, so you suffer the physical consequences of high emotions. Your greatest danger is the tendency to internalize your emotions, especially anger and hostility, which is much more damaging to your health than externalizing it. Exercise plays a critical component in stress reduction and maintaining a healthy emotional balance for Type AB. Dr. D'Adamo recommends a combination of both calming activities and more intense physical exercise to help maintain an optimal balance. For example, three days of aerobic exercise such as running or biking and two days of calming exercise such as yoga or tai chi.

Live Right Mid Brain or Artisan! - Here are Dr. D'Adamo's key lifestyle strategies for people with Blood Type AB:

- Cultivate your social nature in welcoming environments. Avoid situations that are highly competitive.

- Avoid ritualistic thinking and fixating on issues, especially those you can't control or influence.

- Develop a clear plan for goals and tasks – annually, monthly, weekly, daily – to avoid rushing.

- Make lifestyle changes gradually, rather than trying to tackle everything at once.

- Engage in forty-five to sixty minutes of aerobic exercise at least twice a week. Balanced by daily stretching, meditation or yoga.

- Engage in a community, neighborhood or other group activity that gives you a meaningful connection to a group.

- Also carve out time alone. Have at least one sport, hobby or activity that you perform independently of others.

- Break up your workday with some physical activity, especially if your job is sedentary. You'll feel more energized.

You probably notice above that the 4 Genotype Blood Type groups listed the 24 personality recombinations of the Brain.. This controls all life activities including the DNA. Each Blood Type group listed 6 combinations. (6x4=24). These 4 Genotype Blood Types as I mentioned at the beginning of the Chapter creates 6 phenotypes which is the foundation of Dr. D'Adamos Genotype Diet. These 6 clusters or groupings are the genes and its prenatal response to the environment, mother's diet and lifestyle to survive and protect itself. The fetus select 1 out of the 24 recombination's to protect itself from an internal or external threat from the environmental, lifestyle and mothers' diet. Therefore, deciding the dominant sub-brain and the order of the other three sub-brains (the order the nucleotides arranged itself in the DNA to produce proteins according to what's best to protect itself.) – Right, Left, Stem and Mid...etc. This in turn dictates the Blood Type, Body Type, and main Temperament as I have stated above. You have already learned the four main temperaments and the physical characteristics I will discuss that in

the Body Type chapter.

Interestingly, without even knowing about Dr, D'Adamo's phenomenal phenotype research, a review of each cluster or group, you tell their Blood Type, Temperament, Body Type, socially, psychological, physiological and emotional challenges they are prone to, their strength and weakness based on the 24 personalities of the four sub-brains.

Without even having the physical evidence or statistical or clinical data to prove the information in this writing, already existed data is available out there. Reviewing the Human Genetic Code Periodic Table with its 24 sub-brain combinations shows that it appears to be; 24 pairs of chromosomes, 24,000 genes…etc. Also, the properties of the four (4) nucleotides are controlled and managed by each area of the brain..

The order or arrangement of the nucleotides **is determined by sub-brains** which in turn determine the sequence of the amino acids which in turn produced the right protein. Scientist have shown that the four area of the brain - Forebrain [Left/Right], Midbrain and Hindbrain) is visible at about three weeks gestation[162]. The Genetic Code Table below illustrates what I am referring to above. Why am I including this Table in this discussion? It's because whatever medical issues you are experiencing is due to the specific amino acids and proteins not being nourished and cared for with the specific diet or medications… etc. The Table below is based on the OLD Genetic Code from the 64 DNA discovery by Watson, Crick and Wilkins.

The 24 DNA sequences of the Human species is weaved throughout the Tables within this book and represent 24 specific Amino Acids.

1st Base	2nd Base				3rd Base
	G	**C**	**A**	**T**	
G	Gly Gly Gly Gly	Ala Ala Ala Ala	Asp Asp Glu Glu	Val Val Val Val	G C A T
C	Arg Arg Arg Arg	Pro Pro Pro Pro	His His His His	Leu Leu Leu Leu	G C A T

159

	Ser	Thr	Asn	Ile	G
A	Ser	Thr	Asn	Ile	C
	Arg	Thr	Lys	Ile	A
	Arg	Thr	Lys	Met	T
T	Cys	Ser	Tyr	Phe	G
	Cys	Ser	Tyr	Phe	C
	STOP	Ser	STOP	Leu	A
	Trp	Ser	STOP	Lue	T

Dr. D'Adamo said, *"I know that six Genotype exist now, and I can deduce how they developed, but that's the part of the story for which the evidence is still largely circumstantial*[163]*...As it happens, the survival strategies we've worked out with our 30,000 human genes, our common prenatal experience, and our 100,000 years on the planet have fallen into six basic patterns. I can't tell you why there are six any more than I can tell you why there are four blood types – it just happened that ways...*"[164]

The information in this book have the answer to Dr. D'Adamo's concern above. His Genotype (actually phenotype) research has confirm information in this book about the connection between the brain and blood, provides clinical proofs of the six clusters or groups of the 24 personality combinations and their physical characteristics but more so the medical communities with the six Blood Type phenotypes.. The Genetic Code Table (and the 24 sub-brain combinations or sequence) above supports the 6 clusters or phenotypes as you process each DNA grouping based on the sub-brains or Blood Type. There are little variations or differences but not much. You get one gene from each parent (2x3) and you have 6 phenotypes . Your fetus or you choose one Genotype or Blood Type. Actually the sub-brain combinations dictate this. You, fetus knows exactly which of the 24 recombination's is best to protect itself .

This writing will not reinvent the wheel but used Dr. D'Adamo's labeling or titling (**Hunter, Gatherer, Teacher, Explorer, Warrior, and Nomad**) to match its grouping or clusters as they are the same concepts or groups. What Dr. D'Adamo classified as Genotype is what this writing classified as Phenotypes. So, when this writing is discussing Dr. D'Adamo's Genotype Diet, it's really discussing the PHENOTYPE DIET. Please check with **www.GenoTypeDiet.com** for detail information on the Genotype Diet and how he discovered his six genotypes.

The Genotype Blood Type is the dominant sub-brain of both the dominant and auxiliary sub-brains - Right=B, Left=A, Stem=O and Mid=AB. See your Blood Type and Brain combination below amongst the six genotypes with the **24 possible Blood Types and Body Types.**! You will notice that ALL of the 24 sub-brains combinations above or the 4 Genotype Blood Type group above creates the six group of genotypes below of Dr. D A'Damos Genotype Diet.

There are six different patterns that identify the six phenotype and blood types. Again, the six phenotypes or clusters are formed just the way the DNA runs or works. The four DNA bases parallels to each sub-brains.

1			3			4	5
4 Sub-Brain: Right, Left, Stem, Mid			**4 Blood Types:** A, B, O, ABO			6	6
						DSM-IV Treat -ment Model	Genotype DIET
24 Sub-Brains and Personalities			**48 Blood Types (24 MIND/24 BODY) and 24 Body Types**				Dr. D'Adamo
			MIND Geno	BODY Pheno	Body Types		6 Groups
R	L	RLMS	*B+*	A+	EndoE	Axis IV--III	**Gatherer**
		RLSM	*B+*	A+	EndoE	Axis IV-II	**Gatherer**
	S	RSLM	*B+*	O+	EndoM	Axis IV-II	**Gatherer**
		RSML	*B+*	O+	EndoM	Axis IV-I	**Gatherer**
	M	RMSL	*B*	ABO-O	EndoM	Axis IV-I	Warrior
		RMLS	*B*	ABO-A	EndoE	Axis IV-III	Warrior
L	R	LRSM	*A+*	B+	EctoEn	Axis I-II	**Teacher**
		LRMS	*A+*	B+	EctoEn	Axis I-III	**Teacher**
	S	LSRM	*A+*	O+	EctoM	Axis I-II	**Teacher**
		LSMR	*A+*	O+	EctoM	Axis I-IV	**Teacher**
	M	LMRS	*A*	ABO-B	EctoEn	Axis I-III	**Nomad**
		LMSR	*A*	ABO-O	EctoM	Axis I-IV	**Nomad**
S	L	SLRM	*O+*	A+	MesoE	Axis III-II	**Hunter**
		SLMR	*O+*	A+	MesoE	Axis III-IV	**Hunter**
	R	SRLM	*O+*	B+	MesoEn	Axis III-IV	**Hunter**
		SRML	*O+*	B+	MesoEn	Axis III-I	**Hunter**
	M	SMLR	*O*	ABO-A	MesoE	**Axis III-IV**	**Explorer**
		SMRL	*O*	ABO-B	MesoEn	AxisIII-I	**Explorer**
M	S	MSLR	ABO-O	A	MesoE	Axis II-IV	**Nomad**
		MSRL	ABO-O	B	MesoEn	Axis II-I	Warrior
	L	MLSR	ABO-A	O	EctoMe	Axis II-IV	**Explorer**
		MLRS	ABO-A	B	EctoEn	Axis II-III	Warrior
	R	MRSL	ABO-B	O	EndoMe	Axis II-I	**Explorer**
		MRLS	ABO-B	A	EndoE	Axis II-III	**Nomad**

1) **THE EXPLORER GROUP**: Phenotype **Blood Type O+-, B+- A+-, or AB+-,** They are prone to medical conditions described under AXIS III, and AXIS II of the **DSM-IV (Diagnostic and Statistical Manual of Mental Disorder)**[165]. See the Table

above. **Dr.** D'Adamo described the Explorer as muscular and adventurous. The Explorer is a biological problem solver with an impressive ability to adapt to environmental changes and a better-than-average capacity for gene repair. The Explorer's vulnerability to hormonal imbalances and brain strain can be overcome with a balance diet and lifestyles.[166]

2) **THE NOMAD GROUP:** This is **typically phenotype Blood Type A-/+ OR AB-/+.** Their body type is ectomorphic which is abundant of ectoderm tissues. They are prone to medical conditions described under AXIS I and AXIS II of the DSM (Diagnostic and Statistical Manual of Mental Disorder). Dr. D'Adamo described the Nomad as the Genotype of the extremes, with a great sensitivity to environmental conditions-especially changes in altitude and barometric pressures. The Nomad is vulnerable to neuromuscular and immune problems. Yet a well- conditioned Nomad has the enviable gift of controlling caloric intake and aging gracefully. [167]

3) **THE WARRIOR GROUP:** This is typically **Blood Type B- OR AB-** They are prone to medical conditions listed under AXIS IV and AXIS II of the DSM (Diagnostic and Statistical Manual of Mental Disorder).

Dr. D'Adamo described the Warrior as long, lean, and health in youth. The Warrior is subject to a bodily rebellion in mid-life. With the optimal diet and lifestyle, the Warrior can overcome the quick-aging metabolic genes and experiences a second "silver age" of health.[168]

4) **THE HUNTER GROUP:** This is typically **Blood Type O+.** The Hunter is prone to social/spiritual, economic challenges listed under AXIS IV and mental issues under AXIS I of the DSM.

Dr. D'Adamo described the Hunter as tall, thin, and intense with an abundance of adrenaline and a fierce, nervous energy that winds down with age...Vulnerable to systemic burnout when overstressed, the Hunter's modern challenges is to conserve energy for the long haul.[169]

5) **THE TEACHER GROUP:** This typical phenotype Blood **Type A+ and genotype O+** Epigenetic is the deciding factor which Blood Type and Temperament will be dominant in this Group. It may change through life from O+ to A+ or vice versa later in life. Again epigenetic will dictate this. The Teacher is prone to personality challenges listed under AXIS III and social, spiritual, and economic under AXIS IV of the DSM.

Dr. D'Adamo described the Teacher as sinewy and flexible, with an amazing adaptability. The teacher is a balance between opposing and often contradictory forces. Blessed with a tolerant immune system, the teacher can be burdened by excess altruism, leading to problems finding and dealing with the bad guys."[170]

6) **THE GATHERER GROUP**: This typical **Blood Type B+, A+, or O+.** Epigenetic will decide for the Gatherer which Blood Type and Temperament. The Gatherer is prone to challenges under AXIS III and mental listed under AXIS I of the DSM.

Dr. D'Adamo described the Gatherer as they carried humanity on their back during times of famine and scarcity. They are Nature's ultimate survival strategy. Vulnerable to conserving calories as stored fat, the Gathers' modern challenge is to fit their survival programming to the realities of today's overabundance of fats and sugar.[171]

The above information is a summary of the Genotype Diet (or Phenotype Diet) and their relation to Blood Type (Genotype) but more so how the brain works.. You can get detail information about the Genotype Diet at www.GenoTypeDiet.Com.

The following three major diets are great diets. The Ornis Diet is specifically great for Blood Type A- or Nomads. The South Beach Diet is great for B- or Warriors and the Atkins Diet for the O- or Explorer. The other nine Blood Types are a combinations of the above three popular Diets. But, Dr. D'Adamo has simplified it for all of us.

Remember: Your Blood Type (Genotype) is your main Temperament, Attitude, or dominant sub-brains (**DA**). If you are:

1. **Type O, then you are Stem Brain or Guardian.** Your (5 senses) Sensovert attitude is your main tool to manage and control your life.

2. **Type A, then you are a Left Brain or Rational.** Your introvert attitude is your main tool to manage and controls your life.

3. **Type B, then you are a Right Brain or Idealist.** Your extravert attitude is your main tool to manage and control your life.

4. **Type ABO, then you are a Mid Brain or Artisan.** Your emotiovert attitude is your main tool to manage or control your life.

Again, **find your personality combination - EAT, LIVE and follow your BLOOD TYPE (Genotype Diet) or GENOTYPE DIET (Phenotype Diet)!**

The 6 genotype clusters above exhibit 12 (24) physical characteristics or body types which is who we are. (There are actually 12 Genotypes –MIND/BODY. For our discussion, we will stick with 6 phenotypes as this is the one detected by Blood Type test and other physical characteristics.) How is that so? See you in the next chapter.

CHAPTER 12

YOUR BODY TYPE

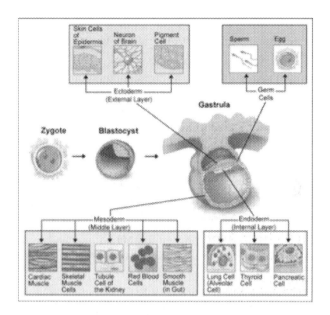

(Picture: Courtesy of **cellular-differentiation.cn.lib.bz/**)

"Like your Temperament, and Blood Type, your Body Type
tells your story while as a fetus/embryo in your mother's womb:
her environment, diet, and lifestyle to keep your alive! It's your
prenatal story but you can change that story"

The **Zygote** (fertilized egg. See picture above) or the single-celled
embryo divides to give rise to a multicelled embryo whose cells
continue to divide until the organism (You) reaches its final size. This
Zygote is made of three basic cell types or tissues which create your
body types. The prevalence of one cell group is dictated by an event or
events during your prenatal life.

Our basic body types are formed from the three different ratios of these
embryonic basic cells or tissues. The **ectoderm** cells form the *nervous
systems, skin, hair, mammary glands and connective tissues.* The **mesoderm**
cells forms *muscles, skeleton, kidney, heart, blood cells, and arteries.* The

endoderm cells forms the *digestive track, glands, lungs, and intestine.* You get 3 of these from each parent (2 x3).

The three basic cells or tissues above formed the three basic body types or somatotypes as a respond to a threat from the environment whether internally or externally. Dr. D'Adamo in his book, the "Genotype Diet", talked about the six genotypes (or phenotypes as this writngs labels) and its three world views. Interestingly, these six phenotypes parallels the six Blood Types (ABO System) as mentioned in the Blood Type Chapter. The three worldviews are the genes respond to the environment to decide which cell or tissues type is needed to protect itself and creates the "six phenotypes" as presented by the Table above or the "Human Genetic Code Perodic Table.".

A **"reactive worldview"** to the environment kicks in the **mesoderm cells** which forms the *muscles, skeleton, kidney, heart, blood cells, and arteries* as dominant and abundant cells or tissues to create the **mesomorph body type** to protect itself. A reactive worldview responds to the environment in an aggressive, proactive, and even hostile way. **Any diet or food for this group MUST nourish these mesoderm tissues or diseases related to these tissues are prevalent among this group**. This is typically the Genotype Blood Type O Group and the Stem Brain controls and manages you. This is the **Hunter** (Pure Blood Type O Diet) **and Explorer (**Mix of Blood Type O+/_, B+/_ and AB+/- Diet) **Genotype.**

A **'thrifty worldview"** kicks in the **endoderm cells** which forms the *digestive track, glands, lungs, and intestine* as dominant to create the **endomorph body type.** The thrifty worldview responds in a cautious way, seeking not to confront threats but to avoid them. Conserve those calories, say this approach. **Any diet or food for this group MUST nourish these endoderm tissues or diseases related to these tissues are prevalent among this group** This is typically the Blood Type B and the Right Brain is in control. **The Genotypes are Warrior** (Phenotype Blood Type B +/-, AB+/-Diet**) and Gatherer** (Phenotype Blood Type B**).**

A **"tolerant worldview"** kicks in the **ectoderm cells** to form *nervous systems, skin, hair, mammary glands and connective tissues* to create the **ectomorph body type.** A "tolerant worldview" is accepting and adaptable, geared to people who had to travel through different environment and confront an ever changing world. **Any diet or food for this group MUST nourish these ectoderm tissues or diseases related to these tissues are prevalent among this group** This is typically the Blood Type A or AB, the Left and the Mid Brain is in control. **The Genotypes are Nomad** (Mix of Blood Type A, O and B Diet) **and Teacher** (Pure Blood Type A Diet).

It's not difficult to predict predisposition to various diseases based on race or ethnic background for now. Western European and many Japanese who are phenotype Body Type Ectomporh are predisposed to disorders of the left side of the brain but more so any disease that may come up. When they were fetuses, their life was less challenging compared to phenotype Body Type Mesomorph and Blood Type B fetuses, therefore, didn't have to built up a strong immune systems. It's internal and external diet, lifestyle and environment were tolerant (tolerant worldview). Therefore, given child vaccinations (or whatever medications), these virus or whatever was introduced in to their body first attacks their predominant (ectoderm) tissues which is the nervous system, hair, skin, mammary glands, and connective tissues.

Next vulnerable group to diseases are the phenotype Body Type Endoderm or "thrifty worldview." These fetuses built up their immunize systems but not as strong as the Mesomorph group. Those of the "thirty worldview" are countries such as Eastern Europeans, East Indians, northern Chinese, and Koreans, a smaller portion of Japanese, Ashkenazic and Serphardic Jews. These cultures were built around conserving food for survival.

And last, the phenotype Body Type Mesomorph group. They have the strongest immune system because as fetuses, they are used to combating foreign invasion of bacteria, versus, stress, you name it. These are the mesoderm built group. When they don't eat the right food to nourish those mesoderm tissues, they are prone to muscle, skeleton, kidney, heart, blood cells and arteries disease. Other Body and Blood Type gets these disease of the above tissues but the Blood Type O suffers from it the most.

Always remember this: *our phenotypes Blood Types(from Blood Type test) , and Body Types are the fetuses respond to the mother's diet,* *lifestyle, and environment to protect itself. It has to choose from 24 choices of sub-brain combination as you already discovered.*

Treatment for Autism (8 out of 10 are boys. Boys are genotypically Blood Type A[ectomorphic] and girls, Blood Type B[edomorphic]) and any other medical challenge lies within the "Human Mind Periodic Table.

In the 1940s, Dr. William H. Sheldon introduced the **theory of Somatotypes.** His theory described three basic human body types: the **endomorph,** characterized by a preponderance of body *fat (a thrifty worldview);* the **mesomorph** *(a reactive worldview),* marked by a well-developed musculature; and the **ectomorph** *(tolerant worldview),* distinguished by a lack of either much fat or muscle tissue. He did also state that most people were a mixture of these types. [172]

New research has confirmed Dr. Sheldon findings of the various body types. The 6 grouping or phenotypes that formed the 24 Personalities Types represent the 12 **basic human body types**. The numerous variations of the 12 body types that we see are due to epigenetic. For example, you will see short or tall people in each of the 12 basic group body types. Whether they are tall or short, but you can tell the specific body type they belong to and confirm also by their phenotype Blood Type. Don't forget your temperament is your genotype Blood Type.

Below you will notice, the three basic Body Type from the three basic tissue types which are the foundation of the 12 Body Types.

ECTOMORPH MESOMORPH ENDOMORPH

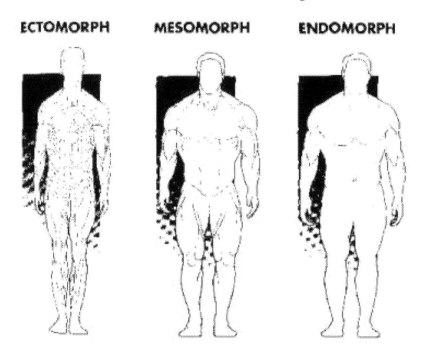

It is this writings objective for you in this Chapter to find your body type and understand that you can not change it. But you can change your current body expression back to what it suppose to be as one of the 12 phenotypes - your basic body type! Just be content and be grateful with it. Work with you body and be kind to it. Hopefully soon, the advertisement world and marketers will understand these specific niches (12 niches) and address them accordingly. For example, ladies if you are an endomorph or a mesomorph, you will never be an ectomorph, the typical model that is shown on TV and advertisement. The same goes for the guys who are ectomorph and endomorphs who wants to be like mesomorphs, the typical muscular model on TV, and advertisements.

When you understand this, it will take away the stress of trying to be something that will never become your reality. The numerous eating disorders that people suffer are because they are trying to be something that will never become their reality. Your body type is your reality and it's your success and happiness to work within that frame work. You should know your body type from Survey results with your phenotype Blood Type and Diet Chapter.

I. MESOMORPH – "HUNTER" - BLOOD TYPE O+ (BODY OR PHENOTYPE), A+/B+(MIND OR GENOTYPE):

MESOMORPH

The above personality is **mesomorph** or **Hunter** and can be defined in one word: *muscular.* If you're a meso or Hunter, your body type can increase your muscle size quickly and easily. The well-developed, rectangular shapes of mesomorphs are representative of their thick bones and muscles. (Before you get too excited about this perfect form, keep in mind that being a meso may also mean you have poor flexibility.) If you are a characteristic mesomorph, you have a well-defined chest and shoulders that are both larger and broader than your waistline. Your abdomen is taut and your hips are generally the same width as your shoulders. Your buttocks, thighs, and calves are all toned and defined.

As muscularly defined, athletic-looking individuals, mesomorphs are full of energy, are physically capable of a lot of activity, and tend to be aggressive athletically. (Usually no couch potatoes in this group.) Although mesomorphs generally store fat evenly all over their bodies, they can become overweight if they are sedentary and consume a high-fat and/ or high-calorie diet.

Cardiovascular disease can be a primary threat to an overweight meso, so if you fit into that category, your best method of prevention is to maintain a healthy diet and a balanced exercise regime. Remember that your heart is a muscle, too, and the best way to keep it fit is to perform cardiovascular activities.

Craving physical activity and constantly seeking action, the mesomorph makes a great athlete. As a meso, you excel in sports that require great strength, short bursts of energy, and lots of power. Mesos are always popular in gym class and at the playground, because people want mesos on their teams. If you're scouting for body types at your local gym (and who isn't?), you will most likely find your fellow mesos lifting weights and avoiding the cardio equipment like step machines or treadmills. Again, as a mesomorph, you are prone to diseases of the follow body tissues - *muscles, skeleton, kidney, heart, blood cells, and arteries if you do not exercise and eat right. Eat the right food and exercise to nourish those tissues!*

II. **ECTOMORPH – "NOMAD" - BLOOD (PHENOTYPE OR BODY) TYPE A-/+,AB-/+ AND A, O (MIND OR GENOTYPE):**

A one-word description for the above four **ectomorph** body type or Warrior is *slim or lanky.* If you're an ecto, mesomorphs and endomorphs usually don't want to stand next to you. It's not that ectomorphs aren't personable, it's just that you're probably a *tall, slender individual* who has trouble gaining weight (oh darn!). As you may have guessed, the perfect example of an ecto is a fashion model.

ECTOMORPH

An ectomorph is relatively linear in shape with a delicate build, narrow hips and pelvis, and long arms and legs. As an ecto, your muscle and bone outlines are usually visible (especially if you are an extremely thin ecto), and you normally have less fat and muscle mass than people with other body types.

Although willowy ectomorphs cover the majority of fashion magazines, nobody's perfect, and ectos do have health concerns. Your primary concern as an ectomorph is your frail stature consisting of small bones and joints that have a tendency to be injured easily during sporting activities. Just remember that you are prone to somatotype diseases related to the following tissues - *nervous systems, skin, hair, mammary glands and connective tissues. Eat the right food and exercise to nourish the above tissues!*

You probably won't be the star of your football team or the next champion gladiator. Don't worry — your body type is naturally suited to perform wonderfully in endurance activities. Just remember: Balancing your activities is the key. Like mesomorphs, ectos have a tendency to stick with what they do best, and ectos excel at cardiovascular training. You find balance in your workouts when you do both aerobic and muscle training.

III. ENDOMORPH – "WARRIOR" - BLOOD TYPE B-/AB- (BODY OR PHENOTYPE) AND B, AB (MIND OR GENOTYPE):

Words that describes the third **endomorph** body types or Nomad is **pear-shaped** *or barrel chested later in life or curves or padded.* The soft, flowing curves of an endo are similar to that of an hourglass in more ways than one. And wouldn't you know it; the sands of an hourglass tend to settle in its bottom half just like the fat in the body. Comparatively, if you're an endomorph, your body fat may have a tendency to settle into the lower regions of your body, predominantly the lower abdomen, hips, and thighs, rather than being distributed evenly throughout your body.

ENDOMORPH

An endomorph body typically has the capacity for high fat storage, and unfortunately puts fat on pretty easily. Although all body types are susceptible to excessive weight gain, as an endomorph, you are more inclined to become obese. The majority of your body weight is either centered in the middle of your body or in your hip and buttocks regions. A metaphor frequently used to describe an endomorph body type is pear-shaped. A pear resembles a body that has more weight in the lower region, like the hips and thighs, than the upper portion of the body. Structurally, as an endo, you have small to medium bones, limbs that are shorter in relation to your trunk, and musculature that is not well defined.

Now for the good news. From top to bottom, your soft swelling curves create full, rounded shoulders, limbs, and a full trunk. Voluptuous and sensual are the descriptions given to many endomorph females whose soft body contours and deep curves create an allure like that of Marilyn Monroe.

A male endomorph (known as an android) tends to have a different fat distribution pattern from a female endomorph (known as a gynoid). Female endos usually collect fat in their butts, legs, and hips, while most males collect fat in their abdomen (the "spare tire" or "love handle" look). Many research studies have shown that abdominal fat deposition is much more dangerous than fat in the leg and butt area. This is primarily due to the danger of heart disease and an increased risk of diabetes, stroke, some cancers, and high blood pressure.

The key to taking the bad with the good and finding happiness with your body type is by balancing all aspects of your life. Your first concern is your health, and your major health concern as an endo is maintaining a healthy body weight. Excessive amounts of body fat can place you in jeopardy of cardiovascular disease. Remember that the risk of such disease is increased if the majority of the fat is carried in the center of your body surrounding your heart. This danger can easily be avoided by maintaining a healthy diet and exercising. The joints of your lower body may be another health concern. Because these joints are already highly susceptible to injury, high-impact sports or activities may be damaging to them, especially if you carry excess body weight.

The Warrior or the Blood Type B- or endomorph person, again you are prone to diseases related to the following tissues - *digestive track, glands (Pituitary, Pineal, Thyroid, Thymus, Adrenal, Pancreas, Testis, ovary), lungs, and intestine.* Again, eating food that will nourished the above mentioned tissues will reduced the many medical problems you are probably experiencing now or may appear in the future. Also, exercise!

IV. ECTO-ENDOMORPH OR ENDO-ECTOMORPH – "EXPLORER" -BLOOD TYPE AB+/_, B+/_, AB+/_:

There are a few combinations of this body from the three main body tissues. This is why you will see various expression of the Explorer somatotypes. **Explorer** is extreme in height as is either tall or short. As an Ecto-Endomorph , you are linear in shape, extremely tall or short, slender, long arms, and legs. You have predominantly characteristics of a Ectomorph and a little of the endomorph. Your body fat may have tendency to settle into your lower region of your body, predominantly the lower abdomen, hips and thighs, rather which evenly distributed

ECTOMORPH   **MESOMORPH**   **ENDOMORPH**

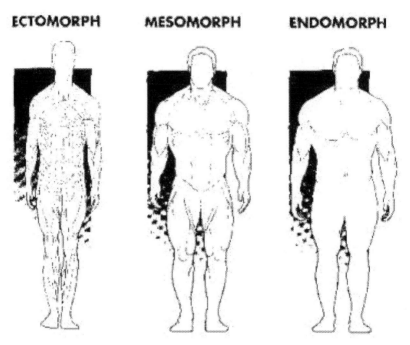

throughout your body. You don't gain weight easily compared to Endo-ectomorph. As an Endo-ectomorph, you are extremely short or tall, pear-shape that has weight in the lower region, like the upper portion of the body. You have broad shoulders. You can gain weight easily.

Explorer expressed itself in various body types as described above. This is another way to describe the Explorer. Just imagine an **Ectomorph** in an **Endomorph's and mesomorph's body** or an **Endomorph** in an **Ectomorph's and mesomorphs body. Which body type the Explorer will have depends on epigenetic. See the pictures above and imagine merging the three in one body.**

The Explorer when have proper health and balance are not prone to obesity, diabetes, or cardiovascular. The reason why because the following tissue are prevalent in your body structure and when they are not properly nourished you are susceptible to disease by those tissues- *nervous systems, skin, hair, mammary glands and connective tissues, digestive track, glands, lungs, and intestine.*

1. ECTO-MESOMORPH OR MESO-ECTOMORPH – "TEACHER" - BLOOD TYPE A+ OR O+:

Like the Gatherer, Teacher expressed itself in two somatotypes – Ecto-mesomorph and Meso-ectomorph. The **Meso-ectomorph Teacher (O+) is muscular and lanky or slim.** Meso-ectomorph takes on the predominate mesomorph characteristics. The Ecto-Mesomorph Teacher (A+) is tall and muscular because it takes on the ectomorph predominate characteristics.. They both posses a low medium body fat percentage, a high metabolism, and a large amount of muscle mass and muscle size. They can be rather large-boned, and the men tend to have asymmetrical, chiseled, craggy faces. Their trunk length is usually longer than their total length, and their upper legs are usually longer than their lower. A lot of left hander's are Explorer. One of the biggest challenges of this group is nourishing the following tissues; *muscles, skeleton, kidney, heart, blood cells, and arteries, nervous systems, skin, hair, mammary glands and connective tissues as they are the ones that caused many of their medical challenges.*

Again, see the picture below and imagine the Ectomorph in a mesomorph body and vice versa. The Explorer is a combination of both the mesomorph and ectomorph. This will give you the picture of what the Explorer looks like.

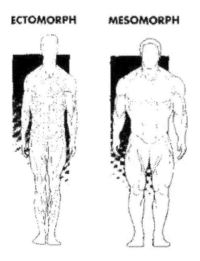

ECTOMORPH   **MESOMORPH**

2. MESO-ENDOMORPH – "GATHERER" - BLOOD TYPE B+ OR O+-:

The **Meso-endomorph (O+) and Endo-mesomorph (B+) are the epigenetic expression of the Gatherer. Gatherer is nature's survival strategy.** They manifest the physical signs of thriftiness. They are not very tall, and their lower legs are shorter than their upper legs. Gatherer woman tend to have visible differences in the size of their breast. Gatherers can easily become overweight, but being a Gatherer in itself is not the same as overweight. Marylyn Monroe was probably a Gatherer, and I've heard anyone refer to her as fat, but rather as lush and voluptuous.[173]

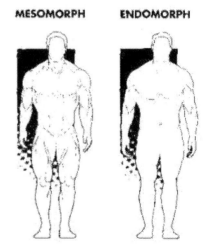

MESOMORPH   ENDOMORPH

If Gatherers metabolic thriftiness is not corrected through diet and proper lifestyle, they can age well. If they do not do it, they welcome numerous health problems which are related to the following tissues - *muscles, skeleton, kidney, heart, blood cells, and arteries, digestive track, glands, lungs, and intestine.* Merged the picture above in your imagination to give you what the Gatherer looks like when they take care of themselves.

The above information highlights but more so emphasized the important of Pre-natal care. As you can see the mother's lifestyle, diet and environment creates the type of child that will be born in to the world or country.

Now, that you are aware that the fetus has 24 sub-brain recombination's to choose from to protect itself (2x12=24 pairs. 24 from each parent) which translate to 12 phenotypes (2x 6=12) and 6 genotypes (2pairs of 3 [Blood Type- A, B, O; Tissues – ectoderm, endoderm, mesoderm; Nucleotides…]) to create YOU!;

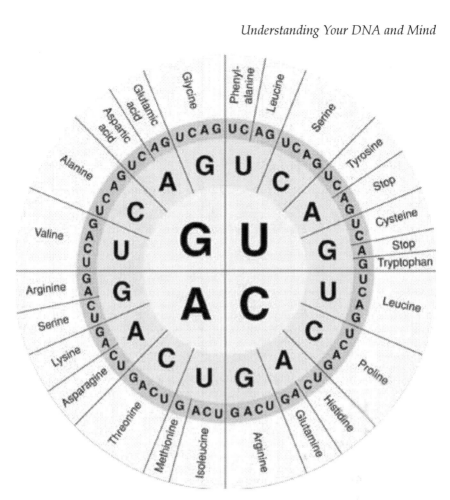

The OLD Genetic Code Chart above illustrates Amino acids controlled by each area of the DNA or four sub-brains. Any medicals issues in you are due to proteins or amino acids in the areas above not being nourished -

5.5   *CONCLUSION:*

The following article from Vic Johnson's eMeditation gives a great conclusion to what you need to do or the bottom line of this book is all about.

> "Only by much searching and mining are gold and diamonds obtained, and a person can find every truth connected with his being, if he will dig deep into the mine of his body." -- As A Man Thinketh

The classic book *Acres of Diamonds* is the story of a person who sold his home and land to travel far and wide in search of diamonds, only to die penniless. As the story goes, the new owner discovered diamonds on the very property that the old owner had ignored.

A lot of times I think we act the same way when we're trying to "fix" something in our life. Whether it's happiness or self-esteem or love that we seek, many times we look outside of ourselves to find the answer. We look to a spouse, a friend, a child, or a parent to fill the void.

Perhaps we expect the answer to come from our pursuit of our occupation or other interests. Or we expect a new home, a new car, or a new boat to satisfy our "hunger."

But, alas, like the poor farmer in *Acres of Diamonds*, our search comes up empty handed, and just like the story, diamonds are waiting to be discovered in our own backyard.

As James Allen points out, the only way to find the gold and diamonds is to "dig deep into the mine of the body."

One of my most favorite authors, Jim Rohn, says, "The greatest source of unhappiness comes from inside." Conversely, that's also where the greatest (and only) source of happiness comes from.

Instead of searching far and wide, spend some time every day searching inside. Instead of expecting something outside to fill you up, learn to fill yourself from within - *LOVE.*

Make a commitment to read more of the materials that will help you discover who you are. Make a decision to grow. As Jim Rohn also says, "What you become directly influences what you get."

> "What you are, so is your world. Everything in the universe is resolved into your own inward experience. It matters little what is without, for it is all a reflection of your own state of consciousness. It matters everything what you are within, for everything without will be mirrored and colored accordingly."--Path to Prosperity

Although we rarely desire to admit it, the world (as we see it) is simply a mirror, reflecting back to us our own inner state. If we are inwardly in turmoil, then we are certain to see a tumultuous world. Just as certainly, a seemingly joyful world is only returning to us our own inward joy.

Those days when everything seems to go wrong from the moment we wake up, usually begins with one bad event (car won't start, alarm didn't go off, etc.) that we allow to affect our state of mind. That leads to another, and then another, and before you know it, the world looks like an ugly place to us.

Put enough of those days together and life can become almost unbearable. Yet, nothing in the world created our misery--it was our response--our own state of consciousness--that created the ugliness.

In the mid-1990s, I allowed a few negative events (brought on by living by the wrong principles) to drastically change my state of consciousness. In the middle of one of the greatest economic expansions in the history of the world, I barely lived above the level of poverty. Where others saw opportunity, I saw lack. It was simply a reflection of my inner state.

By 1998, I had gained control of my inner self and, accordingly, the sun once again began to shine in my world. The same circumstances that had once appeared as lack, now appeared as opportunities. Today there are so many opportunities in my life that I am only able to act on a tiny fraction of them. My table truly over flowed.

During my dark days, I came across a tiny booklet called "12 Ways to Develop a Positive Attitude." The author, Dale Galloway, writes from experience. He was a well-known pastor whose wife suddenly left him one year a few days before Christmas.

One of the many gems he offered was: *"No matter what happens, look for the good and you'll find it. A positive thinker does not refuse to recognize the negative--he refuses to dwell on it. Positive or right thinking is a form of thought which habitually looks for the best results from the worst conditions. It is always possible to look for something good; to expect the best for yourself even though things look bad. And the remarkable fact is that when you seek good, you will find it."*

WOW! IT'S ALL IN YOU! As you know now as science and psychology have isolated the one prime cause for success or failure in life is the hidden self-image of your self or Ego or conscience. It controls your mind, just as your mind controls your heartbeat. The MIND can not act without it and so is the BODY. Again, it links the MIND to the BODY and BODY to the MIND. Both the MIND and BODY can not act without the CONSCIENCE just like the DNA and PROTEIN without the RNA.

Remember, your CONSCIOUS MIND (Left Brain or Cytosine) is the gardener in your field of life. Your futile soil is your SUBSCONSCIOUS MIND(MidBrainorThymine).NaturallawsisyourSUPERCONSCIOUS MIND (Right Brain or Guanine), and your NONCONSCIOUS MIND (Stem Brain or Adenine) is the actual physical elements that make the soil to become futile. Your thoughts are SEEDS that the CONSCIENCE expresses through **images Right), words (left), senses (taste, smell, hear, touch, smell) (Stem) and feelings (mid).** SOW GREAT SEEDS IN YOUR FIELD OF LIFE.

Your Blood Type is who you are. It's your MIND and BODY or BODY and MIND. It tells your life story. Create a NEW story now as you take control of your DNA and MIND by re-training your CONSCIENCE.

Remember, your DNA is your MIND at an organ level and DNA is your MIND at a cellular level.

CHAPTER 13

The understanding of why you do things is in the domain of your four sub-brains. To begin your journey, aside from suggestions in this writing, you may want to seek some professional assistance or help.

MENTAL HEALTH PROFESSIONALS

SUGGESTED SOLUTIONS TO...CHALLENGES

Our emotional, physiological, spiritual, and psychological challenges as studies demonstrated are due to conflicts within your brain. Once when these conflicts are resolved, the issue disappeared.

As one survey by HMO showed, that 84 percent of those who visited health professionals are due to mental or mind conflicts. The diagrams below are just suggestion based on TSF to give you some direction where to begin.

Consult with an appropriate professional in each field. Each power or area of the mind is care for by many specific professionals. Do your homework or research and it is your choice who will be your mentor, role model or helper! Great success to you. Always remember that your choices will create, attract, invite and allow who you want to become.

Note: A Mentor or a Role Model is a professional in the field you are pursing to get help from or conduct business with. A successful treatment **will be a combination of your inferior and tertiary temperaments. Your challenges in life whether socially, psychologically, physiologically, and emotionally is due to your INFERIOR TEMPERAMENT.** That's the culprit why you are not successful in whatever you are pursuing.

Your helping professional will understand the "Human Mind Periodic Table" I presented under each area. **Just understand which area has you brain combination.**

I have re-classified the DSM-IV Categories under each sub-brain as shown below. Also, I have done the same for *Multiaxial System* which will quickly assist helping professionals determined how to help you. Below is the Multiaxial System and their Sub-Brain parallel.

Multiaxial System.

Axis I (Left Brain): *Clinical Disorders other conditions that may be a focus of clinical attention or Mental Disorder.* Some disorders listed here is within the domain of the other sub-brains.

Axis II (Mid Brain): Personality Disorder and Mental Retardation.

Axis III (Stem Brain): General medical conditions or Physical condition disorders.

Axis IV (Right Brain): Psychosocial and Environmental Problems

Axis V (Whole Brain Analyses): Global Assessment of Functioning.

EMOTIONAL – AXIS II

First, if you have the following personality combination and experience emotional challenges, practitioners of the **Psychodynamic School of Psychology** will be the best mental health professionals to help you. *You are prone to social (pessimistic extravert- Right Brain), psychological (pessimistic introvert-Left Brain) and physiological (pessimistic Sensovert-Stem Brain) personality disorders.*

Dominant	Auxiliary	Tertiary	Inferior
100-91 Superior... 81-90 Absent ...	71-80 If symptom.. 61-70 Some mild...	51-60 Moderate.... 41-50 Serious... 31-40 Some...	21-30 Behavior... 11-20 Some... 1-10 Persistence...
Right Axis IV Type B+	Left Axis I Type A⁻	Stem Axis III Type O⁻	Mid Axis II Type AB(O)⁻
Right Axis IV	Stem Axis III	Left Axis I	Mid Axis II
Left Axis I	Right Axis IV	Stem Axis III	Mid Axis II
Left Axis I	Stem Axis III	Right Axis IV	Mid Axis II

Stem **Axis III**	*Right* **Axis IV**	*Left* **Axis I**	*Mid* **Axis II**
Stem **Axis III**	*Left* **Axis I**	*Right* **Axis IV**	*Mid* **Axis II**

Notice that it is your inferior and tertiary personality that is creating your emotional challenges and why you are not successful in what you are pursuing. Disorders listed under **Axis II** are what you are prone to display, followed by your Tertiary Axis disorders. If you balance or harmonized all four areas of your brain then you will create a healthy you.

Your **Global Assessment Functioning** scores within each Axis under each dominancy or weakness MUST fall within the appropriate range; *Dominant: 100-81; Auxillary-61-80; Tertiary: 31-60; and Inferior: 1-30*. For example, the first personality combination above; **Right, Left, Stem, and Mid** – *Mid/Axis II: 1-30, and Stem/Axis III: 31-60*.

Remember, personality is the qualities and traits of being a specific and unique individual. It is the enduring pattern of our thoughts, feelings, and behaviors, it is how we think, love, feel, make decisions and take actions. Personality is determined, in part, by our genetics and also, by our environment. It is the determining factor in how we live our lives. Individuals with Personality Disorders have more difficulty in every aspect of their lives. Your individual personality traits reflect ingrained, inflexible, and maladaptive patterns of behaviors that cause discomfort, distress and impair your ability to function in the daily activities of living. These are the personality you may be prone to; Antisocial Personality Disorder, Avoidant Personality Disorder, Borderline Personality Disorder, Dependent Personality Disorder, Histrionic Personality Disorder, Mental Retardation, Narcissistic Personality Disorder, Obsessive-Compulsive Personality Disorder, Paranoid Personality Disorder, Personality Disorder Not Otherwise Specified, Schizoid Personality Disorder, Schizotypal Personality Disorder,[174] and others.

PHYSICAL – AXIS III

If you have the following personality combination and experience physiological or behavioral challenges, practitioners of the **Behavioral/ Biological/Evolutionary School of Psychology** will be the best mental health professionals to help you. You are prone to developing *medical conditions* describes under AXIS III due to *social (pessimistic extravert), psychological (pessimistic introvert) and emotional (pessimistic emotiovert)* challenges. Obesity is one of those challenges for those whose stem brain as their inferior temperament! Use the Model under Emotion to complete table below. Apply the appropriate Axis for each sub-brain and consult your Mentor/Psychologist.

Dominant	Auxiliary	Tertiary	Inferior
100-91 Superior... 81-90 Absent ...	71-80 If symptom.. 61-70 Some mild...	51-60 Moderate.... 41-50 Serious... 31-40 Some...	21-30 Behavior... 11-20 Some... 1-10 Persistence...
Right **Axis IV**	Left, **Axis I**	Mid, **Axis II**	Stem **Axis III**
Right **Axis IV**	Mid **Axis II**	Left **Axis I**	Stem **Axis III**
Left **Axis I**	Right **Axis IV**	Mid **Axis II**	Stem **Axis III**
Left **Axis I**	Mid **Axis II**	Right **Axis IV**	Stem **Axis III**
Mid, **Axis II**	Left, **Axis I**	Right	Stem **Axis III**
Mid, **Axis II**	Right **Axis IV**	Left **Axis I**	Stem **Axis III**

If you have one of the above personality combinations, you are inclined to the following general medical conditions. Don't panic! See the appropriate helping professional.

General Medical Conditions is for reporting current medical conditions that are potentially relevant to the understanding or management of the individual's mental disorder. The purpose of distinguishing General Medical Conditions is to encourage thoroughness in evaluation/assessment and to enhance communication among health care providers. General Medical Conditions can be related to mental disorders in a variety of ways. First, it is clear the medical condition is directly related to the development or worsening of the symptoms of the mental disorder. Second, the relationship between the medical condition and mental disorder symptoms is insufficient. Third, there are situations in which the medical condition is important to the overall understanding or treatment of the mental disorder.

The following are general medical conditions: Infectious and Parasitic Diseases, Neoplasms, Endocrine, Nutritional, and Metabolic Diseases. Immunity Disorders, Diseases of the Blood and Blood-Forming Organs, Diseases of the Nervous System and Sense Organs, Diseases of the Circulatory System, Diseases of the Respiratory System, Diseases of the Digestive System, Diseases of the Genitourinary System, Complications of Pregnancy, Childbirth, and the Puerperium, Diseases of the Skin and Subcutaneous Tissue, Diseases of the Musculoskeletal System and Connective Tissue, Congenital Anomalies, Certain Conditions Originating in the Perinatal Period, Systems, Signs, and Ill-Defined Conditions, and Injury and Poisoning.[175]

PSYCHOLOGICAL-AXIS I

If you have the following personality combination and experience psychological challenges, practitioners of the **Cognitive School of Psychology** will be the best mental health professionals to help you. You are prone to challenges listed under AXIS I due to social (*pessimistic* extravert), senses (*pessimistic* Sensovert) and emotional (*pessimistic* emotiovert) challenges.

Dominant	Auxiliary	Tertiary	Inferior
100-91 Superior... 81-90 Absent ...	71-80 If symptom.. 61-70 Some mild...	51-60 Moderate.... 41-50 Serious... 31-40 Some...	21-30 Behavior... 11-20 Some... 1-10 Persistence...
Right **Axis IV**	**Mid** **Axis II**	**Stem** **Axis III**	**Left** **Axis I**
Right **Axis IV**	**Stem** **Axis III**	**Mid** **Axis II**	**Left** **Axis I**
Stem **Axis III**	**Right** **Axis IV**	**Mid** **Axis II**	**Left** **Axis I**
Stem **Axis III**	**Mid** **Axis II**	**Right** **Axis IV**	**Left** **Axis I**
Mid **Axis II**	*Stem* **Axis III**	*Right*	*Left* **Axis I**
Mid, **Axis II**	*Right,* **Axis IV**	*Stem* **Axis III**	*Left* **Axis I**

Many challenges listed in this area under AXIS I may classify under other AXIS. For now, if you have the above personality combinations, you are inclined to the challenges listed below.

Clinical (Mental) Disorders is used to report various disorders or conditions, as well as noting other conditions that may be a focus of clinical attention. Clinical Disorders are identified into 14 categories, including Anxiety Disorders, Childhood Disorders, Cognitive Disorders, Dissociative Disorders, Eating Disorders, Factitious Disorders, Impulse Control Disorders, Mood Disorders, Psychotic Disorders, Sexual and Gender Identity Disorders, Sleep Disorders, Somatoform Disorders, and Substance-Related Disorders. Other conditions, known as Adjustment Disorders, may also be a focus of clinical attention include Medication-Induced Movement Disorders, Relational Problems, Problems Related to Abuse or Neglect, Noncompliance with Treatment, Malingering, Adult Antisocial Behavior, Child or Adolescent Antisocial Behavior, Age-Related Cognitive Decline, Bereavement, Academic Problem, Occupational Problem, Identity Problem, Religious or Spiritual Problem, Acculturation Problem, and Phase of Life Problem.

SPIRITUAL/SOCIAL-AXIS IV

If you have the following personality combination and experience social challenges, practitioners of the **Humanist/Sociocultural School of Psychology** will be the best mental health professionals to help you. You are prone to challenges listed under Axis IV due to psychological (*pessimistic* introvert), senses (*pessimistic* Sensovert), and emotional (*pessimistic* emotiovert) challenges.

Dominant	Auxiliary	Tertiary	Inferior
100-91 Superior... 81-90 Absent ...	71-80 If symptom.. 61-70 Some mild...	51-60 Moderate.... 41-50 Serious... 31-40 Some...	21-30 Behavior... 11-20 Some... 1-10 Persistence...
Left **Axis I**	**Mid** **Axis II**	**Stem,** **Axis III**	**Right** **Axis IV**
Left **Axis I**	**Stem** **Axis III**	**Mid** **Axis II**	**Right** **Axis IV**
Stem, **Axis III**	**Mid** **Axis II**	**Left,** **Axis I**	**Right** **Axis IV**
Stem, **Axis III**	**Left** **Axis I**	**Mid** **Axis II**	**Right** **Axis IV**
Mid, **Axis II**	*Stem* **Axis III**	*Left* **Axis I**	*Right* **Axis IV**
Mid **Axis II**	*Left* **Axis I**	*Stem* **Axis III**	*Right* **Axis IV**

You are prone to psychosocial or environmental problem that may be a negative life event, an environmental difficulty or deficiency, a familial or other interpersonal stressor, an inadequacy of social support of personal resources, or other problems relating to the context in which your have developed. Psychosocial and Environmental Problems you are prone to fall into nine categories, including *primary support group, problems related to the social environment, educational problems, occupational problems, housing problems, economic problems, problems with access to health care services, problems related to interaction with the legal system, and other psychosocial and environmental problems that are affecting your ability to function in your daily activities of life.* Also, your personality will experience spiritual challenges and therefore must seek help from your spiritual organizations.

NOTE: Those who have full blown disorder in each category above are attributed to the DOMINANT sub-brain becoming INFERIOR with the rest of the sub-brains! SEE YOUR HELPING PROFESSIONAL! IT'S OKAY TO SEEK HELP. IT'S THE BEGINNING OF YOUR SUCCESSFUL JOURNEY!

If you notice that it is your tertiary and weak or inferior Temperament that is creating ALL the challenges you are experiencing now. The KEY is to use TSF to balance or harmonize all your four sub-brains or Temperaments or Blood Types with help of Mentors and Role models.

PERSONALITY AND LYING – LAW ENFORCEMENT

"The greatest or the BEST evidence in any case whether civil or criminal is the prospect or the accuser or the accused themselves. Our inner Supreme Court will convict or free us! The many physical, emotional, psychological or spiritual ailments that we experiencing are due our inner Supreme Court in session. No one is exempted from this inner trial when guilty or past issues not resolved. Our external activities are just manifestation of our internal trial!"

The numerous physical and psychological abuses that people experienced at the hands of law enforcements officers, whether in the military or civilian is because they (law enforcement officers) don't have a method to determine at the beginning if their prospect is a liar or a criminal or innocent? It's very easy to do that now using the "Human Mind Periodic Table."

Judges in any Court House can now carry out justice if they themselves are not criminal by using the "Human Mind Periodic Table" and techniques learned here.

Different **Temperaments or Blood Types determines the basic style of how we lie.** But our **personalities determine the specific of how we lie.** The helping professionals and law enforcement officers should be very familiar with this as it will make their job easier. But more so you, so that you can see your area of weakness and make an effort to avoid repeating such behavior. This area can hold your success!

Gregory Hartley and Maryann Karinch in their book, **"How to Spot a Liar"** laid the foundation from the works of Jung, Myers-Briggs, David Keirsey and Marilyn Bates about how we lie based on our temperaments. Basically, each temperament has its own method of being untruthful or lying.

The Idealist or Right Brain: This temperament makes good liars when it's an **inferior temperament.** When they anticipate having to lie in a situation, they use their gifts as visual people to conjure up mental picture of the deceit – that is how it happened. They have the ability to picture themselves doing whatever it is the lie is about, and that reduces body symptoms of lying. Idealists are all about creating solutions, helping people and organizations. They focus on process improvement; therefore, they are always picturing new, something that hasn't happened yet. They will lie because it will maintain harmony and good relationship.

This temperament as a dominant does not like to lie or prefer lying as a form of action. They are keenly sensitive to the morality of a lie. It's just that this temperament have a few traits that make them better than the other group of people.

The following **Rationals, Guardians** and **Artisan** with the following personality combination will use the above lying techniques. **Idealist** temperament or the right side is their inferior sub-brain (also prone to disorder listed under Axis IV of the DSM). Therefore, when they are inclined to lie, their inferior temperament is the one that takes over.

They will always have control over their dominant temperament, but not their inferior one.

Left	Mid	Stem,	Right
Left	Stem	Mid	Right
Stem,	Mid	Left,	Right
Stem,	Left	Mid	Right
Mid,	Stem	Left	Right
Mid	Left	Stem	Right

The Rational or Left Brain: Rationals are terrible liars'. They have a clumsy, confessional approach to deceit, first fessing up a little bit, and then spilling the whole truth in response to pressure. They have a fidget body language, they stumble, and they stutter when lying. Because competency and productivity reign supreme for the Rationals, if you catch one in a lie, it's very degrading to him.

Rationals are not accustomed to thinking that they have to lie because they are natural leaders. If they have to lie to move their agenda forward it makes them feel uncomfortable and is not a part of their "leadership persona," or self-image.

The following **Idealist, Guardian** and **Artisan** personality combination are terribly liars (also prone to disorders under AXIS I of the DSM). They will subconsciously use their Rationals temperaments when they are inclined to lie.

Right	Mid	Stem	Left
Right	Stem	Mid	Left
Stem	Right	Mid	Left
Stem	Mid	Right	Left
Mid	Stem	Right	Left
Mid,	Right,	Stem	Left

The Guardian or Stem Brain: Guardians are concrete communicator who collects data through their senses. They would then use a proven methodology to get people together to solve problems. They want to maintain the status quo and they value hard work.

As a rule, Guardian won't lie. They may get legalistic in an attempt to lie, but more likely that they will say, "I can't talk about it." They are rule oriented, so they avoid occasion where they might need to lie. They are easy to read, almost projecting guilt. The following **Idealist, Artisan** and **Rationals** will use this technique of lying (also prone to disorders listed under AXIS III of the DSM).

Right	Left,	Mid,	Stem
Right	Mid	Left	Stem
Left	Right	Mid	Stem
Left	Mid	Right	Stem
Mid	Left,	Right	Stem
Mid,	Right	Left	Stem

The Mid Brain or Artisan: This temperament missions and focus are on enjoyment and action. Artisan will get you in the ballpark of the truth, and that's good enough for them. Their approach to lying is "if I tell a little truth, that's good enough," which translate to "if you ask me what happened on the 10 yard line and I tell you what happened on the 50 yard line, I have told you the truth." You have to keep digging for specifics with a lying Mid brain inferior. Finally, they probably tell you the truth, but the mean time, they won't get uptight about it. For that reason, they can actually turn the lie in to a game or have fun with it. The following **Rationals, Idealist** and **Guardian** will use the above Artisan lying technique (also prone to disorders listed under AXIS II of the DSM).

Right	Left	Stem	Mid
Right	Stem	Left	Mid
Left	Right	Stem	Mid
Left	Stem	Right	Mid
Stem	Right	Left	Mid
Stem	Left	Right	Mid

If you notice in the above write up that the dominant temperament is not the one that uses the specific lying techniques. It's the inferior sub-brain.

Lying is a dysfunctional behavior and therefore, it's the inferior temperament that you used to accomplish it. It's ONLY when the person's dominant temperament using one of the above technique that it is now a severe challenged. When a person's dominant and Tertiary becomes inferior with the other two, then we have a sociopath (Right Brain), psychopath (Left Brain), Sensopath (Stem Brain) and Emotiopath (Mid Brain) This is where various forms of mental pathologies or disorders come into the scene such as sociopath, psychopath, sensopath and emotiopath.

MEDICAL PROFESSIONALS

How do the medical professionals benefit from understanding the "Human Mind Periodic Table?" As I mentioned in the beginning of this Chapter that 84% of those who seek medical help have issues which its origin is in the brain. So, when patience goes to see a Doctor, he or she will see what the patience's Blood Type first, and determine which type of medical challenges they are predispose to. Based on the patience's Blood Type and Body Type, the Doctors will know exactly the type of illnesses the client is predisposed to. Therefore, Doctors will diagnose the patience appropriately.

BUSINESS OR SALES PROFESSIONALS

There are four questions that a person ask themselves or carry an internal dialogue when someone tries to sell them something. The order of these questions depends on the persons Blood Type or how they use their brain. The four questions are related to each part of the brain.

1. What are the benefits (Stem Brain)?

2. What's the cost (Left Brain)?

3. What's the product (Right Brain)?

4. Why should I believe you (Mid Brain)?

The order of how you answered each question is dictated by your Blood Type or sub-brain recombination that you learned from the "Human Mind Periodic Table."

For sales associates, understanding the above concept and knowing their audience increases their sale closures. For an example, if a sales person is selling a product to Google employees which more than likely the majority of them are left brain. Therefore, they begin their presentation by discussing the cost of the product (left), follow by benefits of the products (stem) or what the product is (right) and conclude with discussing the company that make the product. If they start their presentation by talking about the company who makes the product, you will loose the interest of your audience right away. Remember, it's the first thirty seconds that you will make or break your sale.

The same concept above can apply to any form of selling whether online or offline. By knowing your audiences or demographics blood types, you can pretty much increase your closure rate on your sales.

Appendix: I – Complete Survey Sample

How You Use Your Mind Survey

Part I

Complete each section by placing a "1" next to each statement you feel accurately describes you. If you do not identify with a statement, leave the space provided blank. Then total the column in each section.

Section 1

__1__ I easily pick up on patterns
_____ I focus in on noise and sounds
_____ Moving to a beat is easy for me
_____ I enjoy making music
_____ I respond to the cadence of poetry
__1__ I remember things by putting them in a rhyme
_____ Concentration is difficult for me if there is background noise
_____ Listening to sounds in nature can be very relaxing
__1__ Musicals are more engaging to me than dramatic plays
_____ Remembering song lyrics is easy for me
__3__ **TOTAL for Section 1**

Section 2

_____ It is important to see my role in the "big picture" of things
_____ I enjoy discussing questions about life
_____ Religion is important to me
_____ I enjoy viewing art work
_____ Relaxation and meditation exercises are rewarding to me
_____ I like traveling to visit inspiring places
_____ I enjoy reading philosophers
_____ Learning new things is easier when I see their real world application
__1__ I wonder if there are other forms of intelligent life in the universe
__1__ It is important for me to feel connected to people, ideas and beliefs
__2__ **TOTAL for Section 2**

Section 3

__1__ My attitude effects how I learn
_____ I like to be involved in causes that help others
__1__ I am keenly aware of my moral beliefs
_____ I learn best when I have an emotional attachment to the subject
_____ Fairness is important to me
__1__ Social justice issues interest me
_____ Working alone can be just as productive as working in a group
__1__ I need to know why I should do something before I agree to do it
_____ When I believe in something I give more effort towards it
_____ I am willing to protest or sign a petition to right a wrong
__4__ **TOTAL for Section 3**

Section 4

_____ I can visualize ideas in my mind
_____ Rearranging a room and redecorating are fun for me
__1__ I enjoy creating my own works of art
_____ I remember better using graphic organizers
_____ I enjoy all kinds of entertainment media
_____ Charts, graphs and tables help me interpret data
_____ A music video can make me more interested in a song
_____ I can recall things as mental pictures
_____ I am good at reading maps and blueprints
_____ Three dimensional puzzles are fun
__1__ TOTAL for Section 4

Section 5

__1__ I am known for being neat and orderly
__1__ Step-by-step directions are a big help
__1__ Problem solving comes easily to me
__1__ I get easily frustrated with disorganized people
__1__ I can complete calculations quickly in my head
_____ Logic puzzles are fun
_____ I can't begin an assignment until I have all my "ducks in a row"
_____ Structure is a good thing

_____ I enjoy troubleshooting something that isn't working properly

_____ Things have to make sense to me or I am dissatisfied

__5__ **TOTAL for Section 5**

Section 6

__1__ Foreign languages interest me

_____ I enjoy reading books, magazines and web sites

_____ I keep a journal

_____ Word puzzles like crosswords or jumbles are enjoyable

_____ Taking notes helps me remember and understand

_____ I faithfully contact friends through letters and/or e-mail

_____ It is easy for me to explain my ideas to others

_____ I write for pleasure

_____ Puns, anagrams and spoonerisms are fun

_____ I enjoy public speaking and participating in debates

__1__ **TOTAL for Section 6**

Section 7

__1__ I enjoy categorizing things by common traits

_____ Ecological issues are important to me

_____ Classification helps me make sense of new data

_____ I enjoy working in a garden

_____ I believe preserving our National Parks is important

_____ Putting things in hierarchies makes sense to me

_____ Animals are important in my life

_____ My home has a recycling system in place

_____ I enjoy studying biology, botany and/or zoology

_____ I pick up on subtle differences in meaning

__1__ TOTAL for Section 7

Section 8

_____ I learn by doing

_____ I enjoy making things with my hands

_____ Sports are a part of my life

_____ I use gestures and non-verbal cues when I communicate

_____ Demonstrating is better than explaining

_____ I love to dance

_____ I like working with tools

__1__ Inactivity can make me more tired than being very busy

_____ Hands-on activities are fun
__1__ I live an active lifestyle
__2__ **TOTAL for Section 8**

Section 9
_____ I learn best interacting with others
_____ I enjoy informal chat and serious discussion
_____ The more the merrier
_____ I often serve as a leader among peers and colleagues
_____ I value relationships more than ideas or accomplishments
_____ Study groups are very productive for me
_____ I am a "team player"
_____ Friends are important to me
_____ I belong to more than three clubs or organizations
__1__ I dislike working alone
__1__ **TOTAL for Section 9**

Part II
Now carry forward your total from each section and multiply by 10 below.

- Add 1 to 4 and divide by 4. This will give you the true score the for Right Brain area.
- Add 5 to 6 and divide by 2. This will give you the true score for the Left Brain area.
- Add 7 and 8 and divide by 2. This will give you the true score for Stem Brain area.
- 9 is a true score for the Mid Brain.

You will learn all about the Right, Left, Stem, and Mid brain throughout the book and how this is related to your great success.

SECTION	TOTAL FORWARD	MULTIPLY	SCORE	TOTAL SCORE
1	3	X10	30	NA
2	2	X10	20	NA
3	4	X10	40	NA
4	1	X10	10	NA
		Total 1-4	100	/4=25
5	5	X10	50	NA

6	1	X10	10	NA
		Total 5-6	60	/2=30
7	1	X10	10	NA
8	2	X10	20	NA
		Total 7-8	30	/2 =15
9	1	X10	10	NA
		Total 9	10	/1=10

Part III
Now determine your intelligence profile!

Key:
Section 1 – This suggests your Musical strength
Section 2 – This illustrates your Existential strength
Section 3 – This reflects your Intrapersonal strength
Section 4 – This suggests your Visual strength
Section 5 – This indicates your Logical strength
Section 6 – This indicates your Verbal strength
Section 7 – This reflects your Naturalist strength
Section 8 – This tells your Kinesthetic strength
Section 9 – This shows your Interpersonal strength

Remember:

  □ Everyone has all the intelligences!
  □ You can strengthen an intelligence!
  □ This inventory is meant as a snapshot in time – it can
     change!
  □ M.I. is meant to empower, not label people!

© 1999 Walter McKenzie, The One and Only Surfaquarium http://
surfaquarium.com

The Whole Brain Approach			
Right Brain Social Intelligence	Left Brain Intellectual Intelligence	Stem Brain Practical Intelligence	Mid Brain Emotional Intelligence
Sec. 1-4	Sec. 5-6	Sec. 7-8	Sec. 9
25	30	15	10

From the Walter McKenzie table above, input the Total (after division to find the average) Scores in the Form below.

The Whole Brain Approach Here's your TSF below!				
	Dominant	Auxiliary	Tertiary	Inferior
TSF	left	right	stem	mid
Score	30	25	15	10

Input the scores above in to the Form below from the Highest to the lowest score. Highest score is the **Dominant,** next highest is **Auxiliary,** next is **Tertiary** and lowest, **Inferior.**

Appendix II – Ideal Mate

The Love at first sight works because you have met your opposite. You are naturally attracted to that person. You can feel the sparks and chemistry but can not explain it. Now, you have the answer below.

Brain Dominance Intuitive/Creative Brain	Ideal Mate Opposite Attracts
Right, Left, Mid, Stem	*Stem, Mid, Left, Right*
Right, Left, Stem, Mid	Mid, Stem, Left, Right
Right, Mid, Left, Stem	*Stem, Left, Mid, Right*
Right, Mid, Stem, Left	Left, Stem, Mid, Right
Right, Stem, Left, Mid	*Mid, Left, Stem, Right*
Right, Stem, Mid, Left	Left, Mid, Stem, Right
Thinking/Analytical Brain	
Left, Right, Mid, Stem	*Stem, Mid, Right, Left*
Left, Right, Stem, Mid	Mid, Stem, Right, Left
Left, Mid, Right, Stem	*Stem, Right, Mid, Left*
Left, Mid, Stem, Right	Right, Stem, Mid, Left
Left, Stem, Right, Mid	*Mid, Right, Stem, Left*
Left, Stem, Mid, Right	Right, Mid, Stem, Left
Sensing/Practical Brain	
Stem, Right, Left, Mid	*Mid, Left, Right, Stem*
Stem, Right, Mid, Left	Left, Mid, Right, Stem
Stem, Mid, Left, Right	*Right, Left, Mid, Stem*
Stem, Mid, Right, Left	Left, Right, Mid, Stem
Stem, Left, Mid, Right	*Right, Mid, Left, Stem*
Stem, Left, Right, Mid	Mid, Right, left, Stem
Feeling/Successful Brain	
Mid, Stem, Right, Left	*Left, Right, Stem, Mid*
Mid, Stem, Left, Right	Right, Left, Stem, Mid
Mid, Left, Stem, Right	*Right, Stem, Left, Mid*
Mid, Left, Right, Stem	Stem, Right, Left, Mid
Mid, Right, Left, Stem	*Stem, Left, Right, Mid*
Mid, Right, Stem, Left	Left, Stem, Right, Mid

Appendix III

The 12 Steps Model

The reason the 12 Steps Model works when people followed it because it is based on the "**Correct Working Model**" of how your brain suppose to work – *Right, Left, and Stem and Mid for men and the reverse for woman – Mid, Stem, Left and Right.* Men will learn the 12 Steps Model starting at Step 12, and concluded it with the Step 1. When implementing the 12 Steps Model, they start at Step 1 and concludes at Step 12.

For woman, they start learning the 12 Steps Model at Step 1 and conclude at Step 12. But when they implement the 12 Steps Model, they start at the Step 12 and work their way backwards. Its just the way their brain works also.

Make sure you understand your "TI" sub-brains and constantly improve on those two sub-brains of the **12 Step Model.** Then, successes will be delivered to you at will if you decide to do so!

Right Brain	1	**We admitted we were powerless over our addiction - that our lives had become unmanageable**	How It Works. The fact is that most alcoholics, for reasons yet obscure, have lost the power of choice in drink. Our so-called willpower becomes practically non-existent. We are unable, at certain times, to bring into our consciousness with sufficient force the memory of the suffering and humiliation of even a week or a month ago. We are without defense against the first drink. - A.A. Big Book, p. 24 (Substitute your own addiction for drink if your addiction is different than alcohol)
	2	**Came to believe that a Power greater than ourselves could restore us to sanity**	How It Works. When, therefore, we speak to you of God, we mean your own conception of God. This applies, too, to other spiritual expressions which you find in this book. Do not let any prejudice you may have against spiritual terms deter you from honestly asking yourself what they mean to you. At the start, this was all we needed to commence spiritual growth, to effect our first conscious relation with God as we understood Him. Afterward, we found ourselves accepting many things which then seemed entirely out of reach. That was growth, but if we wished to grow we had to begin somewhere. So we used our own conception, however limited it was. We needed to ask ourselves but one short question. - "Do I now believe, or am I even willing to believe, that there is a Power greater than myself?" As soon as a man can say that he does believe, or is willing to believe, we emphatically assure him that he is on his way. It has been repeatedly proven among us that upon this simple cornerstone a wonderfully effective spiritual structure can be built. -*A.A. Big Book p.47*
	3	Made a decision to turn our will and our lives over to the care of God as we understood God	How It Works We were now at *Step Three*. Many of us said to our Maker, *as we understood Him*: "God, I offer myself to Thee-to build with me and to do with me as Thou wilt. Relieve me of the bondage of self, that I may better do Thy will. Take away my difficulties, that victory over them may bear witness to those I would help of Thy Power, Thy Love, and Thy Way of life. May I do Thy will always!" We thought well before taking this step making sure we were ready; that we could at last abandon ourselves utterly to Him - *A.A. Big Book p.63*

Left Brain	4	**Made a searching and fearless moral inventory of ourselves**	How It Works A business which takes no regular inventory usually goes broke. Taking commercial inventory is a fact-finding and a fact-facing process. It is an effort to discover the truth about the stock-in-trade. One object is to disclose damaged or unsalable goods, to get rid of them promptly and without regret. If the owner of the business is to be successful, he cannot fool himself about values. We did exactly the same thing with our lives. We took stock honestly. First, we searched out the flaws in our make-up which caused our failure. Being convinced that self, manifested in various ways, was what had defeated us, we considered its common manifestations. *-A.A. Big Book p.64*
	5	Admitted to God, to ourselves and to another human being the exact nature of our wrongs	How It Works This is perhaps difficult, especially discussing our defects with another person. We think we have done well enough in admitting these things to ourselves. There is doubt about that. In actual practice, we usually find a solitary self-appraisal insufficient. Many of us thought it necessary to go much further. We will be more reconciled to discussing ourselves with another person when we see good reasons why we should do so. The best reason first: If we skip this vital step, we may not overcome drinking. Time after time newcomers have tried to keep to themselves certain facts about their lives. Trying to avoid this humbling experience, they have turned to easier methods. Almost invariably they got drunk. Having persevered with the rest of the program, they wondered why they fell. We think the reason is that they never completed their housecleaning. They took inventory all right, but hung on to some of the worst items in stock. They only *thought* they had lost their egoism and fear; they only *thought* they had humbled themselves. But they had not learned enough of humility, fearlessness and honesty, in the sense we find it necessary, until they told someone else *all* their life story. *-A.A. Big Book p.72-73*
	6	Were entirely ready to have God remove all these defects of character	How It Works We have emphasized willingness as being indispensable. Are we now ready to let God remove from us all the things which we have admitted are objectionable? Can He now take them all, everyone? If we still cling to something we will not let go, we ask God to help us be willing. *-A.A. Big Book p.76*

Stem Brain	7	Humbly asked God to remove our shortcomings	How It Works When ready, we say something like this: "My Creator, I am now willing that you should have all of me, good and bad. I pray that you now remove from me every single defect of character which stands in the way of my usefulness to you and my fellows. Grant me strength, as I go out from here, to do your bidding. Amen." We have then completed *Step Seven*. -*A.A. Big Book p.76*
	8	Made a list of all persons we had harmed, and became willing to make amends to them all	How It Works We have a list of all persons we have harmed and to whom we are willing to make amends. We made it when we took inventory. We subjected ourselves to a drastic self-appraisal. Now we go out to our fellows and repair the damage done in the past. We attempt to sweep away the debris which has accumulated out of our effort to live on self-will and run the show ourselves. If we haven't the will to do this, we ask until it comes. Remember it was agreed at the beginning *we would go to any lengths for victory over alcohol.* -*A.A. Big Book p.76*
	9	Made direct amends to such people wherever possible, except when to do so would injure them or others	How It Works Although these reparations take innumerable forms, there are some general principles which we find guiding. Reminding ourselves that we have decided to go to any lengths to find a spiritual experience, we ask that we be given strength and direction to do the right thing, no matter what the personal consequences may be. We may lose our position or reputation or face jail, but we are willing. We have to be. We must not shrink at anything. -*A.A. Big Book p.79*

Mid Brain	10	Continued to take personal inventory and when we were wrong promptly admitted it	How It Works This thought brings us to Step Ten, which suggests we continue to take personal inventory and continue to set right any new mistakes as we go along. We vigorously commenced this way of living as we cleaned up the past. We have entered the world of the Spirit. Our next function is to grow in understanding and effectiveness. This is not an overnight matter. It should continue for our lifetime. Continue to watch for selfishness, dishonesty, resentment, and fear. When these crop up, we ask God at once to remove them. We discuss them with someone immediately and make amends quickly if we have harmed anyone. Then we resolutely turn our thoughts to someone we can help. Love and tolerance of others is our code. *-A.A. Big Book p.84*
	11	Sought through prayer and meditation to improve our conscious contact with God as we understood God, praying only for knowledge of God's will for us and the power to carry that out	How It Works *Step 11* suggests prayer and meditation. We shouldn't be shy in this matter of prayer. Better men than we are using it constantly. It works, if we have the proper attitude and work at it. *-A.A. Big Book p.85-86*
	12	Having had a spiritual awakening as the result of these steps, we tried to carry this message to other addicts, and to practice these principles in all our affairs	How It Works Practical experience shows that nothing will so much insure immunity from drinking as intensive work with other alcoholics. It works when other activities fail. This is our twelfth suggestion: Carry this message to other alcoholics! You can help when no one else can. You can secure their confidence when other fail. Remember they are very ill. Life will take on new meaning. To watch people recover, to see them help others, to watch loneliness vanish, to see a fellowship grow up about you, to have a host of friends - this is an experience you must not miss. We know you will not want to miss it. Frequent contact with newcomers and with each other is the bright spot of our lives. *-A.A. Big Book p.89*

Appendix Iv

The "Human Mind Periodic Table" below like the Periodic Table in science explains many things. I hope this Table will inspire others to see between the lines and discover more that needs to be discover about the Human Mind.

THE HUMAN MIND PERIODIC TABLE			
Neomammalian	Neomammalian	Reptilian	Paleomammalian
Right Brain (R)	*Left Brain (L)*	*Stem Brain (S)*	*Mid Brain (M)*
Thrifty Worldview	*Tolerant Worldview*	*Reactive Worldview*	*Tolerant/Thrifty Worldview*
Guanine	*Cytosine*	*Adenine*	*Thymine*
Endoderm	*Ectoderm*	*Mesoderm*	*Ecto-endoderm*
digestive track, glands (pituitary, pineal, thyroid, thymus, adrenal, pancreas, testis, ovary), lungs, and intestine.	**nervous system, skin, hair, mammary glands, and connective tissues**	**muscle, skeleton, kidney, heart, blood cells, and arteries**	**digestive track, glands, lungs, and intestine, nervous system, skin, hair, mammary glands, and connective tissues**
Endomorph	*Ectomorph*	*Mesomorph*	*Ecto-endomorph*
Blood Type B	*Blood Type A*	*Blood Type O*	*Blood Type AB(O)*
Extravert	*Introvert*	*Sensovert*	*Emotiovert*
Idealist	*Rational*	*Guardian*	*Artisan*
Superconscious	Conscious	Nonconscious	Subconscious
Social Intelligence	Intellectual Intelligence	Instinctual Intelligence	Emotional Intelligence
Interpersonal, spatial, spiritual, musical, existential Intelligence	*Verbal, Logical-Mathematical Intelligence*	*Bodily-Kinesthetically, Naturalist Intelligence*	*Intrapersonal Intelligence*
Humanist, Sociocultural School of Psychology.	Cognitive School of Psychology.	Behavioral, Biological, Evolutionist School of Psychology	Psychodynamic School of Psychology
Super-Ego	Ego/Conscience	Id	Super-Ego, Ego. Id
Belonging Need	Self-Esteem Need	Physiological Need	Safety Need

Axis IV	Axis I	Axis III	Axis II
PURPOSE	TARGET	ACTION	RESULT
Law of PURPOSE, INTENT	*Law of CLEAR VISION* *Law of FEAR/ FOCUS* *Law of ACTION* *Law of TIME*	*Law of ASSOCIATION* *Law of GRATITUDE* *Law of GIVING* *Law of OPPOSITES*	*Law of DESIRES*

1. Blood Type B
RIGHT Brain: Idealist Temperament
MAIN ATTITUDE: Extrovert

Right-B-	Mid	Left	Stem
RightB-	Mid	Stem	Left
Right B+	Left	Stem	Mid
Right B+	Left,	Mid,	Stem
Right B+O+	Stem	Left	Mid
RightB+O+	Stem	Mid	Left

2. Blood Type A
LEFT Brain: Rationals Temperaments
MAIN ATTITUDE: Introvert

Left A-	**Mid**	**Right**	**Stem**
Left –A-	**Mid**	**Stem,**	**Right**
Left A+B+	Right	Stem	Mid
Left A+B+	Right	Mid	Stem
Left A+O+	**Stem**	**Right**	**Mid**
Left A+O+	**Stem**	**Mid**	**Right**

3. Blood Type O
STEM Brain: Guardian Temperament
MAIN ATTITUDE: Sensovert

Stem O-	*Mid*	*Left,*	*Right*
Stem O-	**Mid**	**Right**	**Left**
StemO+A+	**Left**	**Mid**	**Right**

StemO+A+	Left	Right	Mid
StemO+B+	Right	Left	Mid
Stem O+B+	Right	Mid	Left

4.Blood Type AB(O)
MID Brain: Artisan Temperament
MAIN ATTITUDE: Emotiovert

Mid	Stem	Left	Right
Mid	Stem	Right	Left
Mid -	Left	Right,	Stem
Mid	Left	Stem	Right
Mid	Right	Left	Stem
Mid,	Right,	Stem	Left

The above Table illustrates the four Blood Types under the ABO (A, B, O) system and the 24 Sub-Brain recombination's. To discover your specific phenotype, **check the Human Mind Expanded Periodic Table inside the book**

Cells are the fundamental working units of every living system. All instructions needed to direct their activities are contained within the chemical **DNA (deoxyribonucleic acid).**

DNA from all organisms is made up of the same chemical and physical components. The DNA sequence is the particular side-by-side arrangement of bases along the DNA strand (For example ATTCCGG). The order spells out the exact instructions required to create a particular organism with its own unique traits. Each species have its own unique DNA language or coding.

The **Genomes** is an organism's complete set of DNA. DNA in each human cell is packaged in to 48 chromosomes arranged in to 24 pairs. Each chromosmes contains many **genes,** the physical and functional units of heritary. **Genes** are specfic sequences of bases that encode instruction on how to make proteins.

A great way to understand this whole process is to think of yourself as a book. There are a four (4) main Chapters in your book which is comprised of the four (4) Sub-Brains – Right, Left, Stem and Mid. Within each main Chapters a 6 sub-chapters called **Chromosomes.** Under Chapter One – Right Brain are Sub-Chapter Chromosomes 1, 5, 9, 13, 17, 21; Chapter Two – Left Brain are Chromosomes 2, 6, 10, 14, 18, 22; Chapter Three – Stem Brain are Chromosomes 3, 7, 11, 15, 19, 23; and last Chapter Four – Mid Brain are Chromosomes 4, 8, 12, 16, 20, 24. **Genes** are thousands of stories in each Sub-Chapters. Paragraphs are called **Exons,** interrupted by advertisements called **Introns.** Each paragraph is made up of words called **Codons. Each word is written in letters called Bases.**

Where as English books are written in words of variable length using 26 letters, **genomes** are written entirely in three (3) letter words using four (4) letters A, C, G, and T. There a twenty four (24) words or codons (not 64) that makes up the Human DNA language or coding which is different from other species. The Table below listed the Human DNA language or coding which creates the 24 Blood Types and creates variations in the human species.

Instead of the DNA language written on a flat page, they are written on long chains of sugar and phosphate called DNA molecules to which the Bases are attached as side rings. Each Chromosome is 1 pair long DNA molecule.[177]

The 3 Tables below shows the old coding of the DNA and RNA as it relates to the new 24 DNA/MIND human coding or codons. The 3 Table also demonstrates "how" we have 24 main Blood Types instead of four as currently understood, "how" it relates to the 24 main Body Types, 24 main Personality Types as presented in the book. We may at the fi nal count have only 24,000 genes instead of the current estimated 25,0000. An average of six thousands genes controls and managed by each sub-brain at the organ or each DNA base at the cellular level Also, we have 24 amino acids, instead of 20 as currently discovered.

24 HUMAN DNA AND MIND SEQUENES						
Each Base of the DNA is parallel to a Blood Type: *G=Blood Type B; C=Blood Type A; A=Blood Type O; U=Blood Type AB* *Each Codon represents a Blood Type; 24 Codons =24 Blood Types. For example, GCG=BAB or Blood Type B+…etc.*						
4 Sub-Brains Right, Left, Stem, Mid **24 MIND Sequences**	**4 Bases**: Guanine, Cytosine, Adenine, Thymine **24 DNA Sequence**		**4 Blood Types:** A, B, O, ABO **24 Blood Types(MIND+BODY=48) and Body Types**			
RLMS – RLM		C	GCAT – GCA		A	BA(ABO)O – BA(ABO)	B+/A+
RLSM – RLS			GCTA – GCT			BAO(ABO) – BAO	B+/A+
RSLM – RSL	G	A	GACT – GAC	B	O	BOA(ABO)- BO	B+/O+
RSML – RSM			GATC – GAT			BO(ABO)A – BO(ABO)	B+/O+
RMSL – RMS		T	GTAC – GTA		ABO	B(ABO)OA – B(ABO)O	B/ABO-O
RMLS – RML			GTCA - GTC			B(ABO)AO – B(ABO)A	B/ABO-A
LRSM – LRS		G	CGAT – CGA		B	ABO(ABO) – ABO	A+/B+
LRMS – LRM			CGTA – CGT			AB(ABO)O – AB(ABO)	A+/B+
LSRM – LSR	C	A	CAGT – CAG	A	O	AOB(ABO) – AOB	A+/O+
LSMR – LSM			CATG – CAT			AO(ABO) – AO(ABO)	A+/O+
LMRS – LMR		T	CTGA – CTG		ABO	A(ABO)BO – A(ABO)B	A/ABO-B
LMSR – LMS			CTAG – CTA			A(ABO)OB – A(ABO)O	A/ABO-O
SLRM – SLR		C	ACGT – ACG		A	OAB(ABO) – OAB	O+/A+
SLMR – SLM			ACTG – ACT			OA(ABO)B – AO(ABO)	O+/A+
SRLM – SRL	A	G	AGCT – AGC	O	B	OBA(ABO) – OBA	O+/B+
SRML – SRM			AGTC – AGT			OB(ABO)A – OB(ABO)	O+/B+
SMLR – SML		T	ATCG – ATC		ABO	O(ABO)AB – O(ABO)A	O/ABO-A
SMRL – SMR			ATGC – ATG			O(ABO)BA – O(ABO)B	O/ABO-B

MSLR – MSL		A	TACG – TAC		O	(ABO)OAB – (ABO)OA	ABO-O/A
MSRL – MSR			TAGC – TAG			(ABO)OBA – (ABO)OB	ABO-O/B
MLSR – MLSR	T	C	TCAG – TCA	ABO	A	(ABO)AOB – (ABO)AO	ABO-A/O
MLRS – MLR			TCGA – TCG			(ABO)ABO – (ABO)AB	ABO-A/B
MRSL – MRS		G	TGAG – TGA		B	(ABO)BOA – (ABO)BO	ABO-B/O
MRLS – MRL			TGGA – TAG			(ABO)BAO – (ABO)BA	ABO-B/A

64 UNIVERSAL DNA SEQUENCES					
		2nd Base			
1st Base		T	C	A	G	3rd Base
T		TTT	TCT	TAT	TGT	T
		TTC	TCC	TAC	TGC	C
		TTA	TCA	TAA	TGA	A
		TTG	TCG	TAG	TGG	G
C		CTT	CCT	CAT	CGT	T
		CTC	CCC	CAC	CGC	C
		CTA	CCA	CAA	CGA	A
		CTG	CCG	CAG	CGG	G
A		ATT	ACT	AAT	AGT	T
		ATC	ACC	AAC	AGC	C
		ATA	ACA	AAA	AGA	A
		ATG	ACG	AAG	AGG	G
G		GTT	GCT	GAT	GGT	T
		GTC	GCC	GAC	GGC	C
		GTA	GCA	GAA	GGA	A
		GTG	GCG	GAG	GGG	G
		TTT	TCT	TAT	TGT	

64 UNIVERSAL RNA SEQUENCESS					
		U	C	A	G	
U		UUU	UCU	UAU	UGU	U
		UUC	UCC	UAC	UGC	C
		UUA	UCA	UAA	UGA	A
		UUG	UCG	UAG	UGG	G
C		CUU	CCU	CAU	CGU	U
		CUC	CCC	CAC	CGC	C
		CUA	CCA	CAA	CGA	A
		CUG	CCG	CAG	CGG	G
A		AUU	ACU	AAU	AGU	U
		AUC	ACC	AAC	AGC	C
		AUA	ACA	AAA	AGA	A
		AUG	ACG	AAG	AGG	G
G		GUU	GCU	GAU	GGU	U
		GUC	GCC	GAC	GGC	C
		GUA	GCA	GAA	GGA	A
		GUG	GCG	GAG	GGG	G

Endnotes

Preface:

Anderson. Doug (1998) "Brain Differences - Creativity and the Right Side of the Brain." Retrieved October 1, 2006, from http://tolearn.net/hypertext/brain. htm

Benson. P. J. (1997) "Problems in picturing text: A study of visual/verbal problem solving," *Technical Communication Quarterly,* 6(2), 141-160.

Biography of Ned Hermann," Retrieved October 1, 2006, from http://www.hbdi. com/ned_herrmann.htm

"Brain Mind Bulletin," a publication of The Whole Brain Corporation in Los Angles, CA, V 01.6, No. 4 Aug. 24, 1981.

Herrmann, Ned (1988) Creative Brain. Ned Herrmann Group, Lake Lure, North Carolina.

Herrmann, Ned (1995) The Whole Brain Business Book, McGraw-Hill.

Herrmann International (2005) Retrieved October 1, 2006, from http://www.hbdi. com/ .

Horowitz, Norman H. (1999) "Robert Wolcott Sperry," Retrieved October 1, 2006, from http://nobelprize.org/medicine/articles/sperry

1   "Brain Difference – Creativity and the Right Side of the Brain " by Michael P. Pitek III. at http://tolearn.net/hypertext/brain.htm

2   MacLean, Paul, "The Triune Brain in Evolution: Role in paleocrebral functions, NY, Plenum Press, 1990

3   Scheele, Paul R., "Natural Brilliance," Learning Strategies Corporation, Minnetonka, Minnesota, 1996. page 103.

4   Gardner, Howard, "Frames of Minds: The Theory of Multiple Intelligences." Basic Books, NY New York, 2004.

---"Multiple Intelligences," Basic Books, NY, NY 2006

5   Barton, Bruce, "What Can a Man Believe? Publisher: Grossett & Dunlap, 1927

6   Dispenza, Joe, Dr. "Evolve Your Brain," Health Communications, Inc. Deerfield Beach, FL, 2007.

7   This survey is based on the work of © 1999 Walter McKenzie, The One and Only Surfaquarium http://surfaquarium.com/MI/inventory.htm . I have modified his survey to fit the TSF-24 Model. I'm very grateful for what he had done in the works of multiple intelligence.

Chapter 1:

Anthony, Robert. 50 Ideas That Can Change Your Life!: An Indispensable Guide To Happiness and Prosperity. E-book, Brisbane, Australia: Total Success Publishing.

- - - Advance Formula for Total Success. E-book, Brisbane, Australia: Total Success Publishing.

- - - Betting on Yourself: Step-By-Step Strategies For The Total Winner. E-book, Brisbane, Australia: Total Success Publishing.

- - - Doing What You Love, Loving What You Do: The Ultimate Key To Personal Happiness and Financial Freedom. E-book, Brisbane, Australia: Total Success Publishing.

- - - How to Make the Impossible Possible: Turning Your Life Around Through Possibility Thinking. E-book, Brisbane, Australia: Total Success Publishing.

- - - Magic Power of Super Persuasion: For Top Achievers Who Want To Turn Personal Ideas Into Positive Results. E-book, Brisbane, Australia: Total Success Publishing.

- - - The Ultimate Secrets Of Total Self: Confidence. E-book, Brisbane, Australia: Total Success Publishing.

Johnson, Vic, "eMeditation Series" from **Achieves** February 2005-October 2006. *(Vic has done a phenomenal job writing and recording it to listen to.)* http://www.vicjohnson.com .

8   Bacon, Francis, I don't remember with I wrote this phrase from.

9   Paracelsus,

10   Proverb 23:7

11   Johnson, Vic, "A lesson from Job," August 13th, 2006

12   Quoted from Book of Job

13   Johnson, Vic, "A lesson from Job," August 13th, 2006

14   The Bible

15 Proverb 23:7

16 Jeremiah 17:9

17 Roman 7:14-24

18 Isaiah 40:26

19 Ecclesiastes 1:9

20 Matousek, Mark, "We're Wired to Connect," AARP Magazine, Jan-Feb, 2007.

21 Roberts, Anthony, "Advance Formula for Total Success," Total Success Publishing, Brisbane, Australia.

22 Allen, James. As A Man Thinketh. E-book, St. Augustine, FL: AsAManThinketh. net, 2001.

23 Wattles, Wallace D. The Science of Getting Rich. E-book, St. Augustine, FL: AsAManThinketh.net, 2001.

Chapter 2:

24 Roberts, Anthony, "Advance Formula for Total Success," Total Success Publishing, Brisbane, Australia.

25 Awake, "Your Brain – A marvel of Intricacy," Watchtower Society, NY 1999

26 Garber, Steven D. Biology – A Self Teaching Guide, John Wiley & Sons, Inc. New Jersey, 2002

27 See Appendix "How Woman's Brain Works."

28 See Apendix "How man's Brain Works."

29 Brizendine, Louann MD, "Female Brain," MD Publisher: Broadway; 1 Reprint edition (August 7, 2007)

Schulz, Mona Lisa, MD. The New Feminine Brain: Developing Your Intuitive Genius

30 Society of Neuroscience, "Brain Facts – A Primer on the Brain and Nervous System," pp10

31 C. R. Calladine and Horace R. Dew, "Understanding DNA: The Molecules and How It Works, Academic Press, San Diego 1999

32 Table is based on the Genetic Code Table from "Understanding DNA: The Molecules and How It Works," by C. R. Calladine and Horace R. Dew, pp 11

Stenesh, Jochanan, Biochemistry – Transfer of Genetic Information, Plenum Press, NY and London.

Tudge, Colin, "The Impact of the Gene – From Mendel's Peas to Designer Babies," Hill and Wang, NY 1003, 2000

Watson, James, "DNA- The Secret of Life," Random House, Inc, NY 2003

33 Information from "Understanding DNA: The Molecules and How It Works," by C. R. Calladine and Horace R. Dew, pp 13.

Calladine, C. R. and Drew, Horace, Understanding DNA – The Molecule and How It Works, Academic Press, San Diego 1999

34 Dispenza, Joe, "Evolve Your Brain," Health Communications, Inc. Deerfield Beach, FL, 2007.

35 MacLean, Paul, "The Triune Brain in Evolution: Role in paleocrebral functions, NY, Plenum Press, 1990

36 The write-up in this chapter is from; Dispenza, Joe, "Evolve Your Brain," Health Communications, Inc. Deerfield Beach, FL, 2007.

37 Dispenza, Joe, "Evolve Your Brain," Health Communications, Inc. Deerfield Beach, FL, 2007. pp108-110

38 Ibid pp110-123.

39 Ibid, pp124-126

40 Ibid. pp139-141

41 Ibid, pp129-135

42 Ibid, pp135-137

43 Ibid, pp137-139

44 Goleman, Daniel, "Social Intelligence – Beyond IQ, Beyond Emotional Intelligence," Bantam Book, NY New York, 2007, pp324

- Emotional Intelligence: Why it can matter more than IQ. New York, NY: Bantam Book, 1995.

- - Social Intelligence: The New Science of Human Relationship. New York, NY: Bantam Book, 2006.

Matthews, Gerald. Emotional Intelligence: Science and Myth. Cambridge, Massachusetts: The MIT Press, 2004.

45 Jona, K. (2000) "Rethinking the Design of Online Courses. **ASCILITE 2000**, Learning to Choose, Choosing to Learn," *17th Annual Conference of the Australasian Society for Computers in Learning in Tertiary Education,* Southern Cross University, Coffs Harbour, Australia.

Kerry, Shaun "Education for the Whole Brain." Retrieved October 1, 2006, from http://www.education-reform.net/brain.htm.

Koch, Liz (2005, May 7) "Whole brain learning is a new frontier for science," *Santa Cruz Sentinel,* Retrieved October 1, 2006, from http://www.santacruzsentinel.com/archive/2005/March/07/stvle/stories/01style.htm

"Left Brain/Right Brain, Pathways To Reach Every Learner." By Diane Connell, PhD and Carol Philips, Ed.D, is an associate professor in education at the Harvard Graduate School of Education, where she is designing and directing a professional development *program for teaching fellows.*

Ned Hermann, Participant Memo (Los Angles, CA: The Whole Brain Corporation, (1982).

Society for Neuroscience, Brain Facts – A Primer on the Brain and Nervous System,

46 Dew, Dr. John Robert, **Quality Progress Magazine**, April 1996, pp. 91-93:

47 Numerous research and studies always combine or confuses both learning and behaviors. One deals with senses and the other feelings.

48 Dew, Dr. John Robert (1996) "Are you a Right-Brain or Left-Brain Thinker?" *Quality Progress Magazine,* April 1996, pp. 91-93. Retrieved October 1, 2006, from http://barna.ua.edul-st497/Pdf/rightorleftbrain.pdf .

Chapter 4:

Dohnnann, B. J. (2005) "Whole Brain Learning: The Super Teaching Story," Retrieved October 1, 2006, from http://www.superteaching.org/STMIND2.htm.

Greenberg, Cathy L., Colonel Thomas J. Williams, and Daniel Baker, "Thinking with the Whole Brain." Retrieved October 1, 2006, from http://www.ksg.harvard.edu/leadership/Pdf/ThinkingWithThe WholeBrain.pdf .

49 The above information was from Dr. George Boeree's website http://webspace.ship.edu/cgboer/freud.html

50 Scheele, Paul, "Natural Brilliance," Learning Strategies Corporation, Minnesota, 1996, pp103-104

51 Ibid

52 The above information was from Dr. George Boeree's website http://webspace. ship.edu/cgboer/freud.html

53 The above information or definition of collective consciousness was from Dr. George Boeree's http://webspace.ship.edu/cgboer/jung.html

54 The above information or definition of collective consciousness was from Dr. George Boeree's http://webspace.ship.edu/cgboer/jung.html

55 Jung, C.G. <u>The Undiscovered Self – The Dilemma of the Individual in... society.</u>

---H.G. Baynes (Translator)<u> Psychological Types</u>, Bollingen Series, Princeton U.P. 1971.

56 Dr. Jung's typology suggest that intuitive and sensing are irrationals and thinking and feelings are rational. For the purpose of this writing, I differed with him on this. I believed that sensing and feelings are irrationals and thinking and intuitive are rational.

57 Goleman, Daniel, "Social Intelligence…"

58 Johnson, Vic, "13 Secrets of World Class Goal Achievers, Copyright 2006 Goals-2-Go.

59 Gardner, Amanda, "Study: Brain Region That Fuels Addiction Found," HealthDay News, January 25, 2007.

60 Goleman, Daniel, "Social Intelligence…" pp194

61 Ibid, pp198

62 The following summary of each intelligence was from this website - http://www.infed.org/thinkers/gardner.htm

63 Goleman, Daniel, "Social Intelligence…" pp283-284

Chapter 5:

64 Tracy, Brian. <u>Changing Your Thinking Change Your Life.-- How to Unlock Your Full Potential for Success and Achievement.</u> Hoboken, New Jersey: John Wiley & Sons, Inc., 2005.

65 The following information was from Sternberg's Triarchic Theory of Intelligence at http://wilderdom.com/personality/L2-2SternbergTriarchicTheory.html#Overview

66 Gardner, Howard, "Frames of Minds: The Theory of Multiple Intelligences." Basic Books, NY New York, 2004. pp177

67   http://www.uwsp.edu/Education/lwilson/learning/ninthintelligence.htm The following information was from this website.

68   The following write-up was from **Dr. C. George Boeree website** http://webspace. ship.edu/cgboer/maslow.html on Personality Theories.

69   Robert Sternberg, Triarchic Theory of Intelligence"

70   Merriam Webster Dictionary.

71   Gale Encyclopedia of Childhood & Adolescence. Gale Research, 1998.

Chapter 6:

72   All About Shyness Meredith Whitten, Psych Central, 21 Aug 2001; Accessed 2007-08-02

73   The following information was from Sternberg's Triarchic Theory of Intelligence at http://wilderdom.com/personality/L2-2SternbergTriarchicTheory.html#Overview

74   Sternberg, Robert, "Lessons in Increasing Intelligence," Bottom Line Personal

75   http://www.m-w.com/dictionary/discernment

76   http://www.m-w.com/dictionary/reasoning

77   http://www.thefreedictionary.com/judgement

78   http://www.m-w.com/dictionary/knowledge

79   http://www.m-w.com/dictionary/understanding

80   Sternberg, Robert, "Lessons in Increasing Intelligence," Bottom Line Personal

81   Johnston, Joni E., "Psychology," Penguin Group, New York, NY, 2006. pp 18

82   Ibid

Chapter 7:

83   Sternberg's Triarchic Theory of Intelligence http://wilderdom.com/personality/L2-2SternbergTriarchicTheory.html#Overview

84   Robbins, Anthony, page 150, ""Unlimited Power: The New Science of Personal Development," Free Press, New York, NY, Copyright 1986

85   Ibid

86   Ibid

87   Ibid

88   Ibid

89   Ibid

90   Ibid

91   Ibid

92   Ibid

93   Ibid

94   Ibid

95   Ibid

96   Ibid

97   Ibid, page 157

98   Ibid

99   Ibid

100 Ibid

101 Ibid, page 159

102 Ibid, page 160

103 Ibid

104 Ibid

105 Ibid

106 Ibid

107 Ibid, page 162

108 Ibid, page 162

109 Ibid

110 Robbins, Anthony, page 167, Chapter X, ""Unlimited Power: The New Science of Personal Development," Free Press, New York, NY, Copyright 1986

Robbins, Anthony. <u>Unlimited Power: The New Science of Personal Achievement</u>. New York, NY: Free Press, 2003.

- - Awaken <u>The Giant Within: How to Take Immediate Control of Your Mental, Emotional, Physical and Financial Destiny</u>! New York, NY: Free Press, 2003.

Chapter 8:

111 Doyle, Bob. <u>Wealth Beyond Reason</u>. Duluth, GA: Boundless Living, 2004.

Dyer, Wayne. <u>The Power of Intention: Learning to Co-Create Your World Your Way</u>. Carlsbad, CA: Hay House, 2004.

Murphy, Joseph, Dr.. <u>The Power of Your Subconscious Mind</u>. New York: Bantam, 2001.

112 Roberts, Anthony, "Advance Formula for Total Success," Total Success Publishing, Brisbane, Australia.

113 Freud, Sigmund (1910), "The Origin and Development of Psychoanalysis", *American Journal of Psychology* 21(2), 196–218.

114 Galloway, Tim. "The Inner Game of Tennis." New York: Random House, 1997.

115 Brill, A.A Dr., <u>"The Basic Writing of Sigmund Freud,"</u> 2007. Random House, Inc. NY, NY

Kahn, Michael. PhD<u>. Basic Freud: Psychoanalytic Thought for the 21ˢᵗ Century.</u>

116 Freud, Sigmund (1910), "The Origin and Development of Psychoanalysis", *American Journal of Psychology* 21(2), 196–218.

117 Ibid

118 Ibid

119 All seven definitions were from Alison Thomas-Cottinghan's book, "Psychology made Simple," Broadway Books, NY 2004 p125

120 From the Brain Connection website - http://www.brainconnection.com/topics/?main=fa/emotional-intelligence

121 Ibid

122 Ibid

123 Ibid

124 Ibid, page 56

125 Proctor, Bob, "Your Winners Image," asthemanthinkth.net, St. Augustine, FL, 1995, page 10

Bob Proctor. Power Principles for Creating More Wealth. CD, Toronto, Canada: Proctor, 2006.

- - - You Were Born Rich. Toronto, Canada: Proctor, 1999.

- - - Winners Edges. E-book, Toronto, Canada: Proctor, 1999.

126 Ibid

127 Ibid

Chapter 9:

128 The Temperament list in ALL groups was from http://keirsey.com/handler.aspx?s=keirsey&f=fourtemps&tab=4&c=overview

Keisey, David, Please Understand Me II, Prometheus Nemesis Book Company, 1998.

---Portraits of Temperament, Prometheus Nemesis Book Company, 1997.

---Please Understand Me, Character and Temperament Types, Prometheus Nemesis Book Company, 1984.

Meyers, Briggs Isabel, Introduction to Type: A Guide to Understanding Your Results on the Myers-Briggs Type Indicator, Center for Applications of Psychological Type, 1993.

129 The following list was taken from http://keirsey.com/handler.aspx?s=keirsey&f=fourtemps&tab=4&c=overview

130 From the InterStrenght website, http://www.interstrength.com/curriculum/temperament.html

131 The following write-up was from **Dr. C. George Boeree website** http://webspace.ship.edu/cgboer/maslow.html on Personality Theories.

132 Information from "History of Temperaments" website http://www.personality-project.org/perproj/others/heineman/history.htm by Peter L. Heineman

133 From the website http://www.answers.com/topic/four-temperaments?cat=technology

134 Beren, Linda and Isachsen, Olaf, Working Together: A Personality-Centered Approach to Management, Institute for Management Development, 1995.

135 Information from website http://www.personalitypage.com/four-temps.html

136 From the AdvisorTeam® website, http://www.advisorteam.org/the_four-temperaments/temp_idealist.html

137 From Dr. Peter D'Adamo's "Live Right for Your Blood Type," page 18. Percentage rounded to the next whole number

138 From the InterStrenght website, http://www.interstrength.com/curriculum/temperament.html

139 Information from website http://www.personalitypage.com/four-temps.html

140 From the InterStrenght website, http://www.interstrength.com/curriculum/temperament.html

141 From Dr. Peter D'Adamo's "Live Right for Your Blood Type," page 18. Percentage rounded to the next whole number

D'Adamo, Dr. Peter J, "Cook Right For Your Type," G. P. Putnam's Sons, NY, 10014, 1998.

--- "Live Right For Your Type," G. P. Putnam's Sons, NY, 10014, 2001.

--- "Genotype Diet," G. P. Putnam's Sons, NY, 10014, 2007.

142 From the InterStrenght website, http://www.interstrength.com/curriculum/temperament.html

143 Information from website http://www.personalitypage.com/four-temps.html

144 Ibid

145 From Dr. Peter D'Adamo's "Live Right for Your Blood Type," page 18. Percentage rounded to the next whole number

146 From the InterStrenght website, http://www.interstrength.com/curriculum/temperament.html

147 Information from website http://www.personalitypage.com/four-temps.html

148 From Dr. Peter D'Adamo's "Live Right for Your Blood Type," page 18. Percentage rounded to the next whole number

D'Adamo, Dr. Peter J, "Cook Right For Your Type," G. P. Putnam's Sons, NY, 10014, 1998.

--- "Live Right For Your Type," G. P. Putnam's Sons, NY, 10014, 2001.

--- "Genotype Diet," G. P. Putnam's Sons, NY, 10014, 2007.

149 From the InterStrenght website, http://www.interstrength.com/curriculum/temperament.html

150 From the InterStrenght website http://www.interstrength.com/curriculum/interactionstyles.html

Chapter 10:

151 Information on this Chapter is based from information at http://www.personalitypage.com and http://www.personalitytype.com

152 Ibid

153 Table is based on the Genetic Code Table from "Understanding DNA: The Molecules and How It Works," by C. R. Calladine and Horace R. Dew, pp 13.

Stenesh, Jochanan, Biochemistry – Transfer of Genetic Information, Plenum Press, NY and London.

Tudge, Colin, "The Impact of the Gene – From Mendel's Peas to Designer Babies," Hill and Wang, NY 1003, 2000

Watson, James, "DNA- The Secret of Life," Random House, Inc, NY 2003

154 The five listed personalities were from Johnston, Joni E., "Psychology," Penguin Group, New York, NY, 2006. pp 256-257

155 With the double–stranded DNA there are six possibles reading frames, three in the forward orientation on one strand and three reverse (on the opposite strand).

156 The following summary was from the http://webspace.ship.edu/cgboer/jung.html

157 American Psychiatric Association, "Diagnostic and Statistical Manual of Mental Disorder," 4th Edition- DSM-IV-TR, 2007

Morrison, James, "DSM-IV: Made Easy – The Clinician's Guide to Diagnosis," Guilford Publishing, Inc. NY, NY, 10012, 2006.

Chapter 11:

158 The following explanation of the six genotypes was from http://www.biology.arizona.edu/Human_bio/problem_sets/blood_types/genotypes.html

159 Definition from http://www.brooklyn.cuny.edu/bc/ahp/BioInfo/GP/Definition.html

160 Ibid

161 "Transplant triggers blood change" from http://timesofindia.indiatimes.com/ articleshow/2729227.cms

162 Society for Neuroscience, "Brain Facts – A Primer on the Brain and Nervous System." pp. 10

163 D'Adamo, Peter Dr., "Genotype Diet," Broadway Books, NY, 2007. pp9

D'Adamo, Dr. Peter J, "Cook Right For Your Type," G. P. Putnam's Sons, NY, 10014, 1998.

--- "Live Right For Your Type," G. P. Putnam's Sons, NY, 10014, 2001.

--- "Genotype Diet," G. P. Putnam's Sons, NY, 10014, 2007.

164 D'Adamo, Peter Dr., "Genotype Diet," Broadway Books, NY, 2007. ,pp17

165 American Psychiatric Association, "Diagnostic and Statistical Manual of Mental Disorder," 4th Edition- DSM-IV-TR, 2007

Morrison, James, "DSM-IV: Made Easy – The Clinician's Guide to Diagnosis," Guilford Publishing, Inc. NY, NY, 10012, 2006.

166 D'Adamo, Peter Dr., "Genotype Diet," Broadway Books, NY, 2007. , pp147

167 D'Adamo, Peter Dr., "Genotype Diet," Broadway Books, NY, 2007. pp168

168 Ibid, pp157

169 Ibid, pp116

170 Ibid, pp137

171 Ibid, pp127

Chapter 12:

172 The information in this Chapter was from http://www.dummies.com/ WileyCDA/DummiesArticle/id-488.html and http://www.bodybuilding.com/ fun/becker3.htm

173 D, Adamo, Peter Dr., "Genotype Diet," Broadway Books, NY, 2007. pp132

D'Adamo, Dr. Peter J, "Cook Right For Your Type," G. P. Putnam's Sons, NY, 10014, 1998.

--- "Live Right For Your Type," G. P. Putnam's Sons, NY, 10014, 2001.

Bob Ainuu Afamasaga

--- "Genotype Diet," G. P. Putnam's Sons, NY, 10014, 2007.

174 From http://psyweb.com/Mdisord/DSM_IV/jsp/Axis_II.jsp

175 From http://psyweb.com/Mdisord/DSM_IV/jsp/Axis_III.jsp

Chapter 16:

176 The information in this Appendix VII was copied directly from the "Genomics and It's Impact on Science and Society" Newsletter published by the US Department of Energy Genome Researched Programs: Http://genomics. energy.gov and the book, "Genome" by Matt Ridley which is published by Harper-Perennial, NY.

177 Ridley, Matt, "Genome," Harper-Perenial, NY, NY 2006, pp8

ABOUT THE AUTHOR

Bob Afamasaga is author of *Prepaid Legal Services and Legal Insurance--What CEOS, Human Resource Directors...Should Know,"* the most comprehensive book on prepaid legal services, *and The Ultimate Secret Total Success Formula Exposed.*

Bob received his B.S. in *Criminal Justice, Political Science,* and his *Police Administration Training Certificate* from the University of Wisconsin, and an M.S. in *Administration* from Central Michigan University.

"...an outstanding citizen and a fine representative of his community... performance both in school and the military speak well of his hard work, dedication, and commitment to his fellow man." **Recommendation for appointment as Western Samoan Ambassador to the United Nations,** *Tommy Thompson, former U.S. Secretary of Health Services and Governor of Wisconsin.*

"...is very passionate in whatever he does. He was recognized among the Diablo Magazine's "**Thread of Hope 2000"** award nominees; Recipient of the **Carol Bush Chamber Champion Award**..." *Ambassador of the Month/Year, Pleasanton Chamber of Commerce Business Connection, April 2000/2001.*

"...Leadership: Initiative and innovation have been his hallmark traits for him...has ability, integrity, and drive." *James Hinkle, Brigadier General, USAF.*

"...devoted and loyal, Bob Afamasaga exemplifies the utmost in dedication and integrity..." *David Marcrander, Colonel. USAF.*

Bob Ainuu Afamasaga is proud part Samoan (Malietoa and Mataafa Family), Tongan (Tupou Family), Fijian (Cakobau Family), German (Aull), and others. He was born in Samoa in the South Pacific and has three children. He currently lives in Roseville, California with his son, Vaipou.